T0113459

Yours,
Isaac Asimov

Yours, Isaac Asimov

A Lifetime of Letters

Edited by Stanley Asimov

DOUBLEDAY

New York   London   Toronto   Sydney   Auckland

A MAIN STREET BOOK
PUBLISHED BY DOUBLEDAY
a division of Bantam Doubleday Dell Publishing Group, Inc.
1540 Broadway, New York, New York 10036

MAIN STREET BOOKS, DOUBLEDAY, and the portrayal of a building with a tree are
trademarks of Doubleday, a division of Bantam Doubleday Dell Publishing Group, Inc.

The Library of Congress has cataloged the Doubleday hardcover edition as follows:

Asimov, Isaac, 1920–92
[Correspondence. Selections]
Yours, Isaac Asimov: a lifetime of letters /
edited by Stanley Asimov.—
     p.   cm.
1. Asimov, Isaac, 1920–92—Correspondence.   2. Authors, American—
20th century—Correspondence.   3. Scientists—United States—Correspondence.
I. Asimov, Stanley, 1929– .   II. Title.
PS3551.S5Z48   1995
813'.54—dc20
[B]   95-12967
CIP

Grateful acknowledgment is given to the following for permission to quote from
correspondence with Isaac Asimov: Woody Allen, Polly Bergen, Arthur C. Clarke,
Estate of Norman Cousins, Estate of Lester del Rey, Howard B. Gotlieb, Martin H.
Greenberg, Stephen King, Marvin Minsky, Leonard Nimoy, Estate of Joseph Papp,
Linus Pauling, Fred Pohl, Estate of Gene Roddenberry, Tom Smothers, Estate of
George Vaill, George Wald, Estate of Theodore H. White, Sheila Williams.

September 14, 1966, letter from John W. Campbell copyright © 1987 by AC Projects,
Inc., and used with permission.

July 4, 1983, column by William and Mary Morris copyright © 1983 by the United
Feature Syndicate and used with permission.

ISBN: 978-0-385-47624-9
Copyright © 1995 by The Estate of Isaac Asimov
All Rights Reserved
Printed in the United States of America

144915995

Dedicated to
     My wife, Ruth,
     My love and my life

Contents

Foreword

I've always enjoyed being my brother's brother.

Isaac was 9½ years older and infinitely more famous. But we got along well. He once dedicated a book to me, saying: "To my brother, with whom I have never exchanged a cross word." And that's true.

Of course, that didn't mean we didn't joke with one another or have a laugh at the other's expense. And if it would produce a laugh, Isaac was not above a little exaggeration.

About 20 years ago, he spoke on Long Island at a book-and-author luncheon sponsored by the newspaper *Newsday*. The audience consisted predominantly of Jewish women, and Isaac knew how to win them over. Isaac began:

"I have a Jewish mother, who is sitting in the audience now. Mamma, stand up and take a bow." (Which she did.)

"My brother is also here at the table with my mother. He's Stan Asimov, and he's assistant publisher of *Newsday*. Of course," Isaac continued, "I wouldn't say that my mother plays favorites, for how can a Jewish mother play favorites? Still, I am the firstborn, and you know what that means. For instance, when this luncheon was being planned, my mother said to me:

" 'Isaac, will it be possible for me to sit with you?'

"I said: 'No, Mamma, I'll be on the dais. You'll sit with Stanley.'

"And my mother said: 'Stanley who?' "

The audience burst into laughter, and my mother stood up and shook her fist at Isaac. But it didn't matter. The audience was in his hands. And when I got back to my office, there was a sign on my desk: "Stanley who?"

I not only loved Isaac, but I liked him. He was a fun person to talk to. And if I had a question on a crossword puzzle, I could always call him and get the answer. He was my personal encyclopedia and dictionary.

But the reason that I never felt overwhelmed by Isaac was that I had my own ego. I worked 40 years for *Newsday,* rising from reporter to assistant publisher to vice president in the 1980s. I had my own career and interests.

Isaac died April 6, 1992, about a month before I retired from *Newsday.* Several weeks after Isaac died, Ed Ferman, the editor of *Fantasy & Science Fiction* magazine, asked me whether I would like to look at some of the letters that Isaac had written to him over the years. I said I would, and he sent them to me.

They were wonderful letters, and it occurred to me that, since I was retiring, I might have time to edit a book of Isaac's letters. I mentioned this to Janet, Isaac's wife. She was incredulous. "Impossible," she said, "there are too many." She told me that carbons of Isaac's letters had been donated to the archives at the Boston University library.

"Nonsense," I said, "there can't be that many." So my wife, Ruth, and I drove to Boston to look at them.

There *were* too many. Ruth and I spent two days in the library, and we felt as if we had just put our toes in the ocean of letters.

If I wanted to do nothing else but read those letters ten hours a day, seven days a week in Boston, my guess is that it would have taken me at least four months. So the archivists—Margaret Goostray and Elizabeth Bolton—sent me 30-pound boxes of letters that I could look at in my home on Long Island.

It took me a year.

My estimate is that Isaac received about 100,000 letters in his professional career. And, with the compulsiveness that has to be a character trait of a writer of almost 500 books, he answered 90 percent of them.

He answered more than half with postcards and didn't make carbons of them. But with the 100,000 letters he received, there are carbons of about 45,000 that he wrote. It was more than a half ton of letters. If Isaac had spent his time writing books rather than letters, he could have written another 100 books.

I guess we are brothers. If he had the compulsiveness to write them, I had the compulsiveness to read them. And, after a lifetime of living my own life, I was now living Isaac's.

The most wonderful thing about his letters is that Isaac wrote the way he spoke. In every letter, I could hear his voice. So, during the 18 months that I worked on this book, Isaac was alive for me.

With few exceptions, Isaac wrote brief letters. (Where could he have found the time to write long letters?) There are no long-letter exchanges with correspondents expounding on philosophy or inner thoughts. Instead, all of his ideas poured out of his typewriter into books and articles.

But the letters showed the incredible range of his humor, ideas, opinions, judgments and knowledge.

The people who received his letters included the famous (senators, scientists, entertainment figures) and the less famous (teachers, students, researchers). He wrote to science fiction writers, publishers, editors, fans. He wrote to family members and friends. He wrote to the world.

Over the years, tens of thousands of people received mail from him. And many people saved Isaac's letters and postcards—no matter how mundane the topic.

When word went out in the science fiction world that I was editing a book of Isaac's letters and that I didn't have the postcards, I received copies of postcards from fans everywhere.

One letter came from an Alaska resident who wrote: "I had no trouble finding the postcard; I framed it almost immediately, and it has been one of my treasured possessions." Here's the text of that postcard:

29 March 1973

Will a brief postcard do for the purpose? I'm very glad you like my stuff and I will try to continue pleasing you.

The letters that Isaac received were immensely varied. Naturally, many were typed. But others were printed or handwritten in ink, pencil or even crayon. They came on business letterheads, stationery, scraps of paper, pages torn from notebooks. There were picture postcards, birthday cards, get-well cards, Christmas cards.

Some were brief. Others were l-o-o-o-o-n-g. They came from every state in the Union and virtually every country in the world.

They sent him photographs, drawings, diagrams, scientific ideas, opinions, thanks, awards, poems, parodies, limericks. They requested autographs and photos and asked him to make speeches to their organizations.

They addressed him as Professor, Doctor or Mr. Most frequently, they simply addressed him as Isaac.

With very few exceptions, Isaac's correspondents showered love and appreciation on him for writing books that enriched, inspired, taught and entertained them.

All of Isaac's letters are now back in the special collection vaults of the Mugar Memorial Library, Boston University. His letters, manuscripts, proofs and all his files from the past 30 years are kept in acid-free folders placed in acid-free manuscript boxes. His papers are in 464 boxes that cover 232 feet of shelf space.

The vaults include copies of every book that Isaac wrote, plus a number of foreign translations.

If you were in the vaults, you would see row upon row of immaculate metal shelving holding both books and manuscript boxes. The lights are set to go off every seven minutes to control the amount of light on the boxes.

Isaac's papers share the vaults with the papers of many other prominent people: Martin Luther King, Jr., George Bernard Shaw, Irwin Shaw, Bette Davis, H. G. Wells, Fred Astaire, Dan Rather, Rex Harrison. The library houses the papers of more than 1,600 individuals, and Isaac's papers are among the most voluminous. Several thousand journalists, authors, researchers, scholars and students visit the library each year to look at various files.

Dr. Howard B. Gotlieb, the founder of the special collections section of the library and its longtime director, said this about Isaac:

"He used to claim I had here an exact duplicate of his library, except for a few foreign editions of which he'd been sent only one. He loved to walk up and down the aisles of his books and rub his hands over their spines. He was very proud of his collection."

The letters that you will read in this book are excerpted from the carbons in those files and some family letters. My journalistic training says that a reporter or an editor must never change a quote. But I've made some changes that I must explain.

To keep the excerpts brief and to the point, I have sometimes replaced the pronouns in quoted material with their antecedents. And since Isaac wrote these letters at warp speed, the carbons occasionally contain spelling, grammar or usage errors. He probably corrected these errors in the letters he actually sent. So I've taken the liberty of making the corrections. I've made some deletions of extraneous matter without inserting ellipses. And I've inserted first names so that the excerpt will be clear.

But in no case have I made any changes that have distorted Isaac's words or intent.

Isaac used the British system of dates (i.e., 25 July 1995). So I've retained that form. And because Isaac wrote so many letters, he simplified the normal "Yours truly" to simply "Yours, Isaac Asimov."

In addition, because the contents of the letters stand on their own merits, I have omitted the names of the recipients. Only in those cases where it's vital to understanding the letters have I indicated to whom the letter was written.

So read the letters carefully. One of them may have been written to you.

Yours,
Isaac Asimov

1

Letters

This book was possible because of the vision of Howard B. Gotlieb, Boston University's director of special collections. So let's start with a letter to Isaac from Gotlieb:

October 26, 1964

I write to say that Boston University would be honored to establish an Isaac Asimov Collection. We are in the midst of planning the building of a magnificent new library on our Charles River campus and we hope to make this library a center of study and research in contemporary literature.

An Isaac Asimov Collection would certainly be a distinguished nucleus around which this University could build a great literary center. Your papers would be preserved for future generations.

And this was Isaac's reply to Gotlieb authorizing the collection:

29 October 1964

You take my breath away with your talk of an Isaac Asimov Collection. Although I am not unduly troubled by modesty, I must admit that I have never thought of myself as a candidate for archival material. As a result, I have disposed of my correspondence and my manuscript material as quickly as it was safe to do so. And when I say "disposed," what I really mean is torn up, burned, trash can. Consequently, a great deal of my deathless prose is gone forever.

You are *certainly* welcome to them provided you accept my considered statement that such a mass of trivia you have never seen. My condolences to future generations.

And now for Isaac's letters.

19 November 1964

If you want a good laugh, it seems that Boston University is building a brand-new six-story library, and they want to establish an "Isaac Asimov alcove" or something like that and collect all my manuscripts and galleys and correspondence and meshuggah things like that. I tried to explain that this was ridiculous but they apparently take me even more seriously than I take myself (and that's SERIOUS). I also tried to tell them that if they really want to make things complete and if I continue to produce for the next quarter-century as I have in the last, they will have to build another six-story library, but they don't seem worried.

24 May 1965

I brought in a pile of material to Boston University Library, and I discovered that they were not merely collecting material from Boston University authors but from all authors they could get their hands on. They are trying to make Boston University the center of documentation of 20th-century authors, as Yale is (my librarian says) for 18th-century authors and Harvard for 19th-century authors.

So I asked, blankly, why they wanted me. He said it was because of my influence on 20th-century society. I said, "What influence?"

So he said that, as an example, the current issue of *Life* has an article on some 11-year-old who has been moved from sixth grade into college and is astonishing his professors there with his unbelievable precocity. And, according to the *Life* article, the kid claims he got his start in mathematics by reading my book *Realm of Numbers*.

14 August 1968

I generally like to have a copy of everything for my own complete library of Asimoviana (which is pushing me out of house and home). In addition, though, it seems that Boston University collects my "papers," and they are very anxious to have one of everything, too (together with manuscripts, scrap paper, used stamps and everything I touch).

In late 1968, Isaac got a notice from the IRS that it had questions about his 1966 tax return.

1 November 1968

My accountant kept calming me and calming me and telling me he knew I was honest and the tax people knew I was honest and he would tell them flatly that it was a waste of time to question a man of my integrity etc. etc. Then he looked through my tax return and said, "Aha-a-a-a." And I said, "What, what, what, what, what?" Then, to make it perfectly clear, I said, "What?" (That's a Wodehousian touch.)

In 1966, I was giving my manuscripts and papers to BU, and for the first time, I received a note from them which included a notarized statement from some expert in such matters which gave an evaluation of the worth of my contribution. He placed it at $3,500. BU informed me I could deduct this from my income for tax purposes and so I did.

My accountant said, "Any substantial contribution in something other than money sets off an alarm in the computer and everyone comes running."

I said, "But I had nothing to do with it. I didn't ask for it. I didn't expect it. BU sent it of their own accord, and this guy is a recognized expert employed by them and this is a notarized letter."

And he said, "It doesn't matter. They want to argue it. They're going to question whether the material is worth that much."

I said, "For my part, it isn't worth anything. I used to burn it all up before I started giving it to BU. But the university says it's worth a great deal to them and to future generations of scholars."

He said, "I'll argue it with them and we'll see what happens."

Anyway, I'm not mad anymore because I think this is a legitimate investigation. In my case, I think the deduction is reasonable enough, but I can see where this sort of thing could lend itself to great abuse and the government *should* investigate it. And I'd rather be investigated myself in a careful guard against abuses than to escape it out of the general corruption and inefficiency of the government. Because, to be selfish about it, a rotten government would be far more expensive to me in the long run than the enforced (even unjustly enforced) payment of a few hundred dollars.

Several years later, he wrote Gotlieb:

18 August 1975

Oh my goodness, I didn't know you wasted time *reading* the stuff I send you. Shame on you. You have better things to do with your time. You may not have gotten the best writer in the world, but very nearly the most logorrheic.

Gotlieb once discovered that the library was missing one of Isaac's books. Isaac wrote Gotlieb:

19 February 1985

Thanks for telling me about that missing book. I don't know how I came to leave it out.

I've been slowly giving away copies to deserving individuals, and only this morning, I gave one to be auctioned off at a club to which I belong. When I got your letter, I felt a cold hand clutch at my heart, for I thought that this morning's gift might have been the last copy.

But it wasn't. I had *one* left. I have put it in my "Gotlieb box," and the next time I make up a package for mailing, it will be included and you'll have the missing #229. (My goodness, I've published 85 books since then.)

This book is a testimonial to Isaac's penchant for writing letters. Even he agreed that it was a compulsion.

16 September 1955

Writing at once and answering at once is one of my many compulsions. I do not expect it of others. The pattern of my regular correspondences (as with Sprague de Camp, Cliff Simak and so on) is a letter from them, an answer from me by return mail, an answer from them any time from a month to a year later, an answer from me by return mail and so on. I virtually never write out of turn, so I end up never really bothering anyone.

14 December 1955

I don't send out Christmas cards on principle. (Faugh, mass-produced sentiment.) What I do do is to answer each significant card (i.e., from friends who enclose some sort of personal note or from friends from whom I haven't heard since last Christmas) with a letter.

30 March 1966

I am constantly getting letters couched in the most personal and friendly terms from people I don't know. Either people are naturally friendly or else my informal style encourages them to be friendly toward me. In either case, I am glad because I am a friendly type myself and I feel at ease with informality.

15 February 1967

I am a compulsive answerer of letters, even from the numerous fifth-grade children who write me, and I try hard to be pleasant to all.

30 January 1969

No matter how rich *I* get, I not only answer my own mail, I do so by return mail. Which shows how (nice, stupid—cross out one) I am.

12 January 1970

I use postcards not as an indication that I am being bothered, but merely as a device to save a little time so that I can answer all my letters instead of only some.

16 December 1969

I answer the day's letters *before* beginning the day's work so that I have no letters even two days overdue.

2 September 1971

Receiving as I do 10 to 30 letters a day I have learned to answer most by postcard and the rest on half-sized paper. (I deliberately half-size them to discourage wordiness.)

17 September 1973

I wish I could do more than write a short reply. But I have to choose between writing many books and writing long letters.

Isaac and Janet took a trip to England in 1974, and this was his situation upon his return.

22 June 1974

Coming back I find myself with three weeks of mail filling the office from end to end and floor to ceiling. Aside from reading, sorting, taking care of checks and bills, I have managed to write 38 letters so far (this is the 38th) and there seems scarcely a dent.

22 June 1974

In the last 24 hours, I have written 70 letters (this is #70; that's where it was in the pile; not counting an equal number of objects that I either threw away or kept but didn't answer).

24 June 1974

This is the 112th letter I have written since returning and not one stitch of real work yet. Ah well.

More than letters were dealt with promptly.

27 December 1976

I must say that it is my practice to do everything that must be done as nearly as possible *at once* as I can manage. That means paying all my bills by return mail, for instance. It's no more work to pay a bill or answer a letter a week afterward as immediately. But if you wait a week, it seems to clutter your mind with the feel of "there's something I have to do." That interferes with efficiency, I think.

He expressed amazement at a letter from a fan in the Soviet Union.

14 June 1978

Your letter arrived today, even though it was simply addressed "Isaac Asimov, the well-known writer, USA." I didn't know that the U.S. Post Office knew me so well.

In his next-to-last editorial for Asimov's Science Fiction Magazine, *published in July 1992, after his death, he expressed unhappiness that illness had interfered with his policy of replying to letters:*

I feel guilty about not answering the many letters sent me. The whole experience has made me think more about letters as a unique form of literature. They communicate directly from one person to another, often revealing thoughts and feelings that are sometimes hard to say out loud. In this age of phone conversations, letter-writing has diminished, but my colleagues and fans are literate. Even the messages they wrote on get-well cards were literate, amusing and helpful.

2

Writing

There is nothing in the world that Isaac wanted to do but write. But why?

6 June 1969

I write in order to teach and in order to make people feel good (for I am wedded to the theory that *learning* is the most enduring pleasure). It is nice to make money doing so. However, my chief reason for writing is to please myself, because I myself learn by writing. And that is my pleasure, too.

5 May 1973

I write because I am driven to do so.

29 November 1979

I am so ill-rounded that the ten things I love to do are: write, write, write, write, write, write, write, write, write and write. Oh, I do other things. I even like to do other things. But when asked for the ten things I *love,* that's it.

22 December 1984

My answer to the question "Why do you write" is that I write for the same reason I breathe—because if I didn't, I would die.

7 December 1985

My secret is that I love to write—the mechanical act of it. I guess loving to write isn't a common thing. So I must be the luckiest guy in the world.

27 May 1987

I write primarily for my own pleasure. That I give pleasure to others is a welcome side effect, but they owe me nothing for that.

How did he learn to write?

29 June 1968

It is embarrassing to have to say this, but I must. I don't know anything about writing.

Have you ever heard of a "primitive" artist, like Grandma Moses? Well, I am Grandpa Isaac, the primitive writer. I have never taken a course in writing. I have never read a book on the subject. I don't know a climax from a parenthesis.

All I manage is to "keep doin' what comes naturally" and, thank heavens, it works. I don't dare ask questions, and I am helpless to explain.

17 October 1968

I honestly don't know how to write or to advise anyone else to write. I can *do* it, but that doesn't say I know *how* to do it. I also synthesize DNA in every cell of my body, but I don't know the exact details of how I do that, either.

2 November 1984

Writing is quite analogous to the fact that I can raise my arm through an effort of will, but I don't know what it is my nerves and muscles do that makes my arm responsive to my will.

1 June 1987

I never learned how to write. I knew how from the start.

It all comes to me naturally, and I've been doing it profession-ally for 51 years and non-professionally for seven years before that. I might as well try to explain how to breathe.

How was he able to write so much?

26 April 1965

I have several positive assets. (1) I love to write. I am never so happy as when I am facing the typewriter. (2) I have no competing interests. (3) I have a virtually photographic memory. (4) I apparently have some native talent at writing.

More important, I have one overriding negative asset. Apparently, I lack completely any of the emotional blocks to writing. I have been writing for 27 years and at no time have I ever had "writer's block." There have been a few occasions when something I was writing palled on me, but that only meant I could turn, temporarily, to another project—I have a number in progress at all times. And when I turned back, the pall would be gone.

The lack of emotional blocks not only means I can write at any time. It means I have no worries about what I write. If I write something according to a particular scheme of organization, I accept that as correct. If, after a few seconds of consideration, I choose one turn of phrase rather than another, I am satisfied with it. It is my feeling that I can trust my intuition, and I have no worries in that respect.

In going over my first draft, I make corrections in word order, in spelling. I may cut out a word here, a phrase there, or insert a word here, a phrase there. But I never make major revisions. And after one set of revisions, I make no further changes, except where I detect grammatical errors.

No doubt I could polish further and further to much higher perfection than that which satisfies me, but I lack the desire to do so.

17 April 1968

I am usually amazed (and pleased) at what comes out of the typewriter. Which is why I write so much. I am eager to see what I will say next.

19 March 1973

I don't suffer. I don't agonize. I don't have to drive myself. I just write.

6 June 1979

I start work every day (including Saturdays, Sundays and holidays) at 7:30 A.M. I stop work every evening at 10:30 P.M. The work is continuous except for interruptions which are numerous (telephone, business lunches, social engagements, biological functions, talking to my wife) and which are resented. I work in my apartment and interruptions don't slow me down since at the conclusion of the interruption I begin, full speed, at the point I left off.

3 July 1979

Everything *but* writing is an interruption—including this letter.

6 June 1982

My own leisure evaporated to zero about 35 years ago. Or, as I prefer to put it, my life is 100 percent leisure, since all I want to do is write.

18 January 1984

I always print the first words that pop into my head. I don't know how I decide a beginning or an ending or a title. I just sit down and type and that's that.

13 February 1985

I'm a non-perfectionist. I'm easily satisfied. I don't look back in regret or worry at what I have written.

How was he able to write so clearly?

27 May 1975

I simply make use of the English language. I never use a long word when a short one will do or an involved construction when a simple one will do or literary trickery when plain-speaking will do. Doing all that, I am capable of *convincingly* treating my readers as my intellectual equals, and in return for that, they will go to all lengths to understand me.

Where did he get all that knowledge?

2 December 1968

Rightly or wrongly, I rarely wade through primary material. My references are generally a variety of encyclopedias, dictionaries, textbooks, etc.—in other words, predigested stuff and secondary material.

This would hurt my conscience if I ever pretended to be contributing anything to scholarship, but I don't. I cheerfully admit that I never present anything new. What I have to sell is arrangement and style.

I was once stopped by someone when I was writing one of my books on words because I had a Webster's Unabridged open before me. He said, "Why, you're just getting the material out of Webster's." And I said, "That's right. Here's Webster's and here's what I've written so far. Do you want to continue?"

Where did he find the time to do research?

18 July 1987

As to research, that is done in odd times: reading during meals or in the bathroom or in bed or while I am watching television. Fortunately, I remember what I read and can use it for indefinite periods of time, with slight refreshment when necessary or (sometimes) no refreshment at all. How long that will continue I can't say. For as one ages, one can't help experiencing cerebral deterioration. But I am holding off the decay so far.

Did he have any help?

5 December 1973

I am a one-man operation. I have no typist, no secretary, no partner, no research man, no agent. I do everything myself, first draft, final copy, research, galley reading, indexing—everything.

I type the first draft, correct (very little) and type the second draft. I compose as fast as I type, and I type 90 words a minute.

The point is that I have an orderly mind, I know what I am going to say, have developed an unadorned style and have confidence in my ability to write.

26 November 1975

It is *necessary* for me to do everything myself (including answering my letters myself and answering my own phone). As soon as I hired a staff of people to help me, I would spend most of my time interacting with them. My output would drop to a fraction.

Why weren't there more women in his fiction?

8 April 1985

I am a limited human being. In the fiction I have written, I have not only played down women, I also have virtually no blacks as characters, no Orientals, no Frenchmen, no Englishmen, no foreigners, no Jews, no priests, no rabbis, no farmers, no laboring men. My stories deal almost entirely with white American intellectual males—which is *all I know about.*

11 April 1989

If I try to write about things I know nothing about, I will fail and make myself a laughingstock. This is not prejudice on my part. I am just writing what I know, and I don't know very much.

How did he view his writing?

11 May 1964

I can write straight science without thinking because it requires no thought. I already know it. Science fiction, however, is far more delicate a job and requires the deeper and most prolonged thought.

20 February 1972

What I like about my own writing is: (1) It is intricately and carefully plotted and leaves no untied ends at the close. (2) The heroes are not without flaws, and there are no villains at all. At least there are people who oppose the hero, but usually they are justified in their own eyes and don't feel villainous. I do my best to present their case fairly, even when I disapprove of them personally. (3) My stories don't depend on sensationalism to make their point. They have neither unnecessary sex nor unnecessary profanity nor unnecessary violence. I allow their content to carry them.

10 October 1972

I may not be the best writer in the world, but I can do more different things than any writer who ever lived. And I enjoy demonstrating that.

In Isaac's Black Widower stories, the guest at the monthly dinner is asked, "How do you justify your existence?" An editor once asked this question of Isaac.

30 July 1986

How do I justify my existence? By my writing, I amuse people and make them happy. My writing style is simple, straightforward and upbeat—nothing nasty or horrid or violent or perverse. In this sad world, I think that anyone who spreads happiness automatically justifies his existence.

Nor do I feel guilty that I am not delving into the garbage and muck of human life. There are *lots* of authors who do that. So why should I crowd into said muck with them?

Why did Isaac switch from fiction to nonfiction in the 1960s and 1970s and back to fiction in the 1980s?

31 October 1990

I am given equal acclaim for both my fiction and my nonfiction. So the question arises: Which do I write?

My average novel brings in, quite easily, at least ten times as much money as even my most successful nonfiction book does, so the answer seems clear. Write novels!

However, writing nonfiction is at least ten times as easy and a hundred times as pleasurable as writing novels. (This is a subjective judgment and is not quantifiable.)

Consequently, about 1960, I decided I had enough money. For 20 years, I wrote nonfiction almost entirely and was a happy man.

In the 1980s, however, I returned to novels and have turned out seven of them in eight years. The money has just poured in, a vast flood. Why did I change? I don't need the money. I have nothing to spend it for. My needs and wants are very few.

However, I realized that I was approaching the end of my life. I will leave behind, as survivors, a wife and two children. Consequently, in the 1980s, I bade farewell to ease and happiness and applied myself to laying up financial fat so that my survivors can live through the hard economic times I saw coming as soon as Reagan became President.

The struggle then is between ease and happiness on one side and responsibility and duty on the other. In the 1960s and 1970s, I chose the former. In the 1980s, the latter.

Writing best sellers came late in Isaac's career, but the subject came up from time to time.

14 June 1962

A physical therapist asked me if I had really written 45 books. I said yes. He said, "Very commendable. Very commendable." Then, with a sigh, "I've often thought of writing a best seller, but I never seem to get around to it."

"Really," said I, "I've often thought of writing a best seller, too, and I can't get the swing of it, either. I've missed 45 times now."

And the therapist nodded lugubriously, "I started two best sellers, one fiction and one nonfiction, and never finished them."

"Gee," said I, "could you tell they were best sellers as soon as you started?"

"Sure," said he, with absolute conviction, and wandered off.

I thought of chasing after him to tell him that once I had begun treating patients superbly by means of physical therapy but had not the ambition to complete any cures. But I felt this might just confuse him, so I didn't.

20 December 1967

Oh boy, am I chagrined, and unworthily chagrined too.

Larry Ashmead [his editor at Doubleday] sent me a copy of a column on books that appeared in last Saturday's New York *Post.* One item in it goes as follows: " 'A fantastic sleeper,' says Simon & Schuster of their best-selling encyclopedia, 'The Way Things Work,' published Oct. 18. What woke it up, says S & S, was Isaac Asimov's review in the New York *Times* book section Nov. 19."

Larry was kidding me about creating a best seller for Simon & Schuster, but I am *chagrined.* If a review by me can make someone else's book a best seller, why don't I review one of my own major works and make that a best seller. Or why doesn't someone do for me what I do for them.

I don't enjoy the role of "kingmaker." I would rather be "king."

7 February 1979

You mustn't overestimate the magic of my name. Despite the fact that I have published 200 books, not one of them has been a best seller.

In 1982, Isaac finally made the best-seller lists with Foundation's Edge.

12 November 1982

My book continues on the best-seller lists and is in fourth place, nationwide. This is quite unbelievable and the fact that this has happened (for the first time) after 44 years of professional writing and 262 books qualifies me, I think, as an overnight success.

31 December 1982

Doubleday has stopped counting printings of *Foundation's Edge* at ten, so I don't know what the in-print total is, but the total sale up to Christmas is 225,000.

12 March 1983

Doubleday is suddenly aware of the potential of my novels and is quite determined that I must spend a major portion of my time on science fiction (after 25 years during which a major portion of my time was spent on nonfiction).

23 March 1983

Foundation's Edge is still on the best-seller list after 24 weeks, and I simply don't understand it.

28 October 1983

The Robots of Dawn is *not* getting onto the best-seller list, at least not yet. This has cast me into a deep depression, which shows how peculiar human beings are. For over 40 years, I never dreamed that any book of mine would be a best seller. Now, just because *one* of them made it, I am incredibly disappointed that they *all* don't. Ridiculous.

24 November 1983

The Robots of Dawn did get onto the best-seller lists and it is doing very well indeed. I feel much better.

Isaac enjoyed both reading and writing mysteries.

13 January 1972

I find mysteries entertaining.

5 February 1972

I like the process of solution—all clues exposed, all deduction possible and fair and for me to fail while Hercule Poirot succeeds.

8 August 1972

The great influence on my mystery stories was Agatha Christie. When I write stories, I write Christie—in the mystery field, anyway. I am now doing a series of mystery stories for *Ellery Queen's Mystery Magazine*. I have so far written eight and sold eight, and to my way of thinking, they are pure Christie.

It's a lot easier to develop character in mysteries. You have all the space for it that you don't use up creating an alien society. Mysteries are much easier to write. I can write a good mystery short in six hours (complete from first word of the first draft to mailbox). I wouldn't guarantee a good science fiction short in less than six days. That alien society makes all the difference.

21 January 1974

The policeman in my book *A Whiff of Death is* very much like Colombo, but my mystery was written in 1958!

28 June 1985

I write mysteries merely because I enjoy doing so. But then I also enjoy writing science fiction, fantasy and nonfiction of all kinds. I just enjoy writing.

Did Isaac ever want to write a play?

27 April 1972

I have never considered writing a play, musical or otherwise. Play-writing is a specialized talent which I doubt that I possess, however great my success in other branches of literature. In addition, I doubt that my temperament is such that I can endure interaction with actors, directors and producers over a long period. I am too accustomed to being my own master in my writing, and the habit of autocracy is a difficult one to drop.

When Isaac finished one of his major nonfiction books, it was time to create an index. Using 3 × 5 index cards, Isaac would sit on the floor and spend days preparing it. He loved doing indexes. But they were a lot of work.

12 April 1967

I always do the indexes myself. Whenever I am talked into letting anyone other than myself do the index, I am always bitterly sorry. I'm the best and fastest indexer in the world. Well, anyway, the most conceited.

26 May 1970

I'm index-carding *Troilus and Cressida,* and I wish I hadn't mentioned so many different people. When writing a book and name-dropping all over the place, I never think of what it will mean indexing. Each time, I swear I'll never do it again, and each time I just have to. There's always this wild desire to make the book *perfect.*

10 July 1989

I've just finished a 6,000-item index for a history of science I wrote. (These things make me only about one-fiftieth of the money a novel would earn, but it makes me 50 times as happy to do it. So it evens out.) In any case, I spent ten days on the index and had time for nothing else.

One of Isaac's biggest fans was—Isaac.

25 February 1966

I'm crazy about my own writing, which is most immodest of me, but helps me write a lot and make a decent living.

5 March 1983

I like my own writing—another secret to prolificity, since I can't wait till I write something so I can *read* it.

10 September 1988

I reread "The Lost Dog," and I ended up with tears rolling down my cheeks. I almost never write an emotional story because they always tear me up.

15 February 1989

Please be aware that I am the world's worst proofreader because I cannot make myself look at individual words. Try as I might, I read a phrase at a time. Besides which, it is just about impossible to proofread when my eyes are dripping tears as they always do when I am trapped into rereading "The Ugly Little Boy."

16 May 1989

I did a 400,000-word (maybe more) history of science, which is like no other in existence, I assure you. I loved it, enjoyed it, neglected my most recent novel to finish it.

21 March 1989

I have reached an age and have achieved a reputation that makes it possible for me to write stories entirely for my own amusement. Why not? Since everything I write is published, why not pamper myself?

3

Quantity

While Isaac was most proud of the quality and variety of his books, he was widely known for the quantity of books he had written.

8 November 1961

Last night I attended a banquet. The fellow at my right—an engaging person—caught a reference to a book of mine, and he smiled kindly and said, "Oh, you've written a book?" And I said, "Well, not *a* book." And he said, *"Two* books. Well!" And I said cheerfully, "You're getting warm—42 books." There was the same horrified pause one experiences when one says, "I have 13 children." Then he said, "42!!!!!" And I said, "Well, so far."

30 April 1966

I complained to Houghton Mifflin that a reviewer in discussing my book *The Neutrino* (my 70th) spoke of my "factory production." I said that made it sound as though I had batteries of writers slaving over typewriters with myself walking down the aisles, looking over shoulders and occasionally saying, "I'd put a comma in there if I were you." And it's not so. I'm completely a one-man operation.

I recently was at a panel discussion on writing at Boston College. After my two fellow panelists had filled the air with good advice on how to go about writing and being so discouraging

("You must rewrite 50 times"; "You can't make a living out of writing"; "Such-and-such, a great writer, was so discouraged he almost decided never to publish"), I thought the audience had enough of the blues.

I decided to make them laugh and also show them that it was just barely possible for writing to be fun and easy and a great delight—if they found out what they could do and did it. It went over very well, with everyone laughing and cheering up no end.

The biggest laugh I got was when I said, "For me, writing is as easy and natural as breathing . . ." (ruminative pause) "except once when I had bronchitis. Then, writing was easier and more natural than breathing."

12 April 1967

The Roman Empire is my 80th book, and Boston University library is going to throw a shindig in its honor. I tried to beg off, but they insisted. I will have to show up at a fancy cocktail party and try to be diplomatic to reviewers and publishers and think up clever answers for the inevitable: "How do you manage to write so many books?" I've been asked that a hundred thousand times, and the true answer, "I work like a dog," is not usable because it is so unglamorous. Oh well.

20 October 1969

Don't let the quantity impress you. As a matter of fact, I'm a little bit depressed about the whole thing, for quantity has its disadvantages.

I'm a little tired of being treated as a writing machine. A recent interview that appeared in the New York *Times* has set me to thinking I ought to change my image. Except that I *am* a writing machine. So what can I do?

21 November 1969

I have just finished an article entitled "How to Write a Hundred Books Without Really Trying." It was commissioned by someone who hopes it will prove inspirational to the readers. I suspect he thought I would be giving little hints à la *Reader's Digest* for how to improve yourself. (You know, if you memorize two new words every time you wait for the elevator, you will develop a giant vocabulary. Or, if you practice saying kind things to your wife while you shave, you will save your marriage. Or, if you remember to kiss your typewriter before sitting down at it, you will write a hundred books.)

Well, I can't give them that kind of crap. So after I thought it out carefully, I decided that what I had was the faculty for instant recall, which in turn gave rise to a sense of self-assurance that was transferred to my writing. I also had a deprived childhood which left me no outlet for a vigorous mind but the public library. I also happen to like the act of typing. And I also happen to have something mysterious called writing talent. Which means that if anyone kisses the typewriter before sitting down and happens to have writing talent, instant recall, a liking for the act of typing and a long history of omnivorous reading, he too can write a hundred books.

20 December 1975

The 169 books aren't so much. I just don't do anything else. I write on every subject, science fiction, mysteries, every branch of science, history, literature, humor and so on. And for all age groups—children, adults, textbooks. So there's always something to do.

13 May 1976

It often happens that someone is saddled with some peculiarity of his life and can't shake it. I'm sure Tommy Manville was frequently asked, "What number is your present wife?"

Well, I cannot escape the question: "How many books have you published?" God knows, I hold no record. The late John Creasy published over 500, but of course, they were all mysteries. And my own, a far smaller number, are in every field under the sun. Maybe that makes a difference.

If I keep up my present rate till I am 100 years old, I will catch up with Creasy; otherwise not.

5 February 1981

Some of my books are short, but that is not the secret of my large number, for I have written a 500,000-word *Asimov's Guide to Science,* a 500,000-word *Asimov's Biographical Encyclopedia of Science and Technology* and a 640,000-word two-volume autobiography.

16 July 1983

I know that 99 percent of the population of the Earth have never read one of my over 16,000,000 words in print. I am not ashamed of that. I am, if anything, ashamed that there are probably more people who have read at least one of my words than there are people who have read at least one of Plato's words.

22 September 1983

The worst of writing and publishing 20,000,000 words is that I often don't recognize quotations attributed to me.

But Isaac didn't like being called a workaholic.

19 January 1978

The concept of workaholic offends me. Eisenhower and Bing Crosby spent every minute they could hungrily and blindly playing golf. Crosby even died on the golf course. Why aren't they golfaholics? Some people love to travel and travel every chance they get. Why aren't they travelaholics? Well, I write for the same reason other people play golf or tennis or go fishing or sleep late —because I feel like. Why should I be tabbed with an opprobrious name?

To Houghton Mifflin, he wrote:

26 September 1983

I am sorry my book *Words of Science* is going out of print. It was my first Houghton Mifflin book and was published in 1959. Staying in print for 24 years is not bad for a book of this type.

How many copies of the book were sold altogether in those 24 years? [Houghton Mifflin's reply: 146,589 books.]

When Walker & Company was planning publicity for one of his books, he wrote its promotion department:

21 September 1988

Janet and I, between us, have done 62 books for Walker, the large majority for youngsters. In addition, there are three more in press, two in preparation and many others in the future for as long as we live. I think we have done more books for Walker than any other writer.

So it is quite enough, in our view, if you simply print our names in large letters and say what wonderful people we are.

Isaac's short story, "The Fun They Had" was his most reprinted story.

9 April 1966

The story was first published in 1951. I wrote it as a favor for a personal friend who paid me the magnificent sum of $10 for it. My agent (I had one very briefly at the time) yelled and yelled at me for doing favors for very little money. He was going to *show* me how to make money by being hard-hearted and businesslike.

So I got rid of the agent. I wasn't that interested in money. And what has happened? "The Fun They Had" is by far my most popular story. It has been reprinted, one way or another, at least 18 times that I know of, and it has made me hundreds of dollars.

I'm not sure what the moral is.

That personal friend was Russ Winterbotham, with whom he corresponded regularly in the late 1930s and early 1940s. In 1971, just months before Winterbotham died, Isaac wrote him:

21 January 1971

I've just marked the 40th appearance of "The Fun They Had." Or at least, put it this way. I have 40 different books, magazines, newspaper tear sheets that contain it—including 19 anthologies, seven magazines, a number of foreign translations (including the Hebrew) and so on.

I don't know how much money that little story I wrote for you for $10 has made me over the years, but I estimate not less than $1,500. Who would have thought it back in 1951. Certainly not I.

28 October 1985

"The Fun They Had" has appeared in magazines, newspapers, collections and anthologies over 60 times. I have been paid for it every single time, and it has literally earned me several thousand dollars.

What did Isaac think about vacations?

20 July 1965

You have a vacation when you do something you like better than your work. But there isn't anything I like better than my work. My vacation therefore exists all year long—except when I am forced to go away.

But for a number of summers in the 1970s and 1980s, Isaac and Janet took part in annual seminars at the Rensselaerville Institute in upstate New York. Was it a vacation for Isaac?

29 July 1976

Here we are 70 or 80 of us, surrounded by beautiful countryside in a vacation atmosphere far removed from the cares of everyday life. And how do we spend our time?

It seems to me that most people would ask nothing better than to loll in the sun or to play tennis or to swim, disconnecting their minds and allowing themselves to enter some trance-like state of unreality.

And what do we do? With all the accoutrements of vacation about us, we sit in little rooms and argue out the problems of the world, even some problems the world does not yet face. We propose solutions and warn of dangers and argue about the paths of survival. Then in the auditorium, we present our results and listen to the comments of others.

We do this for four days where others might simply relax and consider us mad that we do not do the same. But we exercise our minds instead and sharpen our thoughts against the thoughts of others and bounce the ball of our words from court to court and immerse ourselves in the heady sea of controversy.

And *we* are the lucky ones.

But as much as he enjoyed the Rensselaerville Institute, it did cause him a problem.

25 August 1973

I've just had a four-day "vacation" in upstate New York running a seminar, and I'm about to have a five-day "vacation" in Toronto being a featured speaker at the World Science Fiction Convention. When do they expect me to do my real work?

Despite getting older, his views on vacations never changed.

7 July 1983

I've never had a voluntary vacation in my life.

22 April 1985

Janet and I just spent three delightful days in Williamsburg, Virginia, but, as usual, I managed to sneak in some writing time and wrote a story. (I can only write fiction when I'm away from my reference library, but fortunately I'm a switch hitter—and can write fiction and nonfiction with equal satisfaction.)

21 July 1985

I was away on one of the mini-vacations I am forced into during the summer months for the crime of having married a normal woman with whom I am deeply in love. (The fact that my whole year, *except* for my "vacations," is a vacation, is considered irrelevant.)

7 July 1988

I am being forced to take a week off for a Bermuda cruise. (But don't worry, I'm sneaking a pen and paper aboard and when no one's looking, I will write.)

How did Isaac celebrate holidays?

25 December 1982

Here it is Christmas Day and what on Earth should a compulsive writer do on this day of great hilarity and solemn religious thought?
   Write an essay, of course!

30 December 1982

I routinely make a lunch date on Yom Kippur. I don't intend to qualify for *any* heaven.

15 February 1987

I hate this system of having holidays come on Monday so that non-working bums can have three-day weekends. It means that I am forever running into Mondays when there is no mail pickup. I work seven days a week and take no holidays—like you're supposed to. If America wants to be "competitive," we had all better do it, grumble, grumble.

3 March 1987

Every day I work is a holiday for me so that I have 365 days of holiday each year (366 in leap years). I know it's un-American, perhaps, to love one's work, but I can't help it.

In addition to all of his books and letters, Isaac also wrote an unknown number of introductions to other people's books.

6 July 1985

Between the odd idea of many that an introduction by me works magic and my own inability to resist the requests of friends, I have probably written more introductions to more books than any writer in history.

When you write almost 500 books, you write almost 500 dedications. Here's one dedication that caused him a problem.

31 May 1966

What with all my books, I have to reach some for dedications. So I dedicated my book *The Roman Republic* to my two editors in the Houghton Mifflin juvenile department—Mary K. Harmon and Walter Lorraine. I dedicated it: "To Mary K. and Walter L., for increasing the pleasantness of life." This, I rather thought, was nice.

However, Walter Lorraine, who is the head of the department, decided he wasn't worth a dedication. So, without telling either myself or Mary K., he crossed out his name. When I received my first copy of the book, I found to my horror that the dedication read, "To Mary K., for increasing the pleasantness of life."

Who can possibly read that and not assume the book is dedicated to my mistress? This is going to make explanations necessary, and the truth sounds so damned phony.

Not only are Isaac's books numerous, but they remain in print for a long time.

5 February 1981

I believe I hold the record for number of books in print at this time, whether you count the hard-cover only, soft-cover only, or both.

6 July 1989

All my fiction and most of my nonfiction is not truly out of print but continues to sell in one form or another. The relatively few books of mine that are truly out of print are in some cases also out of date and in other cases are of limited interest.

Isaac was conscientious. Sometimes, to a fault. He wrote this shortly after he and Janet moved to a new apartment in 1975.

24 March 1975

I am in the midst of moving, and this is the first letter I am writing on my typewriter in the new location. One of the things I carried over today because I wouldn't trust it to the movers was a new manuscript. So I dropped it in a puddle and had to retype parts. Serves me right.

It's obvious that Isaac wrote rapidly.

2 May 1967

I received a request for a quick book, *Galaxies,* and by today—ten days later—I had written the book, mailed it off, received the contract and the advance. I'm not likely ever to improve that record. The reason I did the book in one day was first, it was a *long* day, and second, I had the subject down cold, having written several books and articles on the matter.

22 January 1969

The other day, Walker & Company asked me to do a book called *Space A B C.* You know, "A is for Astronaut," "B is for Block-house" and so on, with about four lines of simple but accurate definition for each (two entries for each letter of the alphabet). I' sat down and did the whole thing in five hours, a new record for a book.

Isaac would squeeze in writing at every opportunity.

3 September 1974

Since I am a good boy and do what nice editors tell me to do, I wrote the food backgrounder on the train ride to Washington. (Longhand, yet.) I have just put it into typewritten form, and it is enclosed.

Then, since I am an overenthusiastic boy and jump the gun, I wrote a weather backgrounder (and a very good one, I thought) on the train ride *back* from Washington. I can submit it on one-day notice.

10 October 1976

I was sitting around this morning after reading the Sunday *Times,* and I had nothing to do other than the four books that are in progress and the six articles currently on order. Time hung heavy on my hands.

"What shall I do?" I thought. And then a brilliant idea came to me.

"I know," I said. "I'll write that piece for *TV Guide* on early theories of disease." So here it is.

Thanksgiving Day
1978

No reason I couldn't do the intro to *The Thirteen Crimes of Science Fiction* in plenty of time. Thanksgiving was my chance. While the Macy's parade is going on outside my window and before my family (brother, his wife and two children and my daughter and her boyfriend) arrive, I did it. And here it is.

13 October 1976

One of the reasons my typing is so poor is that I must aim for speed. I type 90 words a minute or more and cannot afford to stop for errors—unless meaning is subverted.

Would he want to write faster?

25 January 1977

If there were any way I could make my fingers type everything I want to type as fast as I would want to type it, I would do much more than I do. It seems ridiculous that my own overwhelming feeling is one of frustration at not being able to work faster and longer.

4

Typewriters, Word Processors and Computers

Isaac loved his typewriters. Only rarely did they let him down.

30 July 1969

Last weekend, my Selectric IBM typewriter went awry just after IBM service shut down for that weekend. It hit me at 5:30 P.M. With a great deal of self-congratulation, I pushed the typewriter aside and got my backup.

About a year ago, I had paid $500 to get a second identical typewriter with an identical typeface so that when repairs were needed on one, I could use the second. I went right on, scarcely missing a stroke.

Then on Saturday, my backup typewriter went awry, and you should have heard the howl that rent the heavens when *that* happened. I spent the whole Sunday with two, count them, *two,* superbly expensive typewriters out of whack.

Even on Monday I couldn't get a repairman till 1 P.M. At 10 A.M., the doorbell rang and I ran down, expecting the guy from IBM. It was a reporter from the New York *Times* come to interview me—and I said sourly, "Oh, it's *you.*"

25 November 1969

That's no way to speak to a *Times* reporter. I had lots of explaining to do. Fortunately, he was good-humored about it. The repairman came at 1 P.M., administered oxygen to me and repairs to the machines.

25 October 1979

I'm a loner and a semi-recluse, and the only way I can work is as a one-person organization. Well, two, counting my typewriter.

20 May 1980

My IBM Selectric II typewriter is used every day all day. Counting first draft, second draft, correspondence, I should judge I type about 150,000 words a month.

20 December 1980

You bet I personally use the typewriter. This is coming to you on my new Selectric III (albeit one with an old-fashioned ribbon and no correcting feature, because I can't afford to stop to correct. From me they get strikeovers).

27 October 1989

I have been using a word processor since 1981, but I have never abandoned my typewriter, on which I am writing this letter.

But his trusty typewriter needed a ribbon, and Isaac hated to change them even when the print got very light.

21 May 1988

Gee, I need a new typewriter ribbon. When I was a teenager, new ribbons cost 50 cents. And I never had 50 cents. So I had to keep using old ones as long as possible. Now they cost a lot more than 50 cents. But I have lots of money and can easily buy them by the dozen and change them frequently. Old habits die hard. I still have "poor" habits.

23 March 1990

The ribbons on both my typewriter and my printer are growing dim. It is sickening. They don't make ribbons for someone like me who types day and night every day.

7 April 1989

What people should invent is a permanent ribbon that never has to be changed. If we can put a man on the Moon. . . .

For all his reputation as a futurist, Isaac was slow in accepting the use of the word processor. He loved his typewriters.

24 June 1980

I use an electric razor and a color television. However, I hang back from word processing. I'm afraid it would cut down my production.

It would make revision and editing easier, and I would possibly fall prey to both. At the present moment, editing and revision are so difficult on an ordinary typewriter that I have learned to keep both to an absolute minimum. What appears in print is generally the first (or nearly first) careless rapture. If I begin to fall into the habit of polishing, I may lose in both quantity and quality.

17 June 1981

I have a word processor in the apartment and am trying to learn how to use it. It's slow going. At my age, learning new ways isn't so easy.

25 June 1981

The word processor slows me up. But I suppose with time, it may make things easier for me. I don't know. In the last analysis, my brain is still the thing that has to make up everything and arrange the words. No matter what the word processor does, it's only a tool and the same, philosophically, as a pencil.

An article that he wrote for SciQuest *magazine was the first that he created on the word processor. He sent it to the editor with this note:*

3 August 1981

I have been using my new word processor for a month now to correct and print items whose first drafts were produced on my typewriter. This is the FIRST piece that was actually composed on the word processor. I estimate I saved 15 minutes, but there was much more tension. I guess, though, that tension will subside with practice. Also, you've got it without typos.

Eventually, Isaac became a little more comfortable with the word processor.

9 March 1984

As for word processors, I use one. It is a Radio Shack TRS-80. I've been using it for nearly four years, and I am completely pleased with it. I only use it for short essays and for final copies of long essays and books. For the first drafts of the latter, and for correspondence and miscellaneous work, I still use my trusty typewriter.

20 June 1984

The computer hasn't affected my writing. It has speeded it up a little bit in some ways, and it turns out cleaner copy. But I still use my typewriter a lot (I'm using it for this letter), and I intend to continue using it.

It hasn't affected my research techniques or my style. There's no way it could possibly affect my productivity because *long ago* my rate of thinking became the bottleneck. (Thank heaven, my rate of thinking is very high.)

What about computers in general?

8 June 1978

Despite the fact that I write on computers and robots in science fiction and occasionally in science fact, my knowledge of the nuts and bolts of the subject is virtually nil.

22 October 1984

We will never be replaced by computers because they do things we're no good at (playing with figures and symbols deductively). And they can't do things we're good at (guessing, imagining, fantasying, intuiting and other inductive games). I can't conceivably program a computer to write my stories because I don't know how I write them myself.

Even the fax machine baffled him.

1 June 1990

I have trouble figuring out how to use the fax machine. (I am the world's biggest klutz in such things.) Fortunately, I *do* know how to drop an envelope in a mail slot.

Isaac was once asked if he thought computer disks would replace books. He replied:

19 January 1985

I have written about computers now for 30 years. But I don't think books will be eliminated in favor of computer disks. I can carry a book in my jacket pocket and read it while standing in a supermarket checkout line. Tell me what to do with a computer disk under such circumstances. Besides, anyone who has stared at a book for three hours and at a TV screen for three hours knows which is more relaxing.

5

Editors and Publishers

During his entire writing career, Isaac always got along well with his publishers.

                                                    11 February 1964
I have been told often enough, by a number of people, that it is foolish to allow sentiment to enter business arrangements and that mutual benefit is all that should count. However, I have deliberately avoided getting an agent just because the agent is bound to take this view and I would rather not.

I have found, with very few exceptions, that I have been treated kindly and generously by all the publishing houses with which I have been connected. I think that one of the reasons I have been so treated is that they have been able to rely on me to do the "right thing."

                                                       9 April 1977
I'm reminded of a parable told me by an ancient Jewish rabbi:

"The Holy One noted one day as he sat high on his throne in Heaven that writers were indeed a favored lot. They worked whatever hours they wished, on material of their own choosing, unhampered by the hurly-burly of the world.

"He felt (blessed be He!) that this was unfair to others of mankind. So he decided to balance the good things bestowed on writers with an equal quantity of evil. So he gave them publishers."

P.S. I am an exception. I love my publishers.

9 December 1990

I don't know anything about promotion or public relations because I have never interested myself in that. All I ask publishers to do is to publish any manuscript I had and to do so without argument. After that, it's theirs, and I don't care what happens to it.

To tell the truth, I don't even read my contracts. Usually, I can't even find them. I just periodically get checks and put them in the bank. I presume no one cheats me, for I think it is understood that if I ever get the idea that someone is, I don't write for them.

Isaac's books were translated into more than 40 languages. Occasionally, the royalties were in rubles or zlotys and the money could not be taken out of the country. To a Polish publisher, he wrote:

24 January 1985

I understand the difficulties under which you labor, and I am delighted to have the good people of Poland read my stories even without payment to me.

As for the bank account you have opened for me, it is useless. I do not travel, so that I am never likely to visit Poland and will have no use for airline or railroad tickets. It would please me if you take the money and use it for some kindly purpose. Buy meals for poor children or donate copies of the magazine to those who cannot afford to buy them or whatever your good heart tells you to do.

Please, however, do not take this as a precedent for other American writers. Some American writers *do* travel and might intend to visit Poland and might be able to use such money very well. And may the time come when all nations will be friends and all peoples will be one.

The first book that Isaac wrote was published by Doubleday. And Isaac and Doubleday had a special relationship throughout his writing career.

9 December 1968

Doubleday is "family" to me, and in 19 years of association, the firm and all its employees have always been the soul of consideration to me.

20 December 1969

My 20-year relationship with Doubleday has been a most happy one for me. Doubleday has always been extremely generous to me, and I would do anything, within reason, to cooperate with them.

To a publisher who asked him to write a science fiction novel, promising that it would be promoted heavily and be a best seller, Isaac wrote:

20 May 1975

Since our lunch conversation, I have been brooding during showers, automobile rides and sleepless portions of nights. It can't be done. At least I can't do it.

My publisher is Doubleday. I can't leave them. If it were a matter of a contract, that could be broken. But my heartstrings can't be.

11 June 1977

When people say, "Of course Doubleday is nice to you. You're a big author." My answer always is: "In 1949, when I was nothing at all, Doubleday was *just* as nice to me." It's a firm made up of wonderful people and always has been.

24 January 1981

I myself am, as usual, helplessly embroiled in more projects than I can do. Having two large books in preparation for Doubleday, Doubleday also says that for a person like me, two projects won't prevent me from doing a novel. When I say, "But I have two other large books for other publishers," their answer is a calm "We don't want to hear about other publishers."

I walked out muttering and said to the receptionist sadly, "A writer can't walk into a publisher without having contracts forced on him." She answered firmly, "Not *all* writers." She may be right.

29 August 1985

I have been loyal to Doubleday for 36 years, and from my point of view, they have been loyal to me. I can't do anything that would smack of disloyalty to them unless they gave me cause—which they never have. Just the possibility of making more money is *not* cause.

9 December 1990

I've been with Doubleday for 42 years and with Walker & Company for 20 years. In all that time, there have been no changes in their treatment of me. Doubleday is a huge conglomerate, and Walker & Company is a mom-and-pop affair. They both treat me exactly the same. I am also well treated by the 50-odd other publishers I have dealt with directly.

Isaac loved his editors.

24 September 1965

I *am* blessed with genial and cooperative editors. I am happy about that every minute of the day.

He especially loved longtime editor Larry Ashmead.

26 May 1971

Professionally, Larry is one of the brightest of the senior editors at Doubleday. Personally, he is one of the nicest and sweetest guys on the face of the Earth. Not many professional writers are willing to praise their editors, but Larry has been my editor for ten years, and in all those ten years, I have never found one 60-second interval in which I had anything whatever to complain of him.

8 August 1979

He is one of the gentlest, nicest and most good-natured people I have ever met. He is intelligent, hardworking, reliable and a man of his word. I could say a few other things but it would be much easier to run through the dictionary to pick up all the laudatory adjectives. If there's one that doesn't suit him, I haven't discovered it.

And here's how he felt about Jennifer Brehl, the last of his series of editors at Doubleday, in a letter to Jennifer's mother:

5 September 1985

I have a beautiful daughter (Robyn), who has made me happy all the days of her life. But if I didn't have her, I think that Jennifer would more nearly take her place than any other young woman I have ever met. She is such a *good* young lady (an old-fashioned expression, I fear) that I'm happy that you and your husband have had the chance to enjoy her existence and glad that my own daughter exists so that I don't have to feel the pain of envy.

To an editor who requested some changes, he wrote:

20 October 1974

I am delighted to make little changes at your request. You shouldn't sound so defensive. You are used to working with Rotten Writers, who write dumb in the first place and then object to changing. I am, on the other hand, a Nice Writer, who writes fast and good and makes changes on request.

27 November 1985

George Bernard Shaw (and certain s.f. writers, too) did not allow the change of a comma. But I'm an imperfectionist, and I know that my stuff isn't perfect to begin with. So why not let the editors do their job, too.

But he turned down many offers to be an editor. Here's one refusal.

13 May 1968

I cannot accept your offer of a post as consulting editor. I am so compulsive a writer that the thought of editing the books of others in fields which I would like to deal with on my own is, quite literally, a repulsive one.

I admire the editorial function enormously and consider it the most thankless job in the world. All successes are the credit of the author, and all failures the fault of the editor. The editor's help is ignored in successes and bitterly condemned in failures.

None of Isaac's books were ever rejected by a publisher, but on occasion a short story or an article was.

4 April 1966

A rejection of a story is not a rejection of the writer. It is no crime to be rejected or even a sin. Editors do not hate a writer when they reject a manuscript and do not thereafter plot the writer's destruction. Editors can be wrong. Frequently, what one editor rejects, another editor accepts. Or, a piece the author likes cannot be sold, while a piece the author does not like is accepted with rapture.

It is *unprofessional* for the workaday author to either like or dislike his own material. The writer just writes it. It is then up to editors, readers, critics—everyone in the world but the writer—to like or dislike it.

A story is *not* bad merely because it is not perfect. There are two rules here: (1) No story is perfect. (2) Lots of stories that aren't perfect are very good.

25 April 1966

Rejections don't *really* hurt after you stop bleeding, and even a rejection serves to introduce the writer's name to an editor, particularly if a rejected story is competently written.

22 December 1969

I got a rejection from *TV Guide* recently. This proves I'm human, I suppose, though I don't find that kind of proof an occasion for rejoicing.

18 October 1971

I am neither insulted nor disturbed by rejections. No matter how well I write, I don't always hit the mark. For another, rejected material may hit the mark elsewhere. An article rejected by *Cosmopolitan* was accepted by *Construction Man*. An article rejected by *Scanlan's Monthly,* which has since died, was expanded into a book which has sold over 20,000 copies.

8 January 1975

I had a science fiction story in last Sunday's *New York Times Magazine*. It was the first time they had ever published fiction. I'm glad that I was the one who broke the barrier. It was their idea. They came to me for a story, and I wrote one. On the other hand, *Ellery Queen* has just rejected another mystery story of mine. Win a few, lose a few.

17 May 1983

Being a free-lancer means that you accept the fact that the editor is an absolute despot as far as acceptance/rejection is concerned, and that from his decision, there is no appeal. Of course, in my personal case, it doesn't matter. Anything that is rejected can always be put into one or another of my collections. Nothing I have written and completed in 40 years has failed to see print one way or another. This is not to say that everything I write is worth printing, but it has all gotten past some editor or other. So you've got to blame them, not me.

11 January 1991

CBS has recently rejected a script that someone prepared from one of my Black Widower stories. The reason was that it was "too intelligent." If I must have a rejection, that is the kind of rejection I want.

From 1974 to 1987, he wrote a regular column for American Way *magazine. Here's how it started.*

28 August 1974

The editor called Monday to ask if I could have the first article for him by 3 September, and I said, "Oh my, ordinarily I would say certainly, but I have to attend the s.f. convention over Labor Day and I may not be able to."

So he said, all right, but he sounded so disappointed that I just pulled everything out of the typewriter and sat down and wrote the first article. (Only 750 words, after all. At 90 words a minute, it only takes 8⅓ minutes, plus 5 minutes revision, plus 8⅓ minutes final copy, right?)

Two hours after he called, I called him back to say the article was in the mail. The next day, he called to say he had gotten the article and it was *exactly* what he wanted. He wrote me a letter which said: "Our two telephone conversations today have given me an insight into how you have managed to write more than 150 books. Frankly, I'm flabbergasted to know that your first article is already in the mail. Really looking forward to it. Wish I had the good fortune to work with 100 Asimovs every day."

Isaac's books were published in virtually every language around the world. Sometimes he got royalties; sometimes not.

Iran

16 September 1988

Thank you very much for sending me the copies of six of my books on science for youngsters as you have translated them into Farsi. I have long been trying to introduce American children to the beauties and wonder of science. And it gives me pleasure to think that I will be helping Iranian children in the same way.

Hong Kong

1 May 1990

I am delighted that science fiction is flourishing in Hong Kong. I am pleased to appear in a language which is spoken by one-fourth of the world's population.

Korea

10 August 1985

I do not mind being ripped off in places like Korea. I have enough money, actually, and I would rather be read by millions of Koreans than have the money, if it came to one or the other. After all, since I don't believe in personal immortality, the only way I expect to have some version of such a thing is through my books.

China

27 January 1987

It is one of my great sorrows that I do not travel at all so that I will never see China with my own eyes. However, if my books see China, I will be satisfied.

22 April 1987

BUT THEY DON'T PAY ROYALTIES

There's nothing, I think, that's diviner
Than Asimov fans deep in China.
    The land is encumbered;
    A billion are numbered;
That's a readership surely not minor.

6

Limericks and Oddities

In the last 18 years of his life, Isaac wrote hundreds of limericks in books and almost as many to personal friends and even casual correspondents. Here's how it all started.

13 April 1982

The matter of my limerick books started in June of 1974. Until then, I had occasionally tried to toss off a limerick as all red-blooded, two-fisted Americans might, but I never paid any attention to them.

Then in the month mentioned above, my wife and I were returning from England on the *Queen Elizabeth 2,* and we found ourselves in the elegant Queen's Grill, where everyone was on so much their best behavior, I couldn't stand it. No one talked to anyone.

There I was staring out at the ocean and I finally said:

There was a young girl from Decatur
Eyes turned toward me. I smiled and went on:
Who went out to sea on a freighter
Attention was now painfully intense. I said:
She was screwed by the Master
An utter disaster

You could have heard a pin drop. And I finished with a flourish:

But the crew all made up for it later.

There was an explosion of laughter and you have no idea how much the atmosphere was improved thereafter. I was very pleased, since I had improvised the limerick on the spot. For the first time, I wrote one down and took pains not to lose it. I then proceeded to invent and write down others.

Starting in 1975, he began to write limericks to a number of his correspondents. He personalized the limericks by including the name of the recipient.

A fellow member of the high-IQ organization Mensa, Marvin Grosswirth, challenged him to come up with a rhyme for Grosswirth. He wrote:

29 April 1976

Said that aging Lothario, Grosswirth,
To a woman, "Just what is a toss worth?
How much time have we got?
Can I screw you a lot?
Will I get, after all this, my dough's worth?"

To a fan who expressed enjoyment at Isaac's limerick books:

7 June 1976

To her boudoir came young Sydney Gellis,
Having climbed in by way of the trellis.
He said, "This is a bore,
Some go in at the door;
And the ones who do that make me jealous."

To one of his magazine editors:

9 February 1977

There was a young woman named Neale,
Who, whenever she chooses to peel,
    Discloses a skin
    One would love to get in
For the sake of its wonderful feel.

To a woman from British Columbia who sent him a portrait of himself:

25 March 1977

When I think of divine M. L. Ash,
I would be in pursuit like a flash.
    But the distance, you see,
    From N.Y. to B.C.
Is much more than a hundred-yard dash.

Over the years, Isaac's prominence led him to be asked a number of odd questions.

What books does he give at Christmas?

1 November 1968

I try always to tell the truth, and in this case the truth is embarrassing. When I give a book as a gift, whether at Christmas or any other time, it is almost invariably one of my own.

Since I publish six to eight books a year, there is always an ample supply of books which the recipient has not yet read. However, I try to keep such book gifts to a minimum. In general, I prefer to have people buy my books.

Did he have any memories of a certain professor at Columbia University?

5 August 1969

I had one remembered contact with him. I had a lab course in physical chemistry and at one time was asked one question out of a number of possible questions and drew a complete blank. I got a zero.

I came to him afterward and said that the question I was asked was the *only* one of the alternatives I couldn't answer perfectly and that a mark of zero was not a true measure of the state of my knowledge.

He said, "The time will come when you will be asked a question, and it will be the *only* one of a number of alternatives which you *can* answer perfectly. You will then get a mark of 100 and that will not be a true measure of the state of your knowledge either. But you will not complain then, will you?"

Very much against my will, I saw the justice of that and subsided. I kept my zero.

Did he agree with Franz Kafka that upon death, all of one's papers should be destroyed unread?

4 November 1970

Easiest question in the world.

I would under no circumstances make Kafka's mad request, and if I were ever responsible for carrying out such a request, I would most certainly refuse—and without a qualm. Any creative work should be adequately paid for and the creative artist should receive all the money and adulation he deserves. But money or not, adulation or not, the work belongs to mankind.

Back in 1972, a series of New York radio ads featured the "gefilte fish maven." Isaac got a letter from a fan asking him whether he was the radio voice for that ad:

29 March 1972

No, alas, I am *not* the gefilte fish maven. But you have solved a problem that has been haunting me. I have been listening to those commercials with fascination, saying to myself: "Why does that fellow sound like such an intelligent man, so full of humor, so delightful? Why is his voice so resonant? Why does it call to something deep within me?" Now I know.

What was the oddest thing that ever happened to him at a cocktail party?

26 June 1974

I was once at a cocktail party with nothing in my hand, and a woman who was just a trifle the worse for wear looked at me disapprovingly and said, "What's the matter? Don't you drink?" I smiled and said I didn't.

She said, "I'll bet you don't smoke, either." I smiled and said I didn't.

She said, "Well, what the hell *do* you do?" And I said, "I screw a lot."

I was the hero of the party after that, but no woman offered to check the claim.

Would he be willing to be hypnotized?

22 December 1975

NEVER. UNDER NO CIRCUMSTANCES. FORGET IT.

7

The Business Side

Isaac had no agent or business manager. So he had the responsibility to negotiate payment for his writings and then make sure that he received the payment.

2 September 1958

Just got a letter from one of my publishers asking if they had paid me a $250 check they owed me half a year ago because they had no record of it. I laughed and laughed because I keep meticulous books, and no one gets out of paying me $250 checks. So I checked my meticulous books and found to my horror that they had meticulously not paid me. I considered offering to let them keep the money as punishment of myself for letting them do it, but thought better of it. So I contented myself with writing a letter demanding the money instantly.

22 January 1961

I am irritatingly rigid about money matters, chasing down a $5 discrepancy with all the enthusiasm and overemotion that I would chase down a $5,000 discrepancy. The only way I can justify this attitude to myself is by being certain that never, under any circumstances, do I come into possession of money that is not rightfully mine.

3 November 1961

I've been spending the whole morning going over my card files. No matter how I try to keep them up to date and in order, I must do this every once in a while and weed out unnecessary cards, bring necessary cards up to date and write letters to various anthologists and editors (asking them when they are going to pay me what they owe me because, according to my files, they promised last April to pay me in October and here it is November and when will this article appear and so on).

It is time-consuming, but it's got to be done. Besides, it contributes to my reputation as an efficient guy who never lets a deadline pass, either one where I owe somebody or somebody owes me. There are a number of editors who make special efforts to pay me on time, or even early, just because they know that if they're a day late, I'll be on the wire or a letter will be in the mail. And I can get away with it because I'm never late myself and am very reliable.

4 November 1966

I keep meticulous books. It is always with a pang of grief when a publisher sends me a check for which I don't have a little notation: "If check does not arrive on such and such a day, make threatening phone call."

This check caught me completely by surprise. I looked up the contract and discovered the check is not coming to me. I was much relieved, for I would rather be out a grand and a half than feel I was growing senile. Consequently, here is your check back.

21 April 1968

I enclose a check. According to my records, I previously received a check for $35 just ten months ago. I suspect this is a duplicate payment which you shouldn't make. So I am returning it. If I am wrong, let me know.

Since you undoubtedly get called often enough on any payment you don't make, or delay too long, I thought it would be a refreshing change for you to hear from an author who is *returning* a check because you have paid too much.

13 March 1970

You are quite right. I did receive the check. The fault, however, is not my memory, but the increasing complexity of my literary affairs. The trouble was that I received *two* checks almost simultaneously, *both* for "Nightfall" and *both* for anthologization by Bob Silverberg. (Sounds unbelievable.)

Try averaging a check every other day for 10 years or so and see if *you* don't mess up every once in a while. Not that I'm complaining!

Why didn't he use an agent?

9 March 1968

The few years (early on) in which I had an agent were unhappy ones for me because there was always someone between me and the editors. It was like kissing a girl through cellophane. (Ever tried that? Blech-h-h-h.)

Since Isaac made his living by writing and giving lectures, he thought he should be paid for his efforts.

9 March 1968

I was once asked by the editor of a very glossy and high-toned "non-profit" publication to write an article for him free of charge. He explained that the publication was non-profit and could not pay.

I asked him if he donated his editorial services free of charge; if the paper manufacturer donated the paper and the printer his labor; if the artists and designers were not paid. I said if he could assure me all this was so, I would write him an article free of charge. If it were not so, I failed to see why only writers, *only* writers, should be expected to work for nothing.

I never got an answer.

But there were some things Isaac did without charge.

18 September 1987

I have never charged for attending any science fiction convention, not even transportation. It was science fiction fandom that made me what I am and I never forget that.

18 November 1972

I never charge or in any way restrict any production of any writing of mine in Braille. Feel free, please, to convert anything of mine into as many Braille copies as you please. No charge, no restrictions.

Sometimes he was willing to delay receipt of payment.

31 May 1978

I am quite aware of the difficulties of starting a new magazine, and I also recognize that those writers who can afford it should be patient and in this way contribute to the establishment of a new market for themselves and for others. I can afford it, and I will be patient.

And sometimes large payments didn't matter to him.

11 April 1981

You take me aback with your offer of $20,000 for a single page. I can see no possible way in which I could accept such an unfairly large sum. I have in my lifetime frequently done work for little or nothing when the work itself, or the cause for which it is done, pleases me. Nevertheless, to take *more* than the work is worth is impermissible.

If I were to do a one-page introduction for you, I would not wish to accept more than $1 a word—say, $1,000 for a thousand words.

9 July 1990

After I had agreed to give the talk, they told me it was formal and I would have to wear a tux, which I hate. Then they changed the times on me and finally told me I would have to sit through dinner and business and not get to talk till 11 P.M.

I refused flatly. I said that an "after-dinner" talk had been set for 9 P.M. to begin with and I would hold them to that or I would cancel. They wouldn't agree. So I canceled. It was a $20,000 deal, but I've reached the stage in age, health and finances where I can afford to stand on principle.

While Isaac was extremely knowledgeable in a variety of topics, there was at least one area of ignorance.

11 June 1967

We all have our hang-ups, and mine is in the matter of investment.

I come from a non-investing family and have a non-investing bent. I put money in the savings bank. Once, when people yelled at me long enough, I gave some of it to someone to invest for me. He promptly lost most of what I gave him.

I don't have the knack. In fact, if I invest in a company, it will go broke. But if I don't invest in it, it will make millions.

13 May 1971

Financial statements are like poker hands to me. I can't make them out. I'd say Greek, but I can make out Greek.

10 May 1982

I am, psychologically, a poor man as I was, actually, until middle age. I don't wish to spend any time at all figuring out what to do with money. I put it in the bank, and I give it to a broker to buy bonds with. I don't want ever to devote one minute to *think* about it.

2 November 1987

The stock market crash didn't affect me at all. Not a scratch because I had no money in the stock market. (I remember 1929.)

Isaac did not mind paying taxes—as long as the money was being used for good purposes and the system was administered fairly.

5 April 1966

Uncle Sam takes 40 percent of my income, but he's welcome to it. He provides me with a nice country in exchange. If he could only figure out some way to stop with the Vietnam thing and put it all into the war on poverty, into unpolluting the environment and beautifying and conserving the countryside—he could have 50 percent.

5 January 1976

Many Americans have the major share of their taxes withdrawn from their pay even before they see that pay. It is called "withholding tax," and the government can't do without it. If people were required to save enough money to pay their taxes at the end of the year, most of them wouldn't do so and the country would go broke.

I can afford to hire lawyers and accountants to engage in an annual wrestling match with the government to see how little I can pay and yet stay out of jail. Personally, I hate that. I find it demeaning. I would rather have my fair share taken at once and without argument, provided it was true of every other American as well.

I don't want governmental waste and tax abuse, but most of that comes about because individual officials and individual Americans try to gimmick the system for personal gain. I look forward to the day (if it ever comes) when a rigid and unbendable computerization will defy gimmicking and will therefore make dishonesty impossible.

There were some parts of the business of writing that Isaac didn't appreciate.

9 November 1989

I routinely sign contracts without reading them. Always have. I just make it plain to the publishers that the day I feel ill-treated, they will never hear from me again. They are careful not to make me feel ill-treated.

Isaac was pleased to be a free-lance writer.

13 April 1969

I am a free-lance writer which, as far as I am concerned, is the proudest title a man can have and one of the few professions that can lay claim to true independence.

But he conceded that it was a tough business.

24 January 1984

For every writer who makes a good living, there are 50 who simply make a little spare change and 5,000 who go nowhere at all. And there's simply nothing anyone can do about it.

3 March 1986

At least 95 percent of all *successful* writers (who sell books) do not make a living at it. Then why should anyone write?

As nearly as I can make out, people write because they are impelled to, because it gives them pleasure. It's like playing bridge or chess or golf, or going hiking or skiing. You don't make a living in by far the majority of cases. You do it because you want to.

In 1981, the New York Times *published an article about free- lance writing carrying the headline "Average U.S. Author Found to Earn Less Than $5,000 a Year from Writing." A friend sent the headline to Isaac and got this reply:*

17 June 1981

When I saw that headline in the New York *Times,* I rushed into Janet's study and shouted, "We are wiped out! We are wiped out!" Fortunately, she reminded me that I am not average. I hate to tell you how few days it takes for me to reach the average.

8

Prominent People

Over the years, Isaac developed contacts with a number of prominent people.

He had a 30-year correspondence with Nobel Prize winner Linus Pauling. Pauling read Isaac's science articles in Fantasy & Science Fiction *magazine regularly and wrote Isaac whenever he found an error. No writer could ever ask for a more prestigious "editor."*

Here are some excerpts from their letters.

From Pauling to Isaac:

3 June 1963

I was pleased to learn from the July issue of *Fantasy & Science Fiction* that you have included me among the 72 scientists whom you call great.

I looked through the list to see how many of the 72 are still alive, and I found four. This is why I am writing to you. You have indicated one of the four as having died in 1960. The man about whom you have made a mistake is Louis de Broglie. He is still alive. It was his brother Maurice who died in 1960.

From Isaac to Pauling:

11 June 1963

It was a completely unexpected delight to hear from you. Somehow it had never occurred to me that any of the subjects of my article "The Isaac Winners" might see it. But I'm glad you did. At least, it makes quite public my sincere belief that you are one of the four greatest living scientists.

I am quite embarrassed at having mistakenly killed poor de Broglie, and I can assure you I have unkilled him. It was the result of a too hasty reference to my Webster's Biographical Dictionary.

Oddly enough, I have avoided the error elsewhere. I have just completed a 400,000-word history of science in which, I assure you, you are appropriately represented. I checked at once on de Broglie, and I find that there I have kept him alive.

From Pauling to Isaac:

9 August 1978

I am writing now about your article in the September 1978 issue of *Fantasy & Science Fiction.* On page 123, you say that Amontons and Gay-Lussac observed that if a gas at the freezing point of water, $0°$ C, is decreased in temperature to $-1°$ C, then both the volume and the pressure of the gas will decline by $1/273$ of the temperature.

This statement and the rest of the discussion on this page are wrong. What you should have said is that if the volume is kept constant, the pressure decreases by $1/273$, and if the pressure is kept constant, the volume decreases by $1/273$. If for some reason the fractional decrease in volume were kept the same as the fractional decrease in pressure, each of them would be $1/546$.

I hope you are keeping as busy as ever.

From Isaac to Pauling:

21 August 1978

It is always with mingled pride and apprehension that I realize you have your eye on me.

I have been too long away from thermodynamics to remember to specify the variables that must be held constant, and I shall, of course, correct the matter when the essay appears in book form.

You remain my favorite scientist, and may you continue to flourish for seven more decades at least.

From Pauling to Isaac:

17 January 1989

Perhaps it gives me some pleasure to think that you are not infallible.

A little over six years ago, I noticed a mistake in one of your papers. I judge that I decided not to write to you about it, but on running across it again today I decided that I should do so. In *Fantasy & Science Fiction* for October 1982, you have an article in which, on page 135, you say, "To begin with, we must understand that a double bond is weaker than a single bond." [Pauling then describes Isaac's explanation.]

This is all wrong. By various criteria, a double bond is found to be about twice as strong as a single bond. All of this can be found in my book *The Nature of the Chemical Bond*. [Pauling then provides Isaac with a scientific explanation.]

From Isaac to Pauling:

20 January 1989

Chalk up one more mistake I'll never make again. (Unfortunately, I keep thinking up brand-new mistakes.) How fortunate I am to have you as a friend.

From Pauling to Isaac:

26 May 1989

I am pleased to report that I have found another place where you have slipped.

In *Fantasy & Science Fiction* for July 1989, page 102, you discuss the Doppler effect. You mention a train approaching you and say, "All the waves of compression are closer together than they should have been if the train had been standing still. That means that the wavelength is longer and you perceive the pitch as being lower." It should, of course, read, "That means that the wavelength is shorter and you perceive the pitch as being higher."

From Isaac to Pauling:

2 June 1989

My dear wife also caught that error in explaining the Doppler effect.

What happened was that the damned typesetter left out a line or two. I caught it in galleys and inserted the line or two and then the typesetter *ignored the correction.* I don't mind making a mistake and being corrected, but it *does* bother one to have someone else make the mistake and make you look like a fool. But it happens to all of us.

From Pauling to Isaac:

15 October 1991

For years I have admired you for your very broad knowledge of science and ability to present it in a remarkable way to a general group of readers, including your use of excellent English. It is on this last matter that I am now writing to you.

In the [May 1990 issue of *Fantasy & Science Fiction*], you refer to the "escapees," in this case people who are escaping from the cities. I join with authorities on the English language in deploring this usage. Fowler's *Modern English Usage,* second edition, 1965, says, "Escapee is a *superfluous word* that should not be allowed to usurp the place of *escaper.* One might as well call deserters *desertees.*"

Unfortunately, by October 1991, Isaac was no longer well enough to answer letters—even from Linus Pauling. There was no reply to this letter.

For more than 25 years, Isaac and Carl Sagan were good friends.

22 March 1966

Carl Sagan has read half through my book on the universe and has caught one fundamental error so far. In my rendering of Eddington's theories on stellar structure, I talked of radiation pressure. Apparently, I didn't have to. Fortunately, it just means correcting a sentence here and there.

But that's what I need Sagan for. Anything he doesn't catch

isn't there to be caught. If only he were a little faster about it. I said to him that I realized he was awfully busy, too, but then I added with my particular brand of ingenuousness, "But then, what is your work compared to mine?"

And he said, "You say it in such a way that I can take it as a joke. But you really mean it, don't you?"

So I made the best of it. I said, "Yes, I do."

A very smart fellow, that Sagan.

24 August 1966

Tomorrow I will visit Carl Sagan at the Harvard Observatory to see what resources the library has that may help me in possibly putting together a collection of material on the Moon. I asked Carl if there were any youngster at the observatory who wouldn't mind advising me in this respect and he answered, "Yes. Me."

I said I wouldn't think of bothering him for such an unimportant matter, and I really meant some graduate student who would find it fun, perhaps, and wouldn't mind helping out an aging s.f. writer. He said *he* would find it fun and wouldn't mind helping out an aging s.f. writer. So he will.

Here's a sampling of Isaac's letters to Sagan:

15 December 1973

I have just finished *The Cosmic Connection* and loved every word of it. You are my idea of a good writer because you have an unmannered style, and when I read what you write, I hear you talking.

One thing about the book made me nervous. It was entirely too obvious that you are smarter than I am. I hate that.

23 May 1976

I cannot conceive a situation in which I would find myself in disagreement with you on matters of science (and almost on anything else, either).

[Isaac then referred to a draft statement written by Sagan for the International Astronomical Union on astrology that said, in part, that astrology didn't treat humans as individuals and was a "doctrine akin to racism and sexism."]

I find your statement on astrology perfect. It is not as I would have written it. I would have written a savage, contemptuous denunciation. Yours is much better, of course.

15 June 1985

I just heard your talk on nuclear winter on Public Broadcasting. I am so proud of you, I almost burst with it. It was absolutely the sanest best speech I could imagine on the subject. It delighted me so much to find that I was on your side in every sentence of your talk.

And on the occasion of Sagan's marriage in 1980, Isaac wrote him a limerick:

Undated

Three loud cheers for Carl Sagan and Ann
Who today have become wife and man.
    Be your lives bright as day
    As the broad Milky Way
As the Big Bang with which all began.

Here are some letters about or with other prominent people:

From Isaac to actress Polly Bergen:

5 June 1957

To my delight, on yesterday's *To Tell the Truth,* you announced that you were a confirmed science fiction fan. Could it possibly be that in your reading of science fiction, you have read any of my books and/or stories? And if you have, can it possibly be that you enjoy them?

From Polly Bergen to Isaac:

June 21, 1957

Now it's my turn to write a fan letter . . . having recently finished *The End of Eternity.* It was really a provocative experience, and I was amazed at the skill with which you brought a multitude of fantastic situations to such a very successful and satisfying conclusion.

And after Isaac wrote her about an award he had received, Polly Bergen responded:

April 28, 1958

It is indeed good luck to be an Asimov fan. My congratulations for your "Emmy" from the Thomas Alva Edison Foundation. We obviously deserve each other!

From Isaac to Polly Bergen:

1 May 1958

Thank you for the inscribed picture you sent me (and for the delightful inscription). It is framed and on the wall of my writing room and—forgive me, please—but I use it for one-upmanship. If a friend comes in and says, "How come you have a picture of Polly Bergen on the wall," I say carelessly, "A fan of mine!" (Stifling a yawn, you see.) They sneer at me, walk over to the picture, read the inscription—and I just sweep up the pieces.

From Theodore H. White, the author of the Making of the President *series of books on presidential campaigns, to Isaac:*

October 3, 1961

I have just finished reading *The Wellsprings of Life*. I feel I should write and tell you that it is absolutely magnificent! How proud you should be of writing of such complications with such clarity.

From Isaac to White:

11 October 1961

It is very gracious of you to have taken the trouble to write and tell me so. While praise from any source is soothing to the auctorial ego, the considered opinion of a fellow writer of recognized competence has its particular value.

About authors John Updike and Max Shulman:

22 November 1966

I was to a party Friday night, and I met *John Updike*. Yes, indeed, *the* John Updike. I lost my breath for a second. Before I could say a word, he seized me by the lapel and said, "Listen, how do you write all those books, huh?" Then Sunday night at the dedication of Boston University's new library, I saw Max Shulman on the other side of the room. Since I love his writing, I rushed over and introduced myself. Before I could tell him how much I loved his books, he seized me by the lapel and said, "Listen, how do you write all those books, huh?"

For the first time, it dawned on me that I am known among the literary lights of our time—the regular writers, I mean—and that whereas ordinary people are astonished at all the books I write, writers are absolutely thunderstruck. They *know* how hard it is to write. I supposed it wouldn't matter so much if my books didn't get such good reviews and if they weren't on so many different subjects and both fiction and nonfiction.

Of course, I had no answer.

John Updike said something else to me. He said, "You seem to write popularizations on every subject. Tell me, doesn't it feel *funny* to know everything?" And ever since, I've been wondering about that.

From Isaac to Nobel Prize-winning scientist George Wald:

18 January 1967

It was a great and unexpected pleasure for me to have met you at the Faculty Club yesterday. Please accept my apologies for intruding upon the luncheon peace of your wife, your friends and yourself. But I could not resist taking the opportunity to shake hands with one I have admired for so many years.

From George Wald to Isaac:

January 25, 1967

I was delighted to meet you the other day, since I had heard so much of you and have been sending my students to your books. I'm told you are working on the Bible—an obsession of mine! I envy you your capacity to write so much so well.

About Albert Einstein:

8 May 1968

I was recalling my admissions interview at Columbia on April 10, 1935. I remember the day because on that same day, my father and I (he went with me) stopped off afterward at the Metropolitan Museum of Art. We saw Albert Einstein there and looked at him instead of at the art exhibits.

In 1969, the Smothers Brothers show was dropped from television and Isaac told a reporter that he would miss the show. Shortly afterward, Tom Smothers wrote to Isaac:

4 August 1969

The book section of the New York *Times* inferred that "you would miss our show." If inferences can be flattering, Dick and I are flattered. We have been fans of yours for years. If we can convince some daring network that the real threat is not music but rather science fiction, will you write the lyrics for us?

From Isaac to Tom Smothers:

13 August 1969

I assure you no *inference* was intended; nothing so weak. The reporter asked me my favorite show, and I told him. And I *do* miss you. I rather suspect that in losing your show, you found yourself faced with equal mixtures of malice and cowardice on the part of the little men who made the decision. I look forward to another day on which you will return to the medium you enrich.

Isaac himself was a fan of famed British humorist P. G. Wodehouse. Isaac wrote this letter to Wodehouse:

30 June 1972

You don't know me, of course; I'm just a minor scribbler. I am, however, a major reader of your books, having read at least 50 of them at least 50 times each. I quote you as others quote the Bible, and I must be depressed indeed not to cheer up just by thinking of odd passages from the Wodehouse canon.

But I won't waste your time. It is just that you are 90 years old and may decide some decade or other to transfer your field of activity and make Heaven a happier place for one and all. I am not likely to meet you there, being earmarked for the other place, so while we are still here on Earth together, may I thank you for more than you can possibly imagine.

One last word: It is as easy to write something that sounds like you as it is to make brass that looks like gold. I have done it myself. But what I do and what others do is brass. You remain gold.

From Woody Allen to Isaac:

Undated (about
late 1972)

I have co-authored a comedy that I will direct and star in very shortly. The comedy is basically a vehicle for me to be funny. (!?) The idea is a simple one but takes place in the future and much of it is science fictiony.

I am a complete novice in the field of science and science fiction, and I'm certain my story is full of holes and mistakes in areas where I have no knowledge or competence.

One who knows better could, for example, read the story and say, "You describe vehicles, but they'd never be that way. They'd be atomic-powered." Or, "Doorbells wouldn't ring 200 years from now." Or, "No one would catch a cold as your character does on page etc." You get the idea, I'm sure.

Naturally, I'm not Stanley Kubrick and am not looking for an obsessive dramatic accuracy because this is to be a broad comedy and I want to make artistic leaps conceptually rather than obey science to the letter. But I do want to know where I've painted a "wrong" view of the future, either underestimating or overestimating.

There was no letter from Isaac to Allen because, as it turns out, they had a luncheon meeting instead. Isaac described that meeting in the second volume of his autobiography, In Joy Still Felt.

I had lunch with Woody Allen and two of his friends on December 20, and when Allen asked me about the script, I told him flatly that it was terrific.

Did it need changes? he wanted to know. No, I said, it was perfect. Was I sure? Yes, of course I was sure. Allen protested that he knew nothing about science fiction. I said that if he refrained from telling people that, no one could possibly guess.

I was getting a little uneasy, though. After all, I was pushing as hard as I could to get Allen to do the picture and he would be putting the money into it. What if I were wrong?

Allen must have been getting uneasy, too. Did this guy, Asimov, really know what he was talking about? "How much science fiction have you written?" he asked.

Feeling a little nervous, I said, "Not much. Very little, actually. Perhaps 30 books of it altogether." Then, diffidently, I explained in a half whisper. "The other hundred books aren't science fiction."

Allen turned to his friends. "Did you hear him throw that line away? Did you hear him throw that line away?"

Apparently my skill at showmanship (was that what it was?) convinced him. He asked me to serve as technical director for the movie, which meant going to wherever it was he was shooting it. I refused and recommended Ben Bova instead (who took the job and did very well).

The movie, as it happened, was *Sleeper*.

Isaac didn't want any payment for his advice about Sleeper, *but Woody Allen said thanks in a way that was typical of Allen. Two years later, Allen wrote and directed the movie* Love and Death. *In the movie, Diane Keaton was telling Allen about her lovers:*

"Before Alexei, there was Alagorian. And before Alagorian, there was Asimov. . . ."

From Norman Cousins, the longtime editor of Saturday Review, *to Isaac:*

May 28, 1975

You are a master at making the world of science accessible, exciting and acceptable to the lay person.

From Isaac to Norman Cousins:

29 October 1976

I consider myself a member of the *Saturday Review* family. To be sure, I'm polygamous and have many families—of the literary variety, that is.

Isaac has conceded that he knew two persons who were more intelligent than he was—Carl Sagan and artificial intelligence expert Marvin Minsky. Here's a letter from Minsky to Isaac:

December 1, 1978

I'd like to say how much I appreciated the depth and clarity of your lecture on machine intelligence, its relation to the larger issues about the extent of the domain of science, and its complicated connection with the rest of evolution. I enjoyed your views about man's peculiar attitudes about his own finality. And I agree about the importance of expanding into space for the many motives of adventure, variety and (if man is indeed alone in the universe) not to keep all our precious eggs in one basket.

Your message was made most effective and influential, of course, through the skillfully disguised modesty and reasonableness of the presentation.

Isaac wrote this letter to famed architect Buckminster Fuller on the occasion of Fuller's 85th birthday:

22 February 1980

Eighty-five years? That's nothing. That's just quantity. The bristlecone pine can make 5,000. If we're talking quality, however, each one of your minutes is worth ten of the average person's and about a million of the bristlecone pine's.

So by average human standards, you are a minimum of 850 years old and that is something. By bristlecone pine standards, you are at least 85,000,000 years old and that is staggering. Make it a few million more!

Isaac wrote this about Kurt Vonnegut:

30 April 1982

I am proud to be a friend of Kurt Vonnegut. First, personally, because he's a nice guy and his wife took photos of me a dozen years ago and she's a nice gal. Second, professionally, because he has helped place science fiction (even though he doesn't call it that) on the best-seller lists.

On the occasion of purchasing "best seat sponsor" tickets to Shakespeare-in-Central Park, Isaac wrote a limerick to producer Joe Papp:

31 May 1982

A dramatic'ly savvy old chap
Who goes by the name of Joe Papp
　　Flutters here, yon and there,
　　From Shakespeare to Molière,
Letting G & S fill any gap.

Joe Papp responded to Isaac:

June 18, 1982

I have just discovered your letter asking for best seat sponsors and the accompanying limerick. Well, I have always held your verse in great esteem; and more importantly, have always considered *yours* the best seat in the house; so much so, I was tempted to offer you the coveted role of Bottom in our forthcoming *Dream.*

Stephen King wrote this to Isaac on the occasion of the publication of Isaac's 262nd book, which was eventually to become Isaac's first best seller:

September 9, 1982

Good luck with *Foundation's Edge*—not that you'll need it, you dog, you!

From Isaac to King:

14 September 1982

Foundation's Edge seems to show promise, but I am careful not to let my hopes get too high. After all, I get a best seller about as often as you don't get one.

From King to Isaac:

                                          May 29, 1987

I wanted to write a fan letter telling you how much I'm enjoying working my way through *The World's Greatest SF Stories*. I simply refuse to countenance your death until you have reached at least the year 2000.

From Isaac to King:

                                          25 June 1987

I imagine you never expected your life to be *this* crazy because how could anyone not be surprised at finding himself the most successful writer in the history of the world. And so good that you clearly *deserve* to be.

Isaac wrote about Jacqueline Kennedy Onassis in this letter to Vartan Gregorian on the occasion of Gregorian's retirement as president of the New York Public Library:

                                          15 December 1988

I like to think of myself as *not* being a publicity hound, yet even the haughtiest of us doesn't mind a pleasant visit into notoriety now and then.

   You made it possible for me a few years back to be a Literary Lion. That was nice, but something followed that was even nicer.

   On that occasion, I had an opportunity to speak to Mrs. Jacqueline Onassis, and a photo of my doing so appeared in the New York *Times* the next day, with the notation: "What is he saying?"

   What I was saying was, "Now I'll get my picture in the *Times*."

Opera star Robert Merrill once sang at the Dutch Treat Club, a luncheon club of which Isaac was president. Isaac then wrote Merrill:

                                          24 May 1989

There is something about you raising your voice in song that makes me ring like a bell inside. I tell you what. Fix it so that I can sing like that, and I'll let you write a couple of my books.

Isaac, to his distress, once shook the hand of German rocket scientist Wernher von Braun.

21 January 1985

It is astonishing to think of the chain of handshakes that will extend from you to surprising people in the world. Presumably even an ordinary person has shaken the hand that has shaken the hand that has shaken the hand—that has shaken the hand of Ronald Reagan. About four handshakes may well suffice to connect you with anyone in the world.

I once shook the hand (quite unwillingly and only because 800 people were watching at the time and I didn't want to make a scene) of the hand that shook Hitler's. It was the hand of Wernher von Braun.

9

Lectures

Isaac was one of the world's best speakers. He made thousands of speeches in the 40 years that he was lecturing. And he turned down thousands of invitations. His listeners enjoyed these speeches almost as much as his readers enjoyed his books. Here are some of his letters dealing with speeches.

22 September 1965

Recently a "paper" of mine was published in the *New York State Journal of Medicine*. Actually, I gave the paper under the misapprehension that I was delivering a "luncheon talk," and it wasn't until I was actually in the lecture hall that I realized a formal scientific discussion was expected of me. I improvised madly without any sort of visual aid and was told afterward by someone in the audience that it was the first time he had ever seen anyone try to describe the double helix of the DNA molecule with his hands. (Lucky I have Semitic ancestry.) Anyway, once the paper was published, I refused to buy reprints as I could not believe anyone would want the monstrosity. Hah!!! I have as of today received some 300 requests from universities, research institutions, departments of health all over the world—including from behind the Iron Curtain.

18 March 1967

The talk was a howling success. And I mean the howling literally, for the audience was very responsive and laughed uproariously.

When the fellow who introduced me (and who invited me) got up afterward to dismiss the gathering, he looked odd, for his eyes seemed wet. I had the horrible notion that this was not what he had planned and that I had delivered the completely wrong speech. So I turned to his wife in consternation and whispered, "Is something wrong?" And she whispered back, "He laughed so hard, he was crying."

18 March 1967

I am in an anomalous position. Viewed from the outside, I seem to be a typical member of the academic community whose duty it should be to address sections of the academic community for nominal fees. The trouble is that this is inaccurate. For some years now, I have felt that in actual fact, I am a professional entertainer with a highly specialized talent. I can give talks that are both respectably scientific and terribly funny, and I maintain that there isn't a scientist in America who can be as funny as I can, and not a comedian in America who can be as authentically scientific and that, for that, I should command high fees. The trouble is that most of the people who want to hear me talk can't pay high fees, and many of them misapprehend my role.

I *do* consider myself as having higher duties—but not to the academic community. My higher duties are to librarians and science fiction fans. I speak to library groups and librarian associations for fees of $50 or so. And for science fiction fans, I invariably talk for nothing.

30 March 1968

Don't ask me what the talk will be about. I give my talks without formal preparation. But don't let that bother you. I can be wakened at any hour of the night, put on a stage and asked for a talk. I'll deliver.

30 July 1968

Here's one of the nicest compliments I have received so far. I've just completed the second lecture in the Brandeis series. Opposite me is a young Brandeis professor who lectures on architecture, and of course, a number of ladies attend his course rather than mine. One of them stopped me yesterday and said in woebegone fashion, "Can you make your next lecture rotten?"

I looked surprised and she explained. It seems she is interested in architecture and has to attend the architecture lecture (which, I understand, is quite good). The only thing is, she explained, that so many people have been telling her how good my lectures are that she is very aggravated at having to miss them and can only attain peace of mind if I would make my lectures rotten.

8 October 1968

The audience reaction to my speech in New Hampshire was immense. Shortly before I gave the speech, I called Larry Ashmead, and he told me a joke to start my speech with:

It seems that a certain large organization had the chance to join a pension scheme of unlimited benefits that would have been operative only if every member of the organization joined; every member without exception. All signed up eagerly except for one of the janitors who stubbornly refused, saying he didn't understand the value of the scheme. All attempts to clarify the issue failed, and both management and labor were exasperated. Finally, the janitor was called into the office of the president with the head of the union at the side of the president himself. The president put a blank form on the desk, handed a pen to the janitor and said, "Sign or we throw you out of that fifth-floor window."

The janitor nodded and signed without saying a word. The president said, "Well, why the devil didn't you sign before?" And the janitor said, "Because you're the first person who explained it clearly to me."

So, after some thought, I told it to the audience and they howled!!! And when they were finished, I said to them sternly, "And I will now explain the year 2000 clearly to you." And they howled even more. After that, I was home safe.

15 January 1969

I gave a talk at a temple, and they wanted a title. I didn't feel like rattling them by explaining that I never know what I am going to talk about till I get up. So I said, "Oh, just make up a title, and I'll take care of it." So the title they made up is "Science and Faith, or Does the Man in the Moon Wear a Yarmulke?" Now, that's what I call a challenge to my ingenuity. Fortunately, I will meet it as I meet all such challenges.

19 May 1969

Have you ever heard of an extemporaneous commencement address? Have you ever imagined that anyone would have the infinite gall to get up in front of a graduating class, their parents and all the various faculty and officials and make up a talk on the spot? Well, that's the situation into which the State University of New York at Binghamton has now gotten itself into. I have never prepared an address no matter how stately the occasion or how impressive the audience.

20 May 1969

Last night I addressed a dental society. It was my intention to give a funny talk. I began humorously. They faced my humor with unsullied gravity. Now since I don't prepare my talks, I am guided entirely by audience reaction and not even consciously. I just automatically get more and more funny if the audience laughs or less and less funny if the audience doesn't laugh.

This time I got less and less funny and began an increasingly sober discussion of the possible usefulness of the Moon program ending with the hope that the Moon colony would teach mankind how to live an ecologically sane existence, which brought me into the problems of overpopulation and overpollution and I grew very intense indeed. In fact, I don't think I ever gave any talk quite so intense and (if I say so myself) so eloquent. I spoke rapidly and pulled no punches and everyone left shaken up and saying they wouldn't be able to sleep that night.

They should have laughed.

1 November 1969

The fact is that giving talks is purely a side issue with me. I lose money on the deal because I can make more sitting and writing. The only reason I talk is because of non-financial pleasure: listening to my own words, hearing the applause, having people come up afterward to talk and ask for autographs, etc.

9 May 1985

In my immodest way, I like to describe myself as the best off-the-cuff speaker in the world.

Once, about 20 years ago, a young lady said to me, "You're as funny as Bob Hope." And I said, "You mean that I'm as funny as all Bob Hope's writers put together."

Yes sir, my "natural humor" is exceeded only by immodesty.

19 January 1988

I will have neither manuscript nor notes, but don't worry. In 38 years and at least 1,000 talks, I have never fluffed one.

Sometimes people ask whether they can print the text of one of his speeches.

15 January 1970

I have gone over the enclosed transcript and made some minor changes in order to change my words from gibberish to something approaching English. It's amazing how foolishly we speak (even when one is as articulate as I am), yet manage to make ourselves understood. The rhythms of spoken English are altogether different from those of written English, of course, and I hate to see what I speak appear verbatim in written form.

Isaac did not like to give a lecture by telephone, by radio or by using any device that prevented him from seeing the audience.

15 May 1969

I must say that I have given lectures by telephone, and I'm not fond of it. I can't make direct contact with the audience and that results in a kind of loss—like making love while both you and the girl are wearing gloves and raincoats.

4 April 1970

I have decided against appearing on your radio series. I give talks as infrequently as I can and only under specific conditions—as little travel as possible, as high a fee as possible and as large an audience as possible. I need the excitement of a live audience. I don't like to have a microphone as my entire audience. The talk flops and I am unhappy.

Isaac's preference in making a speech was not to be introduced. He would just start speaking. He disliked long, dull introductions that might turn off an audience. He feared funny introductions that might overshadow his talk. And then there was the introduction by Phil Klass, a science fiction writer who used the pen name William Tenn.

22 April 1970

At Penn State, Phil Klass introduced me and gave me a long 15-minute introduction that was very funny indeed; so funny that I began to think grimly that my speech would flop. Fortunately, his last statement was: "Asimov, however, is not truly a Renaissance man. He has never sung *Rigoletto* at the Metropolitan Opera." So when I got up immediately after that, I waited for the applause to die down and began in a resonant tenor: *"Bella figlia dell'amore . . ."* It's the start of the quartet and absolutely brought the house down.

Here's another memorable occasion.

15 September 1988

I spoke at Carnegie-Mellon years ago and that speech was the *only one* in which having left the stage to applause, I was forced to return for a second bow, for the applause would not stop. Standing ovations I have had in plenty, but coming back for a second bow was unique to Carnegie-Mellon.

Over the years, the fees for his talks went up to what seemed astronomical levels. In 1956, his first payment for a talk was $10. But it wasn't until 1974 that he agreed to an exclusive arrangement with a lecture agent, Harry Walker, and began to receive high fees. In a letter to Walker, he described an early lecture that Walker had arranged:

7 November 1979

Back in 1957, I had agreed to give a talk to a group in Swampscott, Mass., for $25. It was the highest fee I had yet received. I had lunch with you on 15 October 1957, our first meeting, and you said you could get me lots of talks at fees of $100, of which you would take $30, leaving me $70. Even what I got under that arrangement would be nearly three times what I got on my own. I agreed and on October 17, you got me a talk for $100 in Fall River, Mass.

And the fees went up.

5 September 1981

I have been a public speaker now for 31 years, and my fees have risen steadily at a rate greater than that of inflation, and you can be sure there must be a good reason for that. My agents will tell you that they have yet to receive an unfavorable report on any talk I have given (quite the contrary) even though I average some 30 a year.

18 December 1981

Listening to me lecture would, indeed, be fun for anyone. Unfortunately, so many people have learned this that the law of supply and demand has driven up the price to ridiculous levels. Not only that, but I don't like to travel at *any* price. The result is that I have an invitation to come to Toronto in June for $10,000—and I'm hesitating.

31 March 1983

I've got to find a price that will let me stay at home.

27 August 1984

It becomes harder to persuade me to speak. I'm thinking of giving some deliberately bad talks to end the nuisance—except that I don't know how.

1 July 1987

It's a combination of reluctance to travel and age. A few months ago, I went to Williamsburg, seven hours by train each way and it took $20,000 to pry me loose. And I regretted it every roll of the train wheels.

10

Science Fiction—I

Isaac will probably be best remembered for his Foundation series. The original three books were written in the 1940s, and there was a gap of more than 30 years before he returned to them.

18 January 1964

I wrote the Foundation series between 1941 and 1949 and only managed to complete one-third of my planned structure. In that ten-year interval, however, I grew ten years older and outgrew the Foundation. The horrible truth is that my mind won't work in the old channels anymore.

During the 30 years between Foundation books, Isaac frequently was asked if he would ever write another.

2 July 1964

There is no possibility of another Foundation book.

13 December 1968

I wrote the Foundation stories as I write everything—with a carefree click-click of the typewriter. Since my typewriter, not I, is the master, that is one reason I am not writing much fiction. The typewriter prefers nonfiction and is currently engaged in a huge work on Shakespeare.

20 June 1965

I regret to have to say there will be no more such stories even though the series is, as you say, not finished.

23 September 1968

I'm afraid it is no longer possible to write any more of the Foundation stories. They were written when I was in my 20s, and that Asimov is gone forever, alas.

7 April 1976

I'm glad you like Foundation so, but I'm not sure I can continue it. Remember that the trilogy was written in the decade of my 20s, and while I am a more polished writer now, I may not have the vigor of youth any longer. Who knows.

Almost all of the declarations about "no more Foundation books" were written to fans on postcards. There may have been hundreds written to Foundation readers, but no record of them exists because Isaac did not make carbons of postcards. But there was a record of the final three letters mentioned above because the recipients returned copies to Isaac in 1982 when Foundation's Edge *was published—the fourth in the Foundation series.*

The fans had kept Isaac's postcards and reveled in the fact that he had finally changed his mind.

In late 1982, here's how Isaac described how the resumption of the Foundation series came about.

23 October 1982

In 1950, I had written the last word of the Foundation Trilogy and was, I thought, through with it. I had been working on little else for eight years and felt it was time to get on to other things— and that is exactly what I did.

It never occurred to me, however, that the stories would be put into trilogy form as three books, for they had appeared originally as items in the magazines, and that the Trilogy, as it now became known, would prove so astonishingly popular.

Over the years, the readers grew louder and louder in their demands for a continuation and, in time, so did Doubleday. I turned a deaf ear, for the longer the interval since the conclusion, the more reluctant I was to turn back. I had written the Trilogy in my 20s and I was growing older. What if I could no longer write in that style? I didn't want to disappoint my readers with an inadequate continuation. I did not want to be the ghost of the Isaac Asimov of the 1940s.

In January 1981, however, Doubleday lost patience at last. They presented me with a non-negotiable demand. I *must* write another Foundation novel or be forced to risk their serious displeasure. That was the stick. They also employed the carrot of offering me an advance just ten times the usual and insisting I take it on the spot, riding roughshod over my feeble protestations.

Having taken the money, however unwillingly, I was condemned to write the book. I reread the Trilogy in one concentrated sitting in order to absorb (or, rather, reabsorb) the milieu and the style—and got to work.

When the manuscript was finished, Doubleday emitted loud cries of glee, and my personal editor confided to me that he was now furious that I hadn't been writing science fiction all along because my judgment to the effect that I "no longer had it" was ludicrously wrong.

As soon as it was published in the United States, it hit the best-seller lists with a loud clang as ravenous readers of the Trilogy waited in line to get their copies.

Foundation's Edge (now the fourth book of a tetralogy) raced through four printings prior to publication, and a fifth by two weeks after publication, and I watched the whole thing in a dumbfounded state. It was my 262nd book, but my first best seller, and I wasn't sure what I was supposed to do about it.

If Isaac wasn't sure what he was supposed to do about it, Doubleday knew.

21 May 1982

Three days ago, Doubleday presented me with another contract and rather forcefully insisted I sign. Furthermore, they made it quite plain that they would do the same every time I finished a novel.

Isaac's famous short story "Nightfall" has been voted in polls of science fiction readers as their all-time favorite story. It is studied in college classrooms, and in 1987, a professor sent Isaac a paper written by two science students challenging its scientific premise. Isaac replied:

22 April 1987

Your young students are completely in the right. But I think, in my own defense, I must stress the fact that when I wrote the story (at a time when I was 20 years old), I knew its scientific shortcomings.

For one thing, in any system of six stars, there are three pairs of stars. One or more pairs may be close together, but each pair is very far from the other pairs. On any planet circling one of the stars, you will see one solar disk, and just possibly two, but never more than that. And of course, if you see even two, the planetary orbit is itself too unstable for life as we know it.

The point of the story, however, was not the astronomical situation but how people might react to something completely outside their experience. It was a psychological story, not an astronomic one.

"Nightfall" was even made into a movie, but not a good one.

15 October 1988

Some time ago, Doubleday sold the movie rights to my story "Nightfall" to some movie producers. They sold it in good faith. They control the subsidiary rights to my science fiction and have every right to make the sale.

The movie people then proceeded to make a movie out of the story—on a shoestring. They did not consult me on any of the details of the script. They never showed me the script. I had nothing to do with it.

Early this year, the movie opened in Tucson, Arizona, I believe. It has never, as far as I know, opened in New York. So I've never seen it. If it ever does open in New York or if it ever appears on television, I plan not to see it anyway.

The thing is I have received a number of letters from fans who are uniformly indignant over what they consider the poor quality of the picture, and some of them seem to show a tendency to blame me. (One actually wanted me to repay him for the money he spent on the tickets.)

May I take this opportunity of telling everyone within earshot that I am a victim, not a criminal, and that this is why I have never shown any interest in sales of my stories to movie people.

My books, good or bad, are *mine*. I take the credit or the blame. Any movies made from my books are *not* mine, and I want to be held guiltless if they are bad. (Or, I suppose, creditless in the case—ha, ha—where they are good.)

Isaac was famous for his robot stories.

27 March 1976

When I first started writing robot stories, I knew nothing at all about any research in computers or cybernetics, and it was to be many years before I met Norbert Wiener. My only knowledge of robots was what I had read (and rejected) in earlier science fiction stories. The three laws of robotics were, in their actual wording, John Campbell's, but he insisted he got them out of the first couple of robot stories.

25 July 1977

Back in 1939, I realized that robots were essentially lovable and were *not* clanking monsters. In less than 40 years, the world caught on, and we have robots such as those in *Star Wars*.

12 April 1978

The embarrassing fact is that despite the fact that I am regarded as the patron saint of robotics (the very word is my invention), I am not, and never have been, active in the field. I am a mere dreamer. The result is that I know nothing of their status and applications today.

25 February 1987

About "Robot Dreams." Byron Preiss [one of his publishers] put together a collection of my stories in order to have a nice illustrated limited edition, and he named it (out of his own head) *Robot Dreams*.

Then he said to me, "I would like an original story for the collection, and I would like to have the story entitled "Robot Dreams."

I said, "With that title, what would it be about?"

"Robot dreams," he said.

"What kind of dreams would a robot have?" I asked.

"You're the science fiction writer," he said. *"You* figure it out."

So I wrote "Robot Dreams."

Here is how Isaac came to write Fantastic Voyage.

23 April 1965

A paperback concern asked me to do the novelization of a forth-coming, very lavishly done science fiction movie. I should have said "no" at once. After all, I have no time for it, and I have no desire to do anything as derivative as novelizing someone else's screenplay. But the editor insisted on having lunch together, and I agreed.

With that instinct that marks the good editor, he sized me up at once as the type of person who will respond to inordinate flattery (or perhaps all writers do) and proceeded to flatter me in huge gobs till I was covered all over with meringue from head to toe. And he inveigled me into just looking at the screenplay. I did, and it is really an elaborate and, in many respects, well done (and certainly very expensive) s.f. movie. It would be a shame not to encourage a good one, but on the other hand I still have no time and there is a logical flaw in the ending big enough to drive a coach-and-four through. They can get away with it in a movie where everyone is concentrating on the special effects and paying no attention to the details, but I couldn't get away with it in a book. Even if the readers didn't notice, *I* would.

17 May 1965

I tried to turn it down, but the people at Bantam Books took turns telling me how great I was, and so impressed was I with their good taste that I finally agreed.

24 July 1965

Yesterday, I finished *Fantastic Voyage*. At the last minute, I had to insert half a page of gobbledygook to make up for a bad flaw in logic that I had not entirely corrected. In the movie, the minia-turized submarine (the size of a bacterium) runs out of air, so it plugs a snorkel into the lung and fills up. But how much air can a submarine the size of a bacterium hold? Enough for men who are much smaller than bacteria? But the individual oxygen molecules are so large in connection with the tiny, tiny submicroscopic lungs that they cannot be utilized.

Therefore, I had to make sure that our heroes could miniaturize the air before they pulled it in. I had to account for Brownian motion and for surface tension on a bacterial scale. I had to explain how a microscopic retina could absorb ordinary light waves and a microscopic eardrum could pick up ordinary sound and so on. Oh boy.

8 January 1966

I tried to sell the serialization of *Fantastic Voyage* to *Fantasy & Science Fiction* for $1,000, which is what I felt was fair payment for *F&SF*. But the guy who owns the story refused to allow it, to my ill-repressed fury, even though I was willing to let him have all the money. He said it wasn't enough, and I said it was fine by s.f. standards.

So now he has taken it and sold it for serialization in *The Saturday Evening Post* next month, and my share alone will be $2,000. And God only knows how much he's getting. (Who the hell would ever have thought the *Post* would be interested?)

20 September 1966

I did not do *Fantastic Voyage* for the money since I received a flat sum of $5,000 plus some additional money from *The Saturday Evening Post* and a very small share of the hard-cover royalties. I'm not complaining. It was just an adaptation.

I did it (a) because of the challenge, I had never novelized a movie script before; (b) because of the chance to use my biochemistry; and (c) because I suspected the movie would be a smash hit. I also did it because it was eight years since I had published a science fiction novel, and I wanted very much to get my name on an s.f. book again even if it was derivative. You don't *know* how hungry a guy can get for s.f.

9 June 1970

Just picked up a copy of *Fantastic Voyage* delivered to my local newsstand. It is the *18th printing* in four years—but I don't get a cent. I had a flat sum to begin with and that's it. Well, I copied it off the movie script, so creativity was minimal and I'm not complaining. But how many other movie-copied novels are still around after four years and in the 18th printing. I must have done more than merely copy. Oh well.

23 November 1973

Fantastic Voyage has done far better than anyone could possibly have expected at the time. After all, 24 printings so far and no sign of an end.

The time eventually came that Isaac wanted to do his own version of Fantastic Voyage.

26 May 1987

In about four months, Doubleday is publishing *Fantastic Voyage II,* which is another version of the plot. This one, however, is all mine, is twice as long and is ten times as good (in my opinion).

Isaac was known for not putting sexual episodes in his science fiction stories.

14 July 1967

Although I engage in sex with enthusiasm (you'll have to take my word for that) and although I carry on a constant ribald flirtation with every girl I meet (you can check that with any publisher's office I frequent, and they are many), I am terribly embarrassed at sexual episodes in books and movies and avoid such things. It is not the sex that embarrasses me, but the cheap treatment of something I consider of awesome and terribly personal worth.

18 May 1973

I came across a letter in which the writer says, "I can't think of an Asimov book where the addition of sexual scenes would help the plot any."

So help me Hari Seldon, I never really thought I'd hear anyone say something as simply factual as that.

It is nice that someone sees I omit sex not because I am a prude, but because the kind of stories I write don't require it. To insert sex when the story does not require it does not help the story. It may help the sales, I suppose, but I take care of that end of it by inserting my name on the title page.

But he did write a "sex" book entitled The Sensuous Dirty Old Man *under the pseudonym "Dr. A."*

19 July 1971

The purpose of the book is to satirize the sexual how-to books now flooding the market. It was my purpose to write a book which was ribald but which did not have a single vulgar word or action in it. It took considerable skill to do this and to do it in a very funny fashion. In my opinion, I succeeded, and I will offer my favorite sentence from the book.

Describing the new summer fashion of wearing a sheer blouse without brassiere, I said: "At a time when President Nixon was making one point very, very clear, the average young girl on the streets of New York was doing exactly twice as well."

With regard to "words at work," the double meaning of the word "point" with respect to an argument and to a physical object is used here magnificently. (Thank goodness, I lack any trace of that unpleasant quality known as "false modesty.")

And there was a significant sexual episode in his book The Gods Themselves.

10 October 1972

When I finished the first part of *The Gods Themselves* (as an independent novelette with no intention of doing more at the time), Doubleday urged me to make a novel of it and showed a copy to a paperback editor while I was thinking. I was told the paperback editor said, "Couldn't he put sex into it?" And Doubleday said, austerely, "Of course not. Asimov never does."

So I did. I put sex into the second part. It is all sex and, I think, sex seriously and decently handled as an integral part of the plot and with no holds barred. It just happened to be extraterrestrial sex.

Was it hard for Isaac to think of all those science fiction plots?

21 January 1968

I have for many years been half amused, half exasperated by shlocks who write me letters saying, "I have a wonderful idea for a science fiction story which I can give you if you will write it up.

Then we can split 50-50." I always write back and say, "I have a better idea. I'll give you a wonderful idea for a science fiction story. You write it up, and we'll split 50-50." My feeling, you see, is that ideas are very easy, and writing is very hard.

4 June 1971

I think of an idea. Then, I think of a problem and a resolution arising from the idea. Then, I think of a beginning. Then I write and make it up as I go along. I never try to look further ahead than the next incident.

16 May 1974

It is almost impossible to think of something no one has thought of before, but it is always possible to add different frills.

22 February 1977

The idea is nothing, or virtually nothing, since all depends on how it is written. A poor idea well written is more likely to be accepted than a good idea poorly written.

28 October 1982

New projects don't present any difficulties for me except that for fiction, I have to get a notion of a plot first. But I don't worry about it. I just try to think of a plot. If nothing comes after a few minutes, I shove it into my unconscious. The next day, I think again. Eventually, something pops up.

Then I just start. I don't make any notes of any kind or do any detailed thinking. I start and keep on going, making it up as I go along. I am never conscious of any particular effort in the process. Presumably, it works itself out in the unconscious while I am doing other things.

7 November 1984

My stories write themselves, and the characters do and say whatever they please without reference to me at all. I am not responsible for them, and their views are not necessarily mine.

18 July 1987

I am a poor sleeper and always have been. Most of my plotting is done when I am trying, and failing, to sleep.

He was once asked by an idea-generating organization whether he could use its services.

8 May 1990

I have been generating ideas for 51 years without stopping, and I would feel ashamed, at this late date, to use artificial aids. I'm afraid that if the day comes when I'm too far gone to think up ideas of my own, I will be too far gone in senility to be able to use anyone else's either.

11

Science Fiction—II

In 1958, after writing the Foundation Trilogy and many other science fiction books, Isaac stopped writing science fiction. He explained his action in this letter to John W. Campbell, Jr.:

16 October 1958

It's been half a year since I've written a word of science fiction. It's not because I'm dried up; or tired of writing. It's just because since the beginning of 1958, I have written a book on the derivation of scientific words, another one on numbers, another one on man's notions of time, another one on blood and its functions, and I'm just finishing one on the solar system. I'm working on a few others, too.

In short, it's all nonfiction, and please don't be angry with me because it was the *Astounding* articles that introduced me to the writing of easygoing nonfiction. You, sir, have corrupted me.

To fellow science fiction writer Robert Bloch, he wrote:

27 March 1959

At Doubleday, I officially canceled the s.f. novel I was supposed to write last year. For an indefinite period henceforward, s.f. and I will have pf-f-ft. The theory is I have to wait for the urge to write nonfiction to subside. The fear is that the urge to write nonfiction will subside, but that the urge to write fiction will nevertheless not return.

Nonetheless, Isaac remained a strong supporter of science fiction.

2 October 1961

This morning I wrote an article entitled "Who Won the Hugo," which is intended for *The New York Times Magazine.* It is on science fiction conventions, and it may not make it. I have a feeling that the editor may be expecting a humorous article poking fun at science fiction fans. In the letter she wrote me, she did say, "We are looking for a tone that is generally on the light, entertaining side."

Well, I made it that. I put in a number of light and entertaining touches. But I also did two other things. I presented science fiction fandom in a rather poignantly heroic light, something like Henry V saying, "We few, we happy few, we band of brothers. . . ." And I also very quietly and gradually led the reader into seeing the true and important significance of science fiction until, by the end, I was speaking in almost a hushed whisper.

It may be that the editor will not want to use the article. If so, the hell with it. I would not write an article making fun of science fiction for the sake of appearing in the New York *Times* or anywhere else and for any price. If, on the other hand, she is tricked by some of my light and entertaining touches into publishing the article, I will be delighted, for it will mean that a first-rate outlet will be printing an essay on s.f. that *does* present it in a poignantly heroic light and I will be so proud.

6 October 1961

I feel a little grim today. I called the New York *Times* to see how my article on conventions was doing, and the silly editor said she loved the piece and others were greatly affected by parts of it, but on the whole it was decided that a piece on conventions was too parochial. That only s.f. fans would be interested.

I said, "But you *asked* for an article on conventions. It was your idea, not mine."

She said, "Yes, it was my mistake."

2 November 1965

As for the Science Fiction Writers of America, I think it is important to remember there are two kinds of writers.

There are the "arrived professionals," who need nothing. There are, however, people less fortunate. Either they are just beginning or else they are (and will remain) marginal writers. Belonging to an organization is not likely to make them better writers or more successful writers; it may not even help them to become shrewder businessmen.

However, it gives them a feeling of belonging. A person who has sold one poor story in the last year has an equal vote with Isaac Asimov. And I think that is just. The situation does not harm me professionally at all (what would I do with two votes?) and bucks up the beginner no end.

1 March 1966

I have always stated that one of the virtues of science fiction is that it can break every taboo without having to be "daring." It is the nature of the medium to break taboos. Now the most taboo of all taboos is mother love. No one must ever say a word against mother love. So I deliberately set out to write a story describing a society in which mother love is disgusting and, therefore, outlawed. The result is my short story "The Deep."

26 September 1966

The people I have met through science fiction—not only the readers but my fellow writers and even my editors—have been uniformly wonderful, warm people. To be a science fiction fan, in whatever fashion, means to be concerned with the future of mankind; even, in a way, to love all men and wish them well in the far-off time when we ourselves have gone our way. I did not know this when I began writing s.f., but nearly 40 years of involvement has taught it to me. I am happy over the choice which, in my innocence, I made so long ago.

5 July 1969

I can't help but think with a certain amazement of the little nine-year-old boy I once was when he fell in love with science fiction. How could he possibly know that the time would come when he would be the biggest single factor in the "respectabilization" of science fiction?

I have probably written more articles on s.f. for "serious" periodicals ranging from the New York *Times* to the *Bulletin of the Atomic Scientists* and been referred to more often as an indication of the "real scientists" who are interested in s.f. and write it than all other s.f. personalities put together. In fact, only good old Arthur Clarke rivals me in this.

11 April 1976

As to being called a science fiction writer . . .

I am not responsible for how others feel, but I have my own self-respect and standards of integrity.

Science fiction readers made me what I am today, and I do not bite the hand that feeds me. Nor do I ever intend to uproot myself.

I *am* a science fiction writer. I will always *be* a science fiction writer. You can *call* me a science fiction writer because I am *not* ashamed of being a science fiction writer.

4 June 1971

There was *nothing* wrong with s.f. when I quit. I was at the peak of my powers and at the peak of my earnings. The last story I wrote before quitting was "The Ugly Little Boy," and it is still my favorite. However, as time went on, s.f. became unsatisfactory and my return (which I always planned) was inhibited. New styles and new authors came in, and my writing became old-fogyish. Yet, I had no intention of altering my style.

My particular strength in science fiction is a very simple one. The reader always knows exactly what is happening and why. Even if not all the motivations are at the moment clear, he has every security that they will be made clear. He also knows that my phraseology will be lucid, that everything in the story will be self-consistent and that it will all wind up logically. My weakness is that I have no "style," no "poetry," no "imagery." And I don't consider that a weakness.

21 December 1972

Science fiction can't die as long as the human imagination lives. Fashions may change, but science fiction remains.

In the 1970s, Joseph F. Patrouch wrote a book, The Science
Fiction of Isaac Asimov. *During his research, Patrouch wrote
Isaac frequently, asking questions about Isaac's books. Isaac answered all of them. Patrouch's book was published by Doubleday, which sent the manuscript to Isaac before publication. Isaac
then wrote this letter to Patrouch:*

28 January 1974

I sat down and read the manuscript at once in one unbroken
sitting. (Why not? I can't conceive a subject more fascinating to
me.) There is not one word (not one word!) that I will suggest
changing for reasons of error of fact.

In fact, I don't even think I would change one word because of
possible error of judgment, either. You are not always compli-
mentary and you do not always like my stories. But you are
always reasonable, and I have a sneaking (and uncomfortable)
feeling that you may even be always right. Except, of course,
when people read my stories, they usually are not as analytical as
you (very rightly) are and are influenced by the general feel of the
story.

I don't suppose that many writers can, while they are still alive,
be made the subject of so careful, so detailed, so reasonable and
so sympathetic a study by a competent critic. I am clearly a very
fortunate person, and I am fully cognizant of that fact.

I trust that the readers of the book, generally, will understand
that in no way did you consult me in any of your judgments and
that in no way did I try to control you and that, in the end, in no
way did I change even as much as a word.

My only fear is that by being my own self, both in my stories
and in my correspondence with you, I managed to be likable
enough to distort your judgment in my favor. I hope not. And I
was *glad* to see you poke holes in me now and then so that I
could tell myself you were not unduly influenced.

I should also tell you (although I am no critic) that it seemed to
me your book was excellently well written.

3 September 1974

I am perhaps the chief apologist for science fiction, but I am
certainly not the father of it. The honor more nearly belongs to

Hugo Gernsback and John W. Campbell, Jr. (Both are dead, so they can't argue.)

                                                    11 February 1975
In my view, the best science fiction, the only valid science fiction and the science fiction I try to write depends on *legitimate* science *rationally* extrapolated. If something is wrong, distorted and illogical, it cannot be categorized as science fiction; any more than noise can be called music or a used paint rag a painting.

In 1984, Isaac was sent several chapters from Alexei and Cory Panshin's history of science fiction, The World Beyond the Hill, *which was eventually published in 1989. Isaac wrote to Alexei Panshin:*

                                                    24 October 1984
Shortly before bedtime, when I had finished my day's work, I thought I would take a look at a few pages before retiring.

Mistake! Mistake! For the first time in many years (one gets blasé and callused with age), I found myself unable to put down a book. I read on till I ran out of pages. When I went to bed (dreadfully annoyed because I didn't want to have to stop), I found I was so full of the manuscript, of what you said and described that I could not sleep. I actually had to take a Valium (something I hate doing) in order to calm down.

Look, this is the best, the *best* history of science fiction I have ever read. You have *everything* right, the people, the s.f. historical background, the world historical background—at least in the section I have read. I am sure you are equally good in the chapters preceding and following the section.

I *must* read it all. You *must* finish the book and get it published. I will buy a copy whatever the price and however many volumes it runs to and read it, the whole thing, word for word, and maybe reread it, too.

Several months later, Panshin sent him the chapter that dealt with Isaac. And Isaac wrote Panshin:

25 January 1985

I've just read Chapter 13, "Shifting Relationships," the one that is all about me. I read it at one long sitting, hoping it would never end. The facts are all exactly right (as they would have to be, for you read my autobiography and other writings so carefully), and your interpretations are so incredibly flattering that it goes beyond credibility that I could complain about a single word.

I said to Janet, "My goodness, Alexei is another one of these guys who think I am superhumanly intelligent."

And Janet said, "But you are superhumanly intelligent."

Who knows? Maybe I'm a minority of one.

Anyway, I'm so glad I wrote you my rave about the book *before* I saw this chapter. Once I read it, I would have been embarrassed to rave about your book, lest you suspect my motive. I simply must live long enough to own your history (and *buy* it—so don't send me one).

Isaac had strong feelings on the abbreviation of "science fiction."

21 July 1980

As to "sci-fi." This is a Hollywood neologism invented as a "witty" analog of "hi-fi," and it grates on the ears of all science fiction writers. Hollywood illiterates may go for that abomination, but the proper abbreviation to all honest science fiction people is "s.f."

In a 1986 column in Amazing *magazine, Robert Silverberg criticized the use of "sci-fi" and praised the abbreviation "s.f." He then asked, "I wish I knew who thought of it." In a letter to* Amazing, *Isaac wrote:*

12 October 1985

Wish no more, Robert. It was thought of by your very own friend Isaac Asimov.

I wrote an editorial in *Asimov's Science Fiction Magazine* in the May–June 1978 issue entitled "The Name of Our Field." Here's the way that editorial ends:

". . . 'Sci-fi' is now widely used by people who don't read

science fiction. It is used particularly by people who work in movies and television. This makes it, perhaps, a useful term. We can define 'sci-fi' as trashy material sometimes confused, by ignorant people, with s.f. Thus, *Star Trek* is s.f., while *Godzilla Meets Mothra* is sci-fi."

12

Campbell and Pohl

John Campbell's influence on Isaac's literary life is legendary. Isaac wrote about Campbell in his autobiography and in many other books. Here's how Isaac described him shortly after Campbell died in 1971.

2 August 1971

The news of John Campbell's death on July 11 clearly marks the passing of an epoch.

John was certainly the most colorful and the most important single personality in the history of science fiction. He was one of the two greatest and most popular s.f. writers of the early 1930s. He was *the* greatest and most influential s.f. editor of all time. He created the modern field by the sheer flood of his ideas and his genius (and incredible industry) in finding and developing the writers who could handle those ideas.

But my loss is not that of science fiction in the abstract. My loss is a personal one. I have lost my literary father, the man who found and molded me, who was the direct and necessary influence in my writing of "Nightfall," of the Positronic Robot Series and of the Foundation Trilogy.

Nothing I have ever written, whether he was directly involved or not, whether it was science fiction or not, fails to carry the impress of his influence—and (however we may have disagreed in our social views at times) of our deep friendship.

And they did disagree on social views. In the 1950s and early 1960s, they had a lengthy correspondence on these issues. Many of Campbell's letters to Isaac are printed in a limited edition, The John W. Campbell Letters with Isaac Asimov & A. E. van Vogt, *edited by Perry A. Chapdelaine, Sr.*

But the vast majority of Isaac's letters no longer exist. Before 1964, when his papers and letters overflowed his files, Isaac would take them out to his backyard barbecue and burn them. In 1964, he began donating all of his papers to the archives at the Boston University library.

A few remain. To provide a flavor of this correspondence, I'm including one of Isaac's letters to Campbell in its entirety. Bear in mind that this letter is in response to a Campbell letter, includes references based on the lengthy series of letters and was written 31 years ago.

30 September 1963

Dear John,

You want the Negroes to "earn" their rights, and there are lots of answers to that. I could say that:

1. Negroes were brought to this country against their will, brutalized in vile slavery for 250 years, stripped of their dignity in so-called freedom for another 100. Perhaps the white American has to do something to "earn" a clear conscience.

2. Groups don't have to earn their group rights. Individuals have to earn their individual rights. The Negroes want their chance to earn rights as individuals. They want an equal chance at schooling, at jobs, at decent homes. *Not* equal schooling, equal jobs, equal homes; equal *chance*.

3. A Nisei's intolerance is not made sacred by the fact that he is a Nisei.

However, maybe you're right. Maybe there's something to this "earning" bit.

There are a whole list of far-out ideas that you and I have talked about over the years: psionics, Dean drive, dianetics, dowsing, Krebiozen. Lots more. [Note: Campbell supported these far-out pseudoscientific ideas, and Isaac thought they were nonsense.]

They have to EARN their right to be heard, John. The AMA won't give them a chance? Tough! The Food and Drug Act turns its back? Tough! Big Science wants to be worshipped as Authority. Tough!

Those outside ideas simply have to make their way against the tide, like the Irish did. Then they, too, will be President of the United States someday. If they don't make their way and get themselves lynched, that just shows they're inferior. And I, for one, won't waste any tears over them.

It strikes me, John, that when the heel is on the face, it depends on whether it's the heel that belongs to you or the face.

Now when we deal with ideas, I'm tough. I own the heel. The new idea has to prove itself against the very harshest opposition. That's the only way we can shake out the good from the crud in the long run.

But when we deal with men, I'm soft. Men have feelings and nerve endings and hearts and minds. They even have constitutional rights. I own the face in that case. You may disagree with me and prefer to be soft on ideas and hard on men. That, of course, is your privilege, but exercising your privilege doesn't make you right.

In fact, when I come to think of it, I don't believe that you are soft on ideas and hard on men.

You will cheerfully reject a bad story, but you don't go around rejecting authors. You don't ask: Is the author a sober man? Is the author a moral man? Is the author a colored man? All authors are the same to you. You ask only: "Did he write a good story?"

But before you can do that, you have to agree to read the stories. Suppose you don't read any stories written by Negroes. In that case, you never know whether one of them has written a good story, do you?

And suppose the NAACP demanded that you read stories submitted to you by Negroes, and you responded that it was unfair to be asked to accept bad stories. And they said, "We're not asking you to accept them, we're asking you to read them and judge them by the same standards by which you judge stories written by white men."

And suppose you said, "Well, the chances of a Negro writing a good story are so small, I won't waste my time looking at them."

And they said, "How do you *know?*"

And you said, "Well, that's what they think in Alabama, and that's good enough for me."

It doesn't sound like you, does it?

In fact, John, I think you're on my side and as soon as you get it through your head that the Negroes are the way-out people facing the authoritarianism of Big Whitedom, you're going to come charging out to fight on the side of the Negro, as you have staunchly borne the standards for everything from dianetics to Krebiozen.

However, don't expect me to return the compliment. However soft I am on men, I intend to stay diamond-hard on ideas.

And here are brief excerpts from letters written to Campbell several months later:

14 February 1964

I reject the following syllogism:

Major premise: Some geniuses have been considered quacks.
Minor premise: He is considered a quack.
Conclusion: He is a genius.

You tell me I *must* judge human beings. Well, as nearly as I can make out that means I must judge whether someone called a quack is really a quack or is really a genius.

I think, John, that you, as a science fiction editor, are a genius and that you, as a human being, are a kind and dear friend. But I also think, John, that you as an exponent of the Hieronymus Machine, etc., etc., are a quack.

8 February 1964

Aside from our various little disagreements, you have all my love and respect.

There was also this brief exchange in 1966. First, a letter from Isaac to Campbell:

10 September 1966

I looked for you before, during and after the banquet and didn't see you. I particularly hoped you were in the audience because the Foundation series, quite to my own surprise, won the Hugo for the all-time best series.

My speech of acceptance was a very short one. It went: "I would like to thank Mr. John W. Campbell, Jr., who had at least as much to do with the Foundation series as I had."

And here was Campbell's reply:

September 14, 1966

I was indeed at the banquet—and I did indeed hear your little speech of acknowledgment.

One thing I think you ought to recognize more clearly, though. If I spot an acorn lying on the ground, and stick it in a spot of good soil, it's hardly being honest to point, a few years later, to the tall oak tree standing there, and say, "What do you think of the tree I made?"

There must be a hundred kids I've seen possibilities in and tried to encourage. I must be doing something wrong; you're the only one who's turned into a really major factor in both science fiction and science.

Must have been you, not me, that brought it about.

When Isaac sent his Campbell correspondence to the Boston University library, he added this handwritten note:

John Campbell died on 11 July 1971. In late years we corresponded little because of deep disagreement on social issues. This is all that is left of a voluminous and, sometimes, acrimonious correspondence.

One of Isaac's lifelong friends was Fred Pohl. In 1979, Isaac was asked to write an appreciation of Pohl for a science fiction convention program.

3 December 1979

What has Fred Pohl ever done for me? Let's see.

When I was 18, I met him as part of the Futurians, and we hung about a lot together, which made me feel right at home in the science fiction fan movement and encouraged me to keep trying to write. Fred went over my rejections and told me they were the best set of rejections he had ever seen, which was encouraging. He gave me advice (good advice) on writing even though he was only a few weeks older than I.

In 1940, he became the editor of *Astonishing Stories* and *Super-Science Stories* and bought half a dozen stories when I needed to make sales most. By the time he had finished his stint as editor, I was strong enough to carry on alone and sell to *Astounding* exclusively.

In 1949, he urged me (indeed, almost forced me) to submit my story *Pebble in the Sky* to Doubleday—thus initiating my career as a book writer. He was my agent till 1953 and was helpful at all times. After he ended his agency, I never had another agent. About 1951, he told me the real money was in writing nonfiction. I didn't believe him, but I didn't forget either.

He has always been my good friend over the decades.

I thought all this over and said to myself, "Yes, but what has he done for me *lately?*"

Pohl's onetime stepdaughter had occasion to write Isaac. In the letter, she asked if Isaac remembered her.

8 December 1967

I remember you well. When Fred Pohl persuaded me to give him the manuscript that eventually became *Pebble in the Sky,* my first book, in order that he might pass it on to Doubleday, I came to his place to deliver it.

He was not home. But you were (you were then his stepdaughter), and I handed it to you.

Considering my general super caution, it is an indication of how little I thought of my chances of selling a book when I tell you I handed the manuscript to a seven-year-old child.

Here are some excerpts of the letters between Pohl and Isaac over the years. The first is from Pohl's letter to Isaac following Isaac's heart attack in 1977.

11 June 1977

Listen, I've given some thought to your situation, and here is what you have to do. You don't have a choice because I have figured out an incentive you can't ignore. If you died ahead of me, I swear I will go to the next s.f. convention there is and make a speech poking fun at you for not smoking or riding in airplanes and being dummy enough to die anyway.

You don't want that, so do the following: (1) Do what the doctors tell you, exactly. (2) Beyond that, learn transcendental meditation and do it. . . .

Meanwhile, thank you for not dying because it would have spoiled all the fun of kidding you.

From Isaac to Pohl:

17 June 1977

Your letter made Janet cry because she says everyone loves me. I didn't want to disillusion her so I said everyone did. But I should think you'd feel ashamed to spread a delusion like that. In any case, I love you.

3 January 1983

I read the new issue of *Starship* and turned first to your column because (I'm not sure I want to say this) I love your columns and consider you the best writer about s.f. there is. (I *know* I don't want to say this.) I think you're better in this respect than I am— by far.

From Pohl to Isaac following Isaac's heart bypass surgery:

29 December 1983

There are those who love you, you know, so please quit worrying us. Slow down. Practice loafing. It isn't a sin. Tell everybody to go screw and take a month off in the sun.

Remember, if I outlive you, it will be widely viewed as a triumph of nicotine and alcohol over clean living and you don't want that. . . . So conserve yourself, Eye, we want you to last a while yet.

From Isaac to Pohl:

22 October 1988

Fred, I'm glad that you and I are still here after 50 years, and I wish I could arrange it so that neither one of us would die first. Let us go at the same moment. Or better yet, not at all.

From Pohl to Isaac:

1 November 1988

All right, let's make a deal. I won't die if you don't. You realize this is a great sacrifice for me. Ray Bradbury and Arthur Clarke can't hold out forever, and you know that if I outlive you, all I get to be is the world's senior s.f. author. But, what the hell, friendship comes first.

From Isaac to Pohl:

24 August 1989

While I read fiction only sporadically these days, if that, I never miss a chance to read any of your commentaries. I know I've praised you before for your nonfiction, but I never tire of doing so. There have been times when I've disagreed with Sprague de Camp, Carl Sagan and Martin Gardner (not often, I admit), but I have *never* disagreed with you.

What I'm trying to say, Fred, is you're my kind of people. Long may you wave.

13

Clarke, de Camp and the del Reys

Arthur C. Clarke and Isaac got along well and had a friendly rivalry. They made an arrangement that they called the "Treaty of Park Avenue."

18 August 1987

Arthur Clarke says I am first in science and second in science fiction in accordance with an agreement we have made. I say he is first in science fiction and second in science.

They respected each other highly, but that didn't stop them from an occasional needle. In 1976, Clarke wanted to include an introduction that he had made of Isaac in a book of essays. He said he would include Isaac's reply and welcomed "any additional insults." He also said he planned to cut down on his writing and lecturing. Isaac replied:

28 June 1976

By all means include both your introduction and my gentle riposte. I wouldn't for the world add more insults, for I love you too much, as you well know. Besides, if I answer gently, everyone will be sorry for me and will hate you.

Delighted to hear you won't be writing or lecturing. I never could stand the competition. Now don't change your mind; I'm going to carry on for both of us. In return, you can have all your royalties forwarded to me. It will be a chore taking care of the money, investing it, paying taxes on it, but what are friends *for?*

Here are some other letters from Isaac to Clarke:

22 April 1978

If you insist on retiring—and if I can get Bob Heinlein to retire, too—then the first three s.f. writers will be Asimov, Asimov and Asimov.

Limericks! You want to challenge me in limericks?

> It may be that Arthur C. Clarke
> Is half-good at sex, in the dark.
>> But by night or by day,
>> Come what might, come what may,
> Isaac always surpasses his mark.

20 February 1982

By a peculiar coincidence, by the way, you are sequeling *2001*, just as I am sequeling the Foundation Trilogy. I'm almost finished, and you and I will have to fight it out for the Hugo and Nebula in all likelihood. If you'll take one, I'll take the other. (What if we both get beaten! Horror!)

Clarke sent a piece entitled "Great Lover" to Asimov's Science Fiction Magazine, *and Isaac replied:*

6 November 1985

The "Great Lover" piece you sent will appear, *in full,* in my editorial, entitled "Persona." I said it was from an unnamed person in Sri Lanka and then added "but the only person I know in Sri Lanka is a minor writer named Arthur C. Clarke, whom I don't suppose anyone else has ever heard of." (Serves you right.)

15 March 1986

I am always glad to hear from you, if only to know that you are alive and well and (I trust) not writing books. Not that it does any good. Half a year ago, Carl Sagan published *Contact* and that knocked half the sales off *Robots and Empire*. (These days, who can afford to buy *two* hard-covers?)

23 March 1987

You and I and Bob Heinlein have been the Big Three for so long that I imagine we'll just continue to hang on, all of us, if only to irritate the others.

5 January 1988

Well, Bob Heinlein has passed his 80th, and you your 70th and I hope you both live forever. However, don't you think that you two should RETIRE. Wouldn't it be nice to let me be the "Big One" for just a little while? After all, I'm a youngster who has just turned 68. Come on, fellas.

19 November 1990

I note that your books disappear the moment they hit the shelves, but I am told this is because the dealers throw them away at once. This news has been kept from you because of your advanced age and debility, but I cannot allow you to live a lie.

In the spirit of equal time, here are three from Clarke. The first was written to the Science Fiction Writers Association when Isaac was named a Grand Master.

26 March 1987

We're both almost as good as we think we are. That's why it's very hard to say anything flattering—and original—about Isaac; he's usually said it first. But at least I've beaten him to the Grand Mastership. Which is why it's impossible for me to say, "It couldn't happen to a nicer guy." It already has, of course.

The next was scribbled on a Time *magazine clipping that quoted the passenger of an airplane that crashed saying that he was reading a Clarke science fiction novel when the crash occurred.*

9 August 1989

He should have read an Asimov book. Then he'd have slept through the crash.

And in a letter to an editor thanking him for a special bound edition of Isaac's short story "Little Brothers" (written in 1934 about his "troubles" with me), Clarke said:

4 November 1989

Many thanks for Isaac's "Little Brothers." I passed it on to my kid brother for his amusement. Tell Isaac that I recognized his style instantly, which shows he hasn't improved after all this time.

Sprague de Camp was one of his closest friends for more than 50 years. Over the years, he wrote de Camp many letters. Here's a sampling.

24 December 1966

I am on a de Camp binge. On impulse I reread *The Bronze God of Rhodes* and enjoyed it tremendously. So I passed on at once to *An Elephant for Aristotle,* and now I am two-thirds through *The Dragon of the Ishtar Gate.* You are undoubtedly the best writer of historical fiction that ever lived. Your stories have verve, your people aren't creaky historical figures—they're moderns like ourselves. What's more, you carefully don't betray your own hindsight. I love you, Sprague.

13 December 1967

Well, old boy, you cost me a day's writing time. I took Robyn to the hospital for a routine checkup and, knowing I would have to wait, I took *The Great Monkey Trial* with me and began reading. I should have known better, for I have had experience with your books. I read and read and read and have just finished and haven't done a stitch of work in the interim. I haven't even taken care of my mail, and you know how compulsive I am about that.

1 December 1969

A few days ago, I idly picked up *The Great Monkey Trial* and began to read it. Of course, I had already read it, but what's the use. Having begun it, I read it through a second time with every bit as much pleasure as the first. My goodness, if everyone loved your writing as much as I do, you'd be rich beyond the dreams of avarice. Thank you, Sprague. There are very few books I have time to read even once these days, and there are very few of *your* books I don't read at least twice.

After the death of a mutual friend in an automobile accident, Isaac wrote:

7 February 1970

Sprague, in case anything happens unexpectedly either to me or to you, can I tell you now that I have loved you for 30 years and that in all that time you have never done anything that has in the least displeased me or made me unhappy; that I have tried never to cause you displeasure or unhappiness, and have certainly never done so wittingly.

Here's what he wrote about de Camp to others.

11 February 1972

Sprague de Camp has discovered a time machine. When I first met him in 1939, he was tall, handsome, dignified and learned. And he still is. People looking at a group photograph taken in 1940 say, "Who's that skinny guy? Asimov? Who's that funny little pointed-chin fellow? Del Rey? Who's that kid? Anderson? And there's Sprague de Camp." There's never any question of Sprague. In 30 years, he hasn't changed. Well, he's grown a beard and it's a little gray, but that's just a detail.

19 March 1976

His rationality is without peer. We do not always agree on the issues of the day, and our temperaments are sufficiently different for us to look at the world, sometimes, in different ways. But even when he disagrees with me, he does so honestly, logically and calmly. Nor has he ever taken umbrage with me for disagreeing with him.

His honesty is beyond question. I have never known him to say anything to me that was not so (within the limits of human failings), take any credit that was not his nor do anything that smacked of unethical behavior however dimly or distantly. If I had a million dollars that required being held for a while and then returned, I would give it to him without a qualm and without asking for a receipt. If I needed someone to lean on, his would be the shoulder of choice.

Since 1940, Isaac and Lester del Rey, the science fiction author and editor, were close friends. Both had quick minds and sharp typewriters. For more than three months in 1974, they conducted a lengthy exchange of long letters even though they lived within several blocks of each other on Manhattan's West Side. Here's a sample of the exchange—from Lester first:

October 28, 1974

You distress me. You making all that fuss about my spelling error in typing abstraction as "abstarction"—which, were I less honest, I really could defend with profound scholarship from an analysis of roots. You, who then type my name upon the envelope as Lester Del Rey. Can this be the man who wrote me years ago saying, "You know what I want? I want you should spell my name right!" Schande über dich!

1 November 1974

I am terribly sorry I misspelled your name. I had forgotten that such is the shyness of your personality you prefer the small *d*.

You explained verbally that *del* means "of" (you are a veritable *mine* of information), and I shall never forget that it should be made lowercase as in Fine & Shapiro's delIcatessen and in the well-known brand of delIcious Apples. No, I guess you should make "del" a separate word as "del Icatessen" and "del Icious." One can't be too careful with these terribly important things.

del Iriously yours,

In sending the stack of letters to the Boston University library archives, Isaac scribbled a little note on top of the last in the series:

A series of spoofing letters between myself and Lester. He the bludgeon. I the rapier.

One of the most brilliant and dynamic women in the history of science fiction was Judy-Lynn Benjamin del Rey. In physical stature, she was a dwarf. In mental stature, she was a giant. She died in 1986 at the age of 43, and Isaac wrote a moving tribute to her shortly afterward.

In that tribute, he wrote of their exchanges of letters as she preyed on his gullibility with pranks and teasing. Both of them loved their relationship. But in all of Isaac's letters, I couldn't find the letters he mentioned. So, instead, let me quote from the tribute, published in Newsday *on April 6, 1986.*

I got a letter telling me that Judy-Lynn had been fired by *Galaxy* [a science fiction magazine]. The letter was written by her replacement, one Fritzi Vogelgesang.

I replied with a most indignant letter, demanding to know how the devil *Galaxy* could let go of a woman such as Judy-Lynn. I was quite caustic about the level of intelligence of anyone who would do such a thing and made threats about never submitting a story to the magazine again.

But Miss Vogelgesang answered so soothingly and sweetly and with such innocent flirtatiousness that my anger seemed to disappear, and in no time at all, I was writing pleasant letters back. By the time I had decided that this Fritzi was every bit as nice as Judy-Lynn, she suddenly disappeared forever. I got a waspish letter from Judy-Lynn:

"So, Asimov, how quickly you forget all about me and take up with my replacement."

She had never been fired. She was Fritzi Vogelgesang.

14

Ellison, Garrett and Greenberg

For many years, the exchange of "insults" between Harlan Elli-
son and Isaac enlivened science fiction conventions. But the rela-
tionship was warm, as seen in these letters to Ellison.

13 September 1967

Without you, a convention is entirely too staid. It is also very pleasant to have *one* person around who is nuttier than myself. Otherwise I stick out like a sore thumb.

27 August 1973

I am constantly asked about my feud with you, and I always answer that you and I are good friends. But it doesn't help. As long as we love each other, however, who cares.

8 November 1985

Janet and I have just this minute finished watching *Paladin of the Lost Hour.* We finished in tears, and Janet's comment was "a masterpiece of acting and of writing." Harlan, you're the best damned writer in the world. I've suspected it on one occasion or another, and now I know it.

I'm so glad to be a writer myself, for, however unworthy, I want to be called by the same name as you.

10 March 1990

Listen, I got *Scartaris* today, and I put it on my office desk to read later on because I was busy at my word processor in the living room. I was curious, though, so I just looked at the first page, *standing up,* because I was all set to walk away.

Then I turned the page, and I turned another page. And I read every one of the 32 pages, *standing up,* because I was too absorbed to remember to sit down. And me standing up all that time after my hospitalization isn't the easiest thing in the world.

Listen, Harlan, you freak, you are one of the greatest writers in the world. You may be obscure at times, you may be violent, you may deal with unpleasant things, but you grip the reader so that he can't let go. For God's sake, for your sake, for the sake of humanity, WRITE, WRITE, WRITE.

But even if they loved each other, they also enjoyed practical jokes. Here's one that Isaac recounted:

21 June 1968

I called Larry Ashmead [his editor at Doubleday] to tell him that I had finished every last bit of my index work and was sending it to him by special delivery. A strange voice got on the line and announced himself as Larry's new assistant. He began to tell me that a check over my book sales had shown that I was doing much worse than had been expected and that Doubleday was going to have to make an agonizing reappraisal about me.

I said he was pulling my leg and to let me talk to Larry. He said he was trying to break the news to me gently and Larry didn't want to talk to me. And I said (getting more nervous by the moment) that I could hear Larry laughing in the background.

It was Harlan Ellison, of course. He was in the office. I just happened to call, and it was his idea of a joke. Oh, boy, talk about picking vulnerable spots. But wait, the opportunity will come, and I will get even.

In 1979, Isaac sang on television. It was "The Clone Song," a parody sung to the tune of "Home on the Range." Here's how he described its origin:

30 August 1979

The first verse and chorus were written by Randall Garrett, the well-known science fiction writer. He handed it to me during a talk I was giving on cloning to a combined meeting of a medical society and a legal society in San Jose, California, on December 12, 1978. I wrote the last three verses myself.

Why Randall wrote it originally, I can't say, except that he is very clever at light verse.

This is what Garrett and Isaac composed:

Oh, give me a clone
Of my own flesh and bone
With its Y-chromosome changed to X
And when it is grown
Then my own little clone
Will be of the opposite sex.

    Clone, clone of my own
    With its Y-chromosome changed to X
    And when I'm alone
    With my own little clone
    We will both think of nothing but sex.

Oh, give me a clone
Is my sorrowful moan
A clone that is wholly my own
And if she's an X
Of the opposite sex
Oh, what fun we will have when we're prone.

My heart's not of stone
As I've frequently shown
When alone with my own little X
And after we've dined
I am sure we will find
Better incest than Oedipus Rex.

Why should such sex vex
Or disturb or perplex

Or induce a disparaging tone?
After all, don't you see
Since we're both of us me
When we're making love I'm alone.

*Isaac later did a parody of the parody for an organization of
Sherlock Holmes enthusiasts, the Baker Street Irregulars. And he
wrote this letter to Garrett:*

6 January 1979

Listen, that "Clone Song" is one of the best things that ever
happened to me. Since I am a member of the Baker Street Irregulars, I saw a chance to do something else. Last night was the night
of the annual banquet, and I asked permission to address the
crowd. I then sang the following:

WATSON'S LAMENT

Oh, give me some clones
Of the great Sherlock Holmes
With their Y-chromosomes turned to X
And when they are grown
Then my Sherlock Holmes clones
Will be of the opposite sex.

　　　Clones, clones of my Holmes
　　　With their Y-chromosomes turned to X
　　　And when I'm alone
　　　With my female Holmes clones
　　　We will all think of nothing but sex.

Oh, give me Holmes clones
Hear my sorrowful moans
Some clones that are wholly my own
And if they are X
Of the feminine sex
Oh, what fun we'll all have when we're prone.

It went over surprisingly well. And when I say "surprisingly
well," the audience did everything but destroy the banquet room.
Of course, there were added inducements. In the first place, I

gave a brief pseudo-learned talk as a prelude in which I discussed Dr. Watson's discoveries in genetics at the turn of the century. And in the second place, I had never been in better baritone voice, and I had a microphone in my hand to sing into.

Nevertheless, they never stopped talking about it and congratulating me and asking for copies. However, and this is the nub, I couldn't get it through their thick heads that while my voice is my own, my words weren't exactly. I gave them a copy and clearly wrote on it "Randall Garrett and Isaac Asimov," and I told everyone I could reach by word of mouth.

But somehow that song is going to spread to all the Baker Street Irregular societies across the country, and something tells me that in one of those great historic injustices, my own name might be the only one mentioned. I'm sorry. I honestly had no idea it would prove such an impossible smash hit.

For the last 19 years of Isaac's life, one of his closest friends was Martin Harry Greenberg, who worked with him on many anthologies. Greenberg lived in Wisconsin, but they talked almost nightly on the telephone.

Their friendship had a strange beginning because Greenberg had the same name as the man who owned Gnome Press and who first published the Foundation Trilogy *and* I, Robot *in the 1950s. Isaac always felt that the earlier Greenberg had cheated him. In 1961, Doubleday got the rights to the four books back from Gnome Press. In his autobiography, Isaac wrote of the earlier Martin Greenberg:*

Sometimes I stop to think of the money Marty could have made if he had made a real attempt to sell them, and had given me regular statements and paid me on time, so that I would write still more books for him. . . . Marty had been sitting on a gold mine and had not been aware of it. He went for the short-term pin money.

That brings us to 1973, when Martin Harry Greenberg wrote Isaac and asked permission to anthologize two short stories. Isaac replied:

29 May 1973

Before I can answer, I must know who you are. Are you the Marty Greenberg who was once publisher of Gnome Press and who published four of my books and anthologized several of my stories?

Or are you someone else? It is important that you tell me this and make the difference, if there is one, or the identity, if there is one, perfectly clear before we can proceed.

From Martin Harry Greenberg, came this letter:

May 31, 1973

I am not what I appear to be! I am (in no particular order), 32 years of age, male, overweight, a college professor, a science fiction fan and editor of science fiction anthologies. We met at the Nebula Award banquet in New York in April, but only for a few minutes.

I am, definitely, not the Martin Greenberg of Gnome Press, but rather Martin Harry Greenberg, son of Max Isador Greenberg of Miami Beach. Could you supply me with any estimates of the odds involved in their being two people named Martin Greenberg who edited, but did not write, science fiction?

And thus began a close friendship. And just to keep things straight in the 1970s, Isaac always addressed his letters to Greenberg:
"Dear Marty the Other."

After working on anthologies with Marty the Other for almost two decades, Isaac made this judgment:

26 January 1989

Marty Greenberg, for my money, is the best judge in the world where science fiction is concerned.

15

Other Science Fiction Friends

Forrest Ackerman

7 November 1966

I met Forrie first in 1939 on the occasion of the First World Science Fiction Convention in New York. I don't think he noticed me. He was the Number One Fan then as he is now, and I was a minute particle on the s.f. scene. He was only 22; I was 19.

Forrie has treated me with the generosity he accords everyone. When he heard that I didn't have a copy of the issue of *Amazing* that contained my very first story (I have tear sheets of the story itself, lest anyone think I am entirely too casual about my career), he sent me—without request and without charge—a copy of the magazine.

He has stood by my side at conventions and kept me from being the only non-smoker and non-drinker in a hostile crowd of hip characters. He has laughed at my jokes with immoderate humor and sent me thank-you letters afterward for entertaining him.

Nelson Bond

22 June 1974

I always enjoyed Nelson Bond's stories when he was writing. I met him only once and that was at the First World Science Fiction

Convention in 1939. My chiefest memory of him is a letter he wrote to me not long after the convention, urging me to stop writing argumentative fan letters to the magazines now that I was a professional contributor. I followed that very good advice, and I have never been sorry. Nor have I forgotten my gratitude to him for his interest in me.

Ben Bova

In 1962, early in Bova's career, Isaac recommended to an editor that Bova be commissioned to write a series of articles. Bova, who recalled this favor at the memorial service after Isaac's death, wrote to Isaac at the time:

> 19 July 1962

I'm sitting down now and offering a heartfelt Thank You Very Much. I've enjoyed doing the articles tremendously. They have bolstered my ego considerably . . . to the point where I'm beginning to think that I might make a name for myself in this business after all. And all this is due to you.

And this was Isaac's reply to Bova:

> 21 July 1962

If you are going to feel yourself bending under a load of gratitude, you will eventually grow to dislike me for subjecting you to it, so please don't! Instead, look at it this way. Any number of people helped me in my time, and it is only my duty to pass some of it onward. If you feel overcome or something, the time will come when you can pass something someone's way and that will be your repayment to me.

Later, Isaac sponsored Bova's membership in the National Association of Science Writers.

> 7 October 1964

Ben falls into the same category as I do. He has written science fiction stories and also some very good science books for the layman. He is thoroughly qualified. He is not, of course, as expe-

rienced or as talented or as handsome as I myself am. But then—
who is?

Ray Bradbury

7 August 1968

Ray and I were born in the same year, took the same path into
science fiction and, as far as I know, share the same political
views. There is, however, one difference. Ray has a pronounced
antipathy and distrust for science, and I have a pronounced sympathy and trust for it. He hates the prospect of a high-machine
future, and I love it.

7 January 1972

Although I am the best writer in the world, I am no Ray Bradbury. "Switch on the Night" simply charmed me to death. I loved
it.

15 October 1988

I heartily concur with the suggestion that Ray Bradbury be
awarded the Grand Master classification by the Science Fiction
Writers Association. He was the first of the magazine science
fiction writers (even counting Bob Heinlein) to be recognized by
the outside world, and his "Martian Chronicles" went a long
way toward putting us on the map. I would have felt uneasy
about accepting my own Grand Master award were I not well
aware that I was half a year older than Ray.

Robert Heinlein

31 July 1976

I can't honestly say that Bob Heinlein inspired my first efforts in
science fiction, for I had three stories published at the time Bob's
first appeared ["Lifeline" in the August 1939 issue of *Astounding*].

However, I know a good thing when I see it. As soon as "Lifeline" appeared, I realized I had a model to copy and I copied as
hard as I could. I never really managed to make myself as good as
Bob (who did?), but it kept me pointed in the right direction. So

I'm grateful to him as we all are—as fans, certainly, and as professionals even more so.

Will Jenkins (Murray Leinster)

27 March 1959

I dropped in on John Campbell and met Will Jenkins there, who admits to 62, and whom I fervently adjured to continue living to 150, if necessary, in order to prevent the mantle of the "dean of science fiction writers" from ever falling on my shoulders.

5 July 1975

Will Jenkins was one of the formative influences in my life. It is hard to believe, considering the number of decades I have been a professional science fiction writer. But when I was just a kid reading the stuff, he was already a science fiction great and was among those whom I idolized.

Fritz Leiber, in a letter to Leiber:

15 November 1958

I have never had the chance to tell you this personally, and I should. Two of the very best s.f. stories I ever read (two of the *very* best) were "Coming Attraction" and "The Night He Cried." I had a story in the same table of contents with each, and in both cases, I just wasn't in the same galaxy with you.

Willy Ley was a fellow science writer whom Isaac admired greatly. He wrote Ley:

25 July 1955

If it weren't that I know you personally, I'd be prepared to bet money that Willy Ley was half a dozen people on the ground that no one person could know as much and be able to write about what he knew so entertainingly.

And some letters about Ley.

31 May 1958

It is delightful to be considered an all-around authority on matters scientific. But Willy Ley is really the guy everyone thinks I am.

25 June 1969

Judy-Lynn Benjamin called me yesterday to tell me about Willy Ley's death. It is very upsetting. He was just 13 years older than I am, and of course I always identified very strongly with him since we both were so alike in some ways. For instance, we both have been writing monthly columns for s.f. magazines for over a decade.

27 June 1969

There was a great deal of friendly rivalry between Willy Ley and myself, but it was *very* friendly. I once introduced him in one of my convention talks as "the second greatest science essayist in the world." Then the next time I got up, I said:

"I have been criticized for saying that Willy Ley was the second greatest science essayist in the world and have been told that that shows unconscionable conceit on my part. There is a demand that I apologize to Willy for this and I think I ought to." So I turned to Willy, who was sitting at the head table with me, and said: "Willy, I apologize sincerely. I am *sorry* you are the second greatest science essayist in the world."

He laughed very heartily, shaking all over.

We would send notes to each other on the subjects we were going to discuss in future issues of our respective magazines, and I think we were both anxious to keep ourselves going for more consecutive issues without missing than the other. Willy was writing his column several years longer than I was, but his magazine was bimonthly for a number of years while mine was monthly throughout. I have always wondered whether I had caught up to him, but kept myself from checking, feeling this was a rather petty attitude that was beneath my dignity.

Anyway, just a couple of months ago, *Galaxy* and *If* were sold to a new publisher, and Willy wrote me a card saying that as a result he was going to be publishing an article a month in *each* magazine, which meant 18 articles a year. Although he did not

124 · YOURS, ISAAC ASIMOV

say so, of course, it seemed obvious to me that there was a satisfaction in the fact that he was going to pull away from me.

His last words to me were: "Yours for a busy future." It just breaks my heart.

10 July 1969

I cannot help but feel that Willy himself would have considered the timing of his death tragic. After his involvement with the space program, after the manner in which he sold rocketry to the whole world even in years when "respectable" engineers would not dream of considering such matters, it seems just too frustrating that he should die three weeks before the lunar landing.

Robert Silverberg, in a letter to Silverberg:

3 March 1970

Listen, your history on Zionism got a very good report in *Publishers Weekly*. I hate you! If you're going to compete with me in quantity and variety and be a dozen years younger than me, can't you at least fall far short of me in quality? It seems to me to be a reasonable request.

In another letter to Silverberg, who was then writing a novelization of Isaac's famous short story "Nightfall":

21 April 1989

To tell you in writing, so that it will be impossible for me to deny it later and say that you must have misled me: I think your outline for the novelization of "Nightfall" is simply superb. Absolutely wonderful. It made me very happy.

Clifford Simak, in a letter to Simak:

12 May 1984

I was 18 years old when we first started corresponding. You were 34. Forty-five years have passed since then, and we are still corresponding, I see. You were already one of Campbell's hopefuls when we started; I had not yet made a sale. Now you are the beloved patriarch of the field and a Grand Master, and I know what it is to have placed straight science fiction books on the best-seller lists. We have come a long way, and I presume neither of us has any complaints.

I have made no secret of the fact that if I have ever deliberately copied anyone's style of writing, it is yours.

I don't suppose you know what you've meant to me, Cliff, and it is difficult to explain. You encouraged me when I was beginning. You wrote me letters that made me feel part of the science fiction fraternity before I was part of it. You were a friend who was always kind and brotherly. I never saw your name on a story or book without feeling warm. And, as you know, I never missed a chance to express my debt to you and my admiration of you in print, right down to the present.

You mean a great deal to Janet, Cliff, quite independently of her relationship to me. You are, by all odds, her favorite science fiction writer and have been since long before she met me. She has every one of your books and keeps them all. Yours are the *only* science fiction novels she not only reads but periodically rereads. (When I say "only," I mean that she does *not* reread mine.)

Ted Sturgeon

8 May 1985

It is now almost half a century since John Campbell took over the editorship of *Astounding* and began the "Golden Age." But I remember it as though it were yesterday. God, what exciting days those were.

Little by little, John gathered a stable of writers and learned the trick of keeping us rubbing our noses against the grindstone. One thing he did, in my case, was to tell me what the other members of his stable were doing.

The one he mentioned with the greatest affection was Theodore Sturgeon. I can see him grinning now as he would hint at the manifold pleasures of something upcoming by Ted.

How I watched for his stories myself. I remember "It" and "Ether Breather" (his first) and "Shottle Bop" and "Yesterday was Monday" and "Killdozer"—and how eagerly I read them and how hopelessly I decided I couldn't match him. And I never could. He had a delicacy of touch that I couldn't duplicate if my fingers were feathers.

Jack Williamson

24 February 1979

I first met Jack in 1939. When my first story, "Marooned Off Vesta," was published, he sent me a postcard congratulating me and offering me a "welcome to the ranks." I cannot say how much that meant to me from one of the writers I respected most. It was typical of his kindness and his gentle heart. I have seen him perhaps five times all told in 40 years, but I wear him always near my heart.

And in a letter to Williamson:

26 January 1989

On 30 January 1939, I received a card from you praising my first published story, "Marooned Off Vesta." Now, on the 50th anniversary of that day (minus four days), I hear from you again (having corresponded in between, of course).

It is tremendous, just tremendous, that after 50 years, we are both still alive, still actively writing, both Grand Masters. Who would have thought it?

He was also generous in his praise of other science fiction writers.

Harry Stubbs

7 April 1969

Harry C. Stubbs writes both science fact and science fiction (the latter under the pseudonym of Hal Clement). He knows as much as I do, or more, about the physical sciences, and certainly knows more than I do about astronomy and geology. He is not quite as facile or fast as I am (nobody is).

John Varley

31 May 1976

He is damn good in my opinion, and it is clear he knows his science, which is, for me, an absolute must for any science fiction writer, whether he uses science in his science fiction or not.

Joe Haldeman

29 March 1987

Joe Haldeman is one of the brightest of the current crop of science fiction writers, one of the most highly thought of by readers and by fellow writers alike.

Harry Turtledove

17 July 1988

He is one of the brightest and best of the new generation of science fiction writers and has an attractive and congenial personality.

Charles Ardai

16 October 1987

Charles Ardai is a very bright young man, and I expect great things of him. I'm glad we're not the same age, in fact. I'd hate to have been in competition with him. I would surely have lost out.

And he wrote these letters to Ardai:

6 January 1989

I don't often meet a young man in whom I recognize something of myself, and I'm depending on your success as a continuation of mine in some spiritual way (even though I am a total materialist in my beliefs).

I believe that you will labor to keep my memory alive. I have done the same for John Campbell for 18 years now, so I know it *can* be done. I was only ten years younger than Campbell, but he rejoiced in my success as I rejoice in yours.

18 May 1990

If I encouraged you, it was simply my duty and my pleasure. Your proper return is to become the best writer you can possibly be and make me proud of you. (I am already proud of you, if it comes to that.)

Barry Longyear, in one of the last letters that Isaac wrote:

12 November 1991

You are one of the best, if not *the* best, science fiction writers to have appeared in recent years. The editors are jerks to reject you, and you're a bigger jerk if you pay any attention to them. Keep on writing as always, *please.*

16

Magazines and Columns

In the spring of 1977, the first issue of Asimov's Science Fiction Magazine *was published.*

24 December 1976

As for the new magazine, having it bear my name was entirely the publisher's idea—to make it match the Ellery Queen and Alfred Hitchcock magazines. Of those two, Ellery Queen is *not* a figurehead but is actively shaping the field. Alfred Hitchcock is a complete figurehead, his only participation being his name and picture.

I will fall in between. I have no editorial expertise whatever, and no time or desire to be an editor even if it were imagined I could learn how. I will participate to the best of my ability.

But Isaac worried that the use of his name might be a problem.

1 March 1976

It is just possible that many science fiction fans would be deeply offended by any magazine bearing the title of a particular science fiction writer. It might strike them as being beneath the dignity of the field, or as being an unendurable example of arrogance on my part. It might even be that science fiction writers (who are, by and large, a very peculiar bunch, with skyscraper egos and no protective skin at all) might be reluctant to write for a magazine that by its very name is boosting the name and career of a competitor.

As it turned out, his worry was unfounded.

7 October 1986

After all since 1950, dozens of science fiction magazines have been started and of them all, *only Asimov's Science Fiction Magazine* managed to survive for ten years (and still counting). We've had good editors and good publishing, but part of it, at least, is the use of my name.

At the memorial service for Isaac after his death, Sheila Williams, the managing editor of the magazine, recalled that she had met Isaac when she was 16 years old after her father had written to Isaac saying that both of them were fans and wanted to meet him at an upcoming Star Trek *convention. This was Isaac's reply to Sheila's father:*

12 February 1973

If Sheila is as sweet as 16-year-olds usually are, there will be no problem at all in having a few minutes of conversation.

They did meet, and Isaac spent time with them. Sheila never forgot it and several months later asked Isaac's advice on which college to attend.

30 October 1973

I taught at Boston University and was always pleased with it. There are numerous science fiction fans in the Boston area, and they could offer a stimulating atmosphere in which to work on writing s.f.

After I sent Sheila copies of her father's and her letters to Isaac and Isaac's replies, she wrote:

10 March 1993

I can't believe you found them in all those letters. By a trick of memory, I'd thought that both letters were written by my father. I certainly wrote my letter requesting information about colleges at my dad's urging. Although I can't believe my audacity, it's great to finally have copies of this interchange that existed ten years before we actually became friends.

Although Asimov's Science Fiction Magazine *will be one of Isaac's legacies, he cherished his relationship with* Fantasy & Science Fiction *magazine. His first letter to editor Anthony Boucher of* F&SF *goes back more than 40 years:*

17 January 1951

Thank you for the kind words for my robot stories, "Mother Earth" and "No Connection." My early days as a writer back in 1939 and 1940 created permanent scars on my soul, and editorial kindness is still mighty soothing.

I have enjoyed *F&SF* tremendously (still do), but must admit that I always thought your editorial bent leant strongly towards fantasy and the emotional or "Ray Bradbury" type of science fiction. It is therefore exceedingly good news to me that you consider my sort of stuff favorably.

One year passed.

18 January 1952

I am anxious to write for *Fantasy & Science Fiction* since it is the one major magazine my byline has not yet appeared in.

Still another year passed, and here is a letter that Isaac wrote to Boucher but never sent:

6 February 1953

I wonder whatever happened to my story "Flies," which you bought months and months ago. I keep watching for it every issue. Of course, I know that each issue has to be put together like a jigsaw and that the turn of "Flies" may not have come up, but—call this crazy, if you like—I keep thinking, "Gee, maybe they changed their minds about the yarn and decided it isn't printable after all."

But then Boucher wrote to him that "Flies" would appear in the June 1953 issue. Isaac replied:

27 February 1953

I'm so glad you wrote to me about "Flies." I was getting quite dismal about it. For your amusement, I'm sending you the carbon of a letter I wrote you on 6 February (the original of which I tore up, after I had sealed it into a stamped envelope).

In the November 1958 issue of F&SF, *Isaac began writing a series of science columns that was to continue for 399 issues. He enjoyed writing these monthly columns more than anything he ever wrote. Following are letters he wrote to Ed Ferman, who became the* F&SF *editor with the December 1964 issue and still holds that position:*

21 February 1968

It is perfectly understood between us that I write these articles for *F&SF* out of love and not for money and that I would write them just as cheerfully for no fee at all. So for goodness' sake, don't ever feel apologetic about what you pay me.

And if I ever missed an issue, no reader or combination of readers could possibly be gloomier than I—although perhaps I wouldn't be gloomy at all. For it seems to me that as long as *F&SF* exists and doesn't fire me, the only reason I would ever miss would be a fatality (or possibly merely a near-fatality) to myself, and I would then be in no position to feel gloom or anything else.

It is my present ambition to reach and pass beyond article #500. In fact, my article #495 (if my calculations are correct) would appear in the January 2000 issue of *F&SF* and wouldn't that be nice.

15 September 1969

Every once in a while, I get letters from high school teachers and even college professors who say they get their students to read some of my *F&SF* articles. It gives me a great kick to get stuff into a science fiction magazine that doesn't ordinarily find its way into the groves of academe itself.

18 January 1971

I am very chagrined. Over the weekend, I planned to do *nothing* because I had just finished a big project on Byron's "Don Juan."

So I picked up a math book and started reading it. Within the hour, I got so restless over what I was reading that I got up, sat down and wrote an *F&SF* essay. But that was not the one I had planned to do next. So I wrote the other one, too. Now I have *two* of them.

This means I now have nothing to do till 10 May, if I can bear to wait so long. Well, I will force myself because I keep creeping up farther and farther ahead of deadline until I have to deliberately wait for you to catch up. How about going semimonthly so I can write two a month? (No extra charge?)

25 December 1976

First issue of my new magazine has just come out. I hope it does well, but even more I hope yours does well. Yours has my essays in it.

21 May 1981

You know, Ed, almost every one of my *F&SF* essays has *something* in it that is completely original with me and that I have never seen used. And no one ever comments on the fact—not the readers, not my fellow scientists, not even my editor.

Sometimes I figure everyone is waiting till I'm dead to say how great I was—so I wouldn't get swelled-headed. And sometimes I think that the mere fact that even after 23 years the readers are not tired of my essays is because they recognize the brilliance and originality even if they don't say so. Well, *I,* never known for my modesty, say so!

4 January 1986

Do you realize that in two months I will complete my 28th year with *F&SF?* When do I get my gold watch? No! That's on retirement, and I don't intend to retire.

4 November 1986

The Los Angeles *Times* Syndicate has talked me into writing a weekly syndicated column for them. So that's a new job for me. I wrote my first column last Saturday morning, and I plan to write one first thing every Saturday morning.

I'm telling you this because the news may get to you, and you may wonder if I'll have time to write my *F&SF* essays if the new job gets pressing. Fear not! If anything shows signs of getting in the way of my *F&SF* column, I drop the anything—*never* the *F&SF* column.

7 May 1988

Sometimes, I'm astonished that I can think up different subjects. It would be nice if I lived long enough to run out of subjects, because then I think I would live forever.

His final Fantasy & Science Fiction *column appeared in the issue of February 1992. Isaac died April 6, 1992.*

Isaac's Los Angeles Times *Syndicate column also gave him a lot of pleasure. Here are several letters he wrote to Don Michel, his editor at the syndicate:*

19 March 1988

If you wonder sometimes if I'll get tired of doing the column, fear not. I've gotten so used to waking up early Saturday morning and doing my column before breakfast that the weekend wouldn't be the weekend without it.

18 May 1990

I've done my syndicated column, and now I can do my setting-up exercises and shower and do some of the other work I have to do. I hate setting-up exercises but doing the column cheers me up and makes it possible for me to face the dull aspects of life. Then when I finish I can get back to work—where I belong.

For several months in late 1991 and early 1992, he and Janet wrote the column jointly. Since his death, Janet has continued writing the column on her own.

17

More Limericks
and Oddities

Isaac's occasional partner in writing limericks was John Ciardi, the poet. He met Ciardi at a writers' conference in 1950, and they became fast friends. The friendship was marked by mutual teasing and good-natured insults.

13 April 1982

One of my good friends is John Ciardi, who tells everyone he is a poet. Overcome with envy at the way in which I had exploded onto the poetic scene, he challenged me to a contest and, as a result, *Limericks: Too Gross* and *A Grossary of Limericks* was put out.

25 August 1979

Ciardi wrote half the limericks in *Limericks: Too Gross*. His are gross. Mine are clever.

And here are several letters to Ciardi:

4 September 1984

I have just published a little book called *Limericks for Children,* 42 *clean* limericks. (I know you don't know what they are.)

11 April 1981

It is a constant wonder to me how you can possibly turn out books as urbane, as eloquent, as witty and as delightful as you do. The inevitable conclusion is that your wife writes the books.

20 April 1981

I was fascinated by your book *A Browser's Dictionary* and loved it. Thank you so much for letting me see it. Anyone who knew you only from your books would think you a delightful and incredibly intelligent fellow. That I think so after having met you numerous times in person is probably a terrible reflection on my taste.

And now more limericks.

To Mary Manningham, past president of the Massachusetts State Poetry Society:

11 May 1977

The genesis of my light verse? I scarcely know. I simply think hard. For instance, suppose I wanted to do a limerick around your name and involve John Ciardi. I would start:

> *"John Ciardi?" said Ms. Mary Manningham,*

Then I think of a possible rhyme:

> *"Why, everyone seems to be panning him,*

Then I just have to finish it off.

> *And reading his verse*
> *(Which couldn't be worse)*
> *Let's vote on the chances of banning him."*

See, no problem.

To Sylvia Smith, who was my secretary from 1967 to 1985:

3 June 1977

> A certain girl, Sylvia Smith,
> Once startled her kin and her kith
>   By saying, "You know,
>   My virtuous show
> Is nothing at all but a myth."

To Elizabeth and Ben Lieberman, who printed some personalized get-well limericks for him:

21 June 1977

Three cheers for Eliza and Ben,
Whose achievements are far past my ken.
    They print; I just write.
    Can I match them? I might.
Then they'll do more and beat me again.

To Harry Walker, his longtime lecture agent:

13 January 1978

Here's a toast to old grandfather Walker,
Raised on high by a fellow New Yorker.
    And you'll find the rhyme fine,
    If your accent's like mine.
He's my agent and I am a talker.

To the wife of a friend who had died:

14 January 1978

AVE ATQUE VALE

Alas for the friends of Bill Sloane,
Now that he is off on his own.
    Where his soul finds its place
    In the vastness of space
And has left us all sadly alone.

To a fan who asked him for a souvenir to sell at a fund-raiser:

22 August 1978

There was a fine fellow named Ray,
Who said to I. Asimov, "Hey,
    It would be very fine
    If you wrote us a line
We could sell on our fund-raising day."

To a college-age fan who wanted to correspond regularly with him, he declined and instead wrote her a limerick:

13 October 1978

As to lechery, no one is keener
Than my freshman friend, sweet young Sakina.
    And they say (though it's lewd)
    She's a knockout when nude.
My goodness, I wish I had seen 'er.

To a Mensa member:

19 March 1979

One must vary; not stay with the same mix.
All that work makes you dull, try a play mix.
    Brigitte, Andress, Raquel?
    Have they bored you? Oh, well.
Try the best; have a Meredy Amyx.

To an old friend from his days at the Philadelphia Navy Yard in World War II:

13 October 1979

I saw the fine verse of friend Meisel.
To your feet, everyone, won't you rise all?
    Let the cheering ring out
    With a laugh and a shout.
We'll all toast him; the gals'll; the guys'll.

To a friend at a charitable organization:

15 April 1980

There is a young woman named Edie,
A delectable charmer and sweetie.
    When I see her, you know,
    My heart beats, like so,
And all of my thoughts get so greedy.

To friends who were getting married:

25 April 1980

There's a marriage for Howard and Jacqueline,
And with pleasure we're all of us cacklin'
    If I weren't a coward
    And afraid of old Howard,
I wouldn't mind some of the tacklin'.

And now for some more odd questions.

Did he want to offer a selection to be included in a book entitled
The Book I Never Wrote?

27 December 1975

I cannot contribute. Fortunately for myself, I write fluently and prolifically and all my books are published. Any book I want to write, (1) I have already written or (2) I am writing or (3) I will write as soon as I get to it. I turn my literary dreams into literary acts.

What did he spend money on when he first felt rich?

21 May 1976

When I first began to feel rich (that is, when I felt I could spend money as I pleased without worrying), here is what I did:
   (1) I began to hail taxis when I wanted to go places and gave up buses and subways. (2) I began to make long-distance calls whenever I was too lazy to write a letter. (3) I began to buy electric typewriters whenever I felt like it.

Could he contribute a favorite recipe to a cookbook?

11 September 1976

The trouble is that I don't cook and have no gourmetish tendencies. I eat a lot, but that just means I am a glutton.

What is he most afraid of?

9 March 1977

Philosophically: That I will live long enough to be sure that civilization will not endure. *Personally:* That my life may outlast my brain and that I will grow senile and be able to recognize it in lucid moments. *Family:* That I will live long enough to witness disaster to wife or children. *Neurotically:* Heights and flying.

What did he dislike most about New York City?

13 August 1978

What I most dislike about New York is that its preeminence as a stimulating place to live has made it a target for the scorn and envy of all those who cannot measure up or who have used it as a footstool to reach the point where they can "escape." To all within sound of my voice, I say this: New York, even in decline, bears a ravaged beauty that still marks its greatness, and what it has been, no other place will ever be.

What kind of world are we leaving our children?

23 February 1979

It is one in which almost all the leaders are concerned with short-range goals: the next election, the next diplomatic coup, the next step in outreaching the neighboring power economically, militarily or both. The number of leaders who are primarily concerned with the vast interlocking problem of human survival seems to be zero.

In such a world of short-range goals only, it may be that the long-range goal of survival will be lost and our children with it. It is that sad possibility our children are inheriting.

How did he relieve stress?

21 February 1985

I have no mental exercises to relieve stress. Where my writing is concerned, I never feel stress. Where my non-writing life is concerned and stress is coming on, I sit down and write. And then there is no stress.

What were some of his most famous quotations?

30 October 1980

(1) Violence is the last refuge of the incompetent. (2) I'm not a speed reader. I'm a speed understander. (3) I am the beneficiary of a lucky break in the genetic sweepstakes. (4) If there were fewer fools, knaves would starve. (5) Never let your sense of morals keep you from doing what is right.

What would he write for his epitaph?

25 March 1981

It's not dying I mind. It's having to stop writing.

16 January 1982

Wait, I'm not finished!

18

Science

Isaac was a scientist and proud of it.

12 February 1962

Some physics researcher got interested in an article of mine in *F&SF* in which I posed the question of the maximum possible temperature. As a result, he switched his line of research and began investigating the temperatures of supernovae and came up with a new theory of supernovae formation based on neutrino production. Well, a little story on it appeared in the 2 February issue of *Time* magazine. (No mention of me, of course, but *I* know I'm involved, and I feel so proud.)

In my years of writing, I have frequently heard from youngsters who have told me that because of my stories and articles, they are going to enter science. That has pleased me very much because it makes me feel as though I'm doing my bit in the recruiting game. However, this is the only case (that I know of) where an established scientist has been chivvied into doing a particular piece of work because of one of my speculations and has done it fruitfully.

Even 30 years ago, he knew what he wanted to achieve.

1 April 1963

In science writing, my dreams are limitless. I intend to be *the* unquestioned popularizer of 20th-century science. This is easy, and I think I will accomplish it. But there is another part of my dream which is not in my power to accomplish but for which I must depend upon the world.

I want science writing, science communication, science translation to be recognized as a contribution to *science*. And if it is done well enough, I want the science writer (me) to be recognized as a scientist, even as a great scientist, despite the fact that his contribution is by typewriter and not by test tube. Oh, my ambition may o'er-vault itself, but what's the good of an ambition if it isn't at the farthest limit of your reaching fingertips?

Many of the persons who wrote to him asked him questions on science. And he frequently responded with scientific explanations. Here are just two samples.

The first is from a Western Australian writer who sent him $10 and asked him: "In the autumn when the days are shortening, why is it that the daily time difference in the sunrise is much greater than that of the sun setting? The same inequality, in reverse, is seen in the spring."

13 March 1984

For simplicity's sake, successive "mean noons" are set exactly 24 hours apart. This would be correct in actuality if the Earth's orbit were perfectly circular and there were no axial tilt.

But there is an axial tilt, and the Earth's orbit is slightly elliptical. As a result, the *real* noon time is sometimes ahead of mean noon and sometimes after it—by as much as 15 minutes. The amount of before and after is indicated by the "analemma," the figure-eight thing on large globes. As a result of this swing, the time of sunrise creeps forward faster than sunset one half the year and vice versa the other half, but it all comes out even in the end.

I don't charge for answering questions. So here's your money back.

Here's an answer to a mother who was writing on behalf of her six-year-old son.

19 November 1985

I can't answer all your questions, but here are some. A "googol" (horrible name) is 10^{100}, or a 1 followed by 100 zeroes. The number that is one order of magnitude smaller is 10^{99}, or a 1 followed by 99 zeroes. 10^{99} is "1 duotrigintillion." That means the proper name of a googol is "10 duotrigintillion." There are names for numbers all the way up, but it is useless to know them. Scientists always say 10^{100} or 10^{99}.

Incidentally, Webster's unabridged has a list of names of numbers, under the word "numeration." They only go up to "vigintillion," which is 10^{63}, but it gives you the idea for how to go higher.

Isaac was frequently asked about his vision of the future. Sometimes, he was pessimistic.

14 August 1970

I wish that I could say I was optimistic about the human race. I love us all, but we are so stupid and shortsighted that I wonder if we can lift our eyes to the world about us long enough not to commit suicide. I keep trying to make people do so.

But on other occasions, he was optimistic.

11 September 1969

In considering the future society, let us assume that (1) there will be no nuclear war; (2) the population will increase but not disastrously; and (3) the trend toward automation will continue.

In that case, the kind of work that will be done in the future will tend to be more and more that of supervision of the machinery that does the real work. Work will become increasingly administrative and managerial. Men and women who can run the machines and repair them will be in great demand. Because the type of work will be just as applicable to women as to men, the trend toward sexual equality will be accelerated.

This means there will be more and more leisure in the world, and the leisure will have to be filled because doing nothing is a terrible chore and very painful for any mind above that of an idiot. This means there will be a great emphasis on creativity and the purveying of amusement. Hobbies will be in great demand (all sorts of leisure-time activity from mountain climbing to stamp collecting), and there will be a huge and increasing industry catering to these hobbies.

Then, too, every form of show business will increase mightily in all its ramifications. I suspect that in the 21st century, one-third of the human race will be engaged, directly or indirectly, in supplying amusement for the other two-thirds. And that is a conservative estimate.

3 June 1978

A century from now there will be two prime sources of energy—nuclear fusion and solar power collected in space.

Either one can be used to produce electricity more or less directly. Either one can also be used to combine water and carbon dioxide to form hydrocarbons and oxygen. The hydrocarbons and oxygen then recombine to do all the things that oil does today without any pollution whatever and without anything being used up but heavy hydrogen and sunlight, each of which can last billions of years. There will be other comparatively minor energy sources but these are the two basics.

Isaac was an environmentalist.

30 October 1990

A major environmental issue is the question of lowering carbon dioxide emissions to ameliorate the greenhouse effect.

Those who profit from foul air and a poisoned atmosphere will profess to worry about more expensive automobiles. But I see no percentage in gloating over a few hundred dollars saved while dying of lung cancer and emphysema, and while the Earth warms, the ice caps melt and the coastal regions drown.

But he always tried to be realistic.

28 August 1979

I was at a talk in which the speaker said, "We must give up our automobiles and get closer to nature." I was the only one in the audience who didn't applaud because I was the only one who wasn't a hypocrite. Not one intended to give up an automobile.

What kind of credentials did Isaac have for his predictions?

12 October 1984

I speak of a future in which human beings are increasingly freed of non-creative work and at the same time brought up *from birth* in a computerized system of education that no one in the past or present has ever experienced. It is impossible to judge the effects except by intuition—but then my "intuition quotient" is high. I spoke of robots of the type now being planned for the future as long ago as 1939, and I described a pocket computer with considerable accuracy (the outside at least) as long ago as 1950.

Isaac's predictions were of the distant future. He didn't want to guess in 1984 about the changes expected in the world by 1994.

19 June 1984

Frankly, I don't know what changes will take place by 1994, and I hate to give the idea that the future is cut and dried.

Isaac always believed in the need to reach the Moon, explore it and eventually build Moon colonies.

6 January 1966

I've just written an article that briefly states my thesis that it is important to start a Moon colony, for they will show us how to *really* construct a managed economy, and it will be on them that the brunt of further space exploration will fall. The peroration is: "Why spend billions to place a man on the Moon? If we don't, we may lose the Earth. If we do, we may gain the universe. You couldn't ask for better odds."

20 July 1969

This is Man-on-the-Moon month. In fact, today is Man-on-the-Moon day. I had to write articles and give interviews. Last Thursday and Friday, I was interviewed five times, and Saturday I went into hiding. I think I liked it better when I was a crackpot for thinking people would go to the Moon someday.

25 July 1969

To think of all the fuss everyone is making about the Moon trip. I told them all about it 30 years ago, and they *laughed* at me. Oh well, Jules Verne told them 100 years ago.

Isaac believed in the space program.

23 July 1969

I got a letter from a reader who wrote to berate me on the expense of the space program and telling me I ought to be ashamed for not spending the money on the cities and the poor.

I wrote back to say that the people of the United States spend exactly as much money on booze alone as on the space program. And if you add tobacco, drugs, cosmetics and worthless patent medicines (and chewing gum, suggests Carl Sagan), then we spend far more on these useless-to-harmful substances than on space exploration.

I asked her if she indulged in any of these vices and if she would consider sponsoring a movement to have the people give up these things and donate the money equivalent to the cities. (Of course, this would throw a hell of a lot of people out of work, which shows how difficult it is to do *anything*.)

1 October 1969

Relieving the plight of the poor and of the cities is of paramount importance, and if the only source of the money required for this were the space program, I would say to dismantle the space program.

However, it is a shame to do one constructive act at the cost of another when there are much better alternatives available. The billions of dollars we spend on defense could, in my opinion, be cut considerably by clamping down on waste and graft, without in the least impairing national security. The money thus saved could support *both* the cities *and* the space program.

26 June 1974

I believe many planets circling other stars bear life. Short of going there and seeing, we can prove it only by receiving information-carrying radio waves sent out by civilizations more advanced than our own.

19 June 1975

What has been done so far, the manned voyages to the Moon and the unmanned probes to other planets, were projects that already strained the resources of the two most technologically advanced nations on Earth. To attempt to do more would overstrain those resources. For projects such as the colonization of the Moon, manned flights to Mars and so on, we need not only an international but a truly global pooling of resources.

Not only will such a global effort be necessary if space exploration is to continue, but if mankind can learn to live together in peace and can disband all the military machines that disfigure our world, the "war" against the universe, the "battle" to wrest knowledge from space, the "campaign" to expand man's position in the solar system will supply the emotional triumph and excitement that war has brought us in the past. It will also form a noble and enormous goal which will help mankind obtain a sense of unity, since all will be contributing as "Earthmen."

19 January 1978

Future exploration of space should be done with *both* manned and unmanned probes.

In the near future, unmanned probes are much the more feasible, for sending human beings out on many-months-long voyages to Mars, for instance, would be economically and psychologically difficult.

Once we establish the shuttle as a working space vehicle, the expense of flights will drop. And once we establish space settlements, the psychology of long flights will be less formidable. *Then* we can switch to manned probes, since as of now and for the foreseeable future, human beings are more versatile than machines.

Isaac's opinions on space issues were solicited by senators and congressmen of both parties. Here is an excerpt from a letter to Adlai E. Stevenson III, then a Democratic senator from Illinois.

18 November 1979

I believe the exploration and exploitation of space would not only be of advantage to the United States but is absolutely imperative if human civilization is to be preserved.

It is from space that we will get the material resources, the energy and the gains in technology that will be needed to allow humanity to continue to grow and expand. Confined to Earth, we have reached our limits.

Furthermore, international cooperation must be made a reality. War must be abolished. This can only be done if we lose our localisms in a great, unifying project. Space offers the only such project.

Isaac detested and opposed President Reagan's "Star Wars" program.

28 March 1986

I have been pro-space since I was a child—as is obvious, since my first professional science fiction sale, 47½ years ago, involved a wrecked spaceship.

However, I am disturbed at the increasing militarization of the shuttle in particular and of space in general. I do not see eye to eye with Ronald Rambo Reagan in this, and I have every intention of saying so publicly, loudly and often.

2 April 1983

I won't speculate on space wars in reality (as opposed to fiction). The only weapons I want in space are NONE, either offensive or defensive. The only weapons I want on Earth, except for the minimum required in both number and quality to maintain civil peace, is NONE.

19

Fans

Of the 100,000 letters that Isaac received in his career, more than half came from fans—fans of his science fiction and fans of his science fact. The overriding tone of these letters was appreciation, respect and, in so many ways, love. Perhaps the most unusual aspect of his relationship with his fans was that he wrote back.

First, here are some letters that he wrote about fans.

13 March 1961

A senior at Williams College wrote me: "I am majoring in chemistry here, but your book *The Intelligent Man's Guide to Science* has taught me as much in three days as my major has in four years. Your book has reawakened in me a forgotten joy in learning."

Isn't that nice? I am absurdly gratified whenever someone tells me that the book has "reawakened a forgotten joy in learning" because that is what I try to do; that is my mission; only how do I go about saying so without sounding priggish and mawkish? We live in a society in which it is impermissible to be idealistic; where to wish to do good and to help one's fellow man in any way is so laughed out of court that those who most wish to do so (for the very selfish reason that it makes them feel good and gives meaning to their life) must live constantly in fear of being accused of hypocrisy or worse.

11 December 1961

I attended a meeting of the Harvard Humanists, a student group of non-religious people. The people who agreed to attend were professors and other functionaries of Harvard, including the president of Radcliffe. I went with alacrity because I figured I would spend an evening with a bunch of other big brains and improve myself with their conversation.

I walked in, was given my name card, and a group of solemn undergraduates closed in on me—every one of them a science fiction fan. I broke away eventually on some excuse and headed purposefully for some of the big brains I could see talking on every side, but I was hemmed in again. After several more attempts, I gave up.

10 October 1962

There was a letter from a professor of English at Columbia who is preparing a Shakespeare anthology. He remembered having read a little story about Shakespeare being brought into the present, taking a course in Shakespeare and flunking, only he couldn't remember who wrote it. So he wrote to Groff Conklin [a science fiction anthologist], who didn't know. So Conklin wrote to me, and of course I said, "Why, Groff, I wrote the story." It is "The Immortal Bard," and it was included in my collection *Earth Is Room Enough*.

The professor goes on to say, "My wife and I have long wanted to tell you about the many hours of delight you have provided for us in recent years."

Oh, I *wish* I could have known back in 1935 when I first took an English class at Columbia (I was only 15 then) that the day would come when Columbia English professors would send me fan letters. It would have made me feel so good.

7 December 1969

I have had to write and mail, yesterday and today, 40 pieces of mail, very little of which was really business. Still, how can I complain about my fan mail when so much of it is wildly adulatory?

9 June 1976

The amount of fan mail I get is hard to say—perhaps five to ten letters a day is the average. Usually, the fans tell me how much they like my stories (very rarely that they dislike one), ask me to explain contradictions or to answer questions.

And now for some letters to fans.

28 March 1968

I am grateful to you for being so enthusiastic a purchaser and a little ashamed that I make it so hard for you by writing so many books.

17 October 1969

It is extremely satisfying to know that people I have never met and may never meet in the future are nevertheless made a little happier by what I do.

16 December 1969

My fan mail is handed over to Boston University, which collects *all* my papers for posterity. So generations unborn will be reading that letter of yours.

17 September 1974

Thank you for liking my stories. It all sneaked up on me. By the time I stopped thinking of myself as not-really-a-writer, I found I was getting letters like yours without really knowing how to handle the praise. If I could make this letter blush, I would.

To a fan whose middle name was Read, he wrote:

27 July 1979

There's no question but that you must be every writer's ideal reader. Your middle name was clearly chosen out of some divine inspiration. Thank you, thank you, for your letter is inspirational and delightful on every line.

Isaac gave a number of his books to a young fan, Robert Esposito, who had decided to collect every book that Isaac had ever written. Here are some letters that Isaac wrote to him:

31 May 1980

I'm not sure I ought to encourage you in your project of getting all my books. It will fill your bookcases and impoverish you.

4 February 1982

There are many people who claim to be my "Number 1 Fan," but if I leave out people with an interest transcending the literary —such as myself, my wife, my daughter and so on—then I think that I will hereby appoint you as my Number 1 Fan.

25 February 1984

Undoubtedly, you have the best collection of Asimoviana of anyone in the world except for myself and Boston University.

Isaac did not like posing for photographers or sending out photos of himself to fans.

4 September 1981

I hate the process of being photographed. I hate the time it takes, and I hate the silliness with which the whole process is imbued. And I am not enamored of the results. I do not consider myself photogenic, and I cannot believe that anyone would consider it the least important to have my mug immortalized.

15 December 1982

It is not my face that I sell, only my writing.

3 February 1988

I'm afraid you're confusing me with Madonna or Michael Jackson. I am not in show business. I am just a writer. I have no pretty pictures to send out.

To a person who wanted to illustrate the publication of Isaac's remarks at a commencement with a photograph:

1 March 1984

Why not just use a photograph of Robert Redford or the young Cary Grant and put my name on it. I wouldn't mind.

To an associate who wanted to distribute a half dozen autographed photos of Isaac to his friends:

18 January 1987

How about I should give them nice autographed paperback books instead. On the one hand, they might read them and give their reading muscles exercise. Then, too, if they should like them, they might do the right thing and buy my books—which is how I make my living.

After all, if they like my picture, what will they do? Buy different poses?

And then there was the strangest photo request.

24 September 1984

I wrote an article on Ellis Island for *TV Guide*. Now they want photos of myself as a little child with my mother and father and stagger back in disbelief when I tell them that no such things exist. Sixty years ago, immigrants arriving in steerage did *not* have photographs taken of themselves except for the passports. And I don't have those.

On autographs:

25 July 1969

My policy on autographs is to give them graciously when asked for and to force them on people when they are not asked for.

31 March 1972

I will be perfectly willing to autograph and oblige my readers in any way possible. I don't know what other writers are like, but I am always aware that it is from my readers that my income ultimately derives.

4 August 1975

I don't charge for autographs. (If I did, and if people were willing to pay, I'd be rich, rich. . . .)

19 September 1989

Last Sunday, they celebrated "New York Is Book Country," and I stayed there six hours signing my name over 1,000 times.

23 July 1990

I have been doing this for over half a century, and I am heartily tired of it. I hate the appearance of my own signature. I resent having to sign my checks.

Frequently, Isaac received in the mail manuscripts of short stories or books with a request that he read or evaluate them. He always returned them unread.

14 June 1983

The explanation of my caution in not reading unsolicited manuscripts is a simple one. Our American society is a litigious one, and every established writer runs the daily risk of nuisance lawsuits in which he is accused of plagiarism. Even when this is thrown out of court with contempt, legal costs are high. The best defense is an established reputation of not reading unsolicited manuscripts, something I try to make sure people know is true in my case.

What did he tell a beginner who wanted to get started as a writer?

12 March 1984

I don't tell them anything because I don't know how to get started as a writer. I got started 46 years ago just by writing and submitting until I sold something. But if I tell young writers that that's all there is to it, they won't believe me and will think I am hiding a secret.

The trouble is that when I was getting started, I never looked for good advice because it never occurred to me to do so. I've spent my whole life writing by instinct, and there's no advice I can give.

But over the years, he occasionally did give advice.

16 March 1969

1. *Read.* Read everything you can get in that branch of writing in which you feel you would like to write yourself. Read with care, trying to understand what the writer has done and how he has managed to achieve the effect upon you that he has achieved. (Or why he has failed to achieve any useful effect.)

2. *Write.* Write and rewrite. Submit fearlessly and accept rejection courageously. But despite rejection, continue to write.

26 February 1973

To break into the science fiction field, all one must do is (1) keep writing science fiction stories and (2) keep sending them to the various magazine editors. The editors are desperate for good stuff (they really are), and they read *everything* and publish anything they see any hope in at all. If you get a rejection, try again. If you get another rejection, try again. And so on.

26 November 1968

In any profession, you must expect a period of training. If you wanted to be a doctor, you would expect to spend four years in college and four years in medical school, wouldn't you?

Well, if you want to be a writer, you have to expect to spend a period of time in training before you can succeed. The way you train is to write. So keep on writing and if your stories aren't very good to begin with, just consider it part of your education. They will get better.

19 June 1971

Never judge your own writing. You're not fit to do so. Always allow others to do so—preferably professionals, like editors. If they don't like it, maybe they'll like the next one. In any case, *they* won't tear it up but will send it back to you intact.

15 February 1974

Getting started in literature is like starting your car at 40 below.

12 May 1980

When I am asked what is the best strategy for breaking into the field of free-lance writing, I always answer: "Keep your job."

20

Young People

Isaac's lectures and books always had a great appeal to young people. Though Isaac got older, he always had a young audience.

7 July 1962

I just got back from a brief trip to New Hampshire, where I gave a talk before 150 people attending a conference on "Information Retrieval."

The talk was a success, and the nicest comment I received was from one of the listeners who had forced his 14-year-old son to attend against the latter's will. The son insisted on sitting in the last row so he could sneak out when things got too bad. Apparently, he stayed through the entire talk, laughed and applauded like mad, then came to his father at the end and thanked him for making him come. I beamed with foolish delight when the story was told to me.

8 January 1966

So pure is my fiction that although *Fantastic Voyage* was written for adults, the Teen-Age Book Club is going to distribute a hunk of the paperback issues and is apparently in ecstasy over the fact that it has nothing offensive in it. They did ask permission, however, to excise half a dozen "damns" and a couple of "son of a bitches." I told them, wearily, to go ahead and excise if it meant that much to them, but asked them sardonically if they'd ever heard teenagers talking.

A tenth-grade student in Michigan once wrote Isaac saying that he had gotten a low mark on a paper dealing with one of Isaac's stories. The student said the teacher disagreed with the student's interpretation. He asked Isaac who was right.

26 September 1968

I suspect that your teacher did not give you a C– just because you two disagreed on the theme of "The Feeling of Power." A good story often has a great deal to say—sometimes even more than the writer consciously intended—and different readers may interpret it differently, depending on their own feelings.

For that reason, there is sometimes no *true* theme to a story. It depends on the reader.

I must say, though, that when I wrote the story I happened to be much more interested in the sorry way in which great scientific discoveries are turned toward destruction than in whether man was superior to the computer or not. In that sense, I would prefer your interpretation of my story to your teacher's.

However, I have a feeling your teacher gave you a C– for other reasons and that this letter won't change matters, except that it may make you feel a bit better.

Over the years, Isaac wrote a number of books for children. One of his biggest appeals is that he didn't write down to them.

12 November 1970

I don't have any philosophy about children's books, nor do I write them any differently from my adult books. It's just that publishers call some adult and some juvenile and my readers read them indiscriminately, the adults reading the "juveniles" too and the kids reading the "adults" also.

At the age of 12 or 13, kids are as bright as they'll ever be and just pile up experience thereafter. So they can read and like any well-written "adult" book. ("Well-written" is the key word.)

When Isaac was writing textbooks for youngsters in the early 1970s, there was some discussion of the "level of comprehension" in the books.

17 September 1972

While it is of first importance to be clear and, if possible, elegant in style, it is also important not to talk down.

This generation is the first that grew up after Sputnik had made America conscious of the necessity of making science an important part of the high school, junior high school and even grade school curriculum. The result is that never before have there been so many teenagers conversant with science.

What may seem "too hard" for youngsters in the opinion of middle-aged men is, really, a judgment that it would have been too hard for them when *they* were youngsters. It is generally not too hard for youngsters today. Heaven knows that in the case of my science books for the general public, I dread most of all the bright 13-year-old. His eye for the careless mistake is unerring, and his eagerness to write you a letter about it and beat you over the head with it is frightening.

7 October 1974

Actually, I don't give a damn what the critics say. I am writing for bright kids in the 10- to 13-year range, who are generally rather smarter than the critics who see my books.

The important thing is to introduce them to hard things. They can get the pap in any other book in the market.

A publisher planned to use one of Isaac's stories in an anthology being sold to schools and asked permission for "damn" to be changed to "darn."

3 February 1978

Yes, of course you can change "damn" to "darn" and make any other changes to reduce the small bits of profanity that creep into my stories. Actually, to be cynical about it, I have lived near a junior high school, and I have heard the lighthearted badinage exchanged by the dear young things (both sexes) at the tops of their 13-year-old voices, and if they ever said "damn," they would be ashamed of themselves for saying anything so feeble and pallid.

23 October 1987

The praise of youngsters is the truest and the least likely to have ulterior motives. I am delighted that at my own increasingly advanced age, I am still able to reach them.

Isaac got a letter from an astronomer who thanked him for having had a "profound influence" on the astronomer's life and career. Isaac replied:

22 December 1986

I frequently refer to myself as a signpost that points the way, but stays in one place. I sometimes mean it literally, for I do not fly and hate to travel. Though I talk about all the marvels of far places (to the very outermost quasar), I nevertheless don't budge from Manhattan.

More figuratively, the youngsters I reach in my writings sometimes move on to important positions in science and to important deeds there, while I remain behind to reach new youngsters. Believe me, every case like yours warms my heart.

A father of a ten-year-old boy with cerebral palsy asked Isaac to write a letter to his son who was a "fine student with the heart of a lion and who would not be defeated."

3 August 1981

I hear from your father that you are in the fifth grade and doing well. That's great.

You know everyone has a handicap of some sort or other. Some people lack will or are ridden by fear or aren't very bright. Those are the really bad handicaps because they are almost impossible to overcome.

If, on the other hand, one has will and courage and, most of all, has a brain, other handicaps can be overcome.

Best wishes on your overcoming.

And then there was a letter that Isaac once received from a nine-year-old. Here is the text of that letter:

January 25, 1983

Dear Mr. Asimov,

My name is Isaac and I am 9. Sometimes I hate my name because kids at school joke about it. You are the only other Isaac I ever heard of who is famous. My teacher told me about you. I hope that is OK. Where did you get your name from? Will you be my friend? I sure need one.

Your friend,
Isaac V.

P.S. What do your friends call you? Did you ever get so mad you wanted to punch somebody?

And this was Isaac's reply:

31 January 1983

Dear Isaac,

I was named for my mother's father, my grandfather, who died before I was born. My friends all call me Isaac and they're used to the name now and don't think it's funny.

Actually it's a good name and there are a number of famous Isaacs.

Eight hundred years ago, there were two Isaacs who reigned as Emperor in Constantinople. One of the most beautiful buildings in the city of Leningrad in Russia is the Cathedral of St. Isaac.

The greatest scientist who ever lived was Isaac Newton. The greatest violin player in the world is Isaac Stern. Another writer besides myself, one who has won a Nobel Prize, is Isaac Bashevis Singer.

Someday you may be famous and then you will be proud to have a name that isn't so common it is meaningless.

Your friend,
Isaac

21

Travel

Isaac hated to travel and was especially afraid to fly. Here's how he viewed it.

24 May 1974

Those who know me know I do not willingly travel. Not for me the urge to cross the hill and penetrate the horizon in order to learn what lies beyond. I am perfectly content to sit at home and let my mind wander. And wander it does—very effectively. In the course of the books I have written, it has wandered from the dawn of the universe to its end and from here to the farthest star. It has wandered over almost every field of human knowledge without ever growing footsore.

Naturally, then, when invited to visit this or that distant land, one time Sweden, let us say, another time New Jersey, I hesitate and generally say "no." If it is distant enough to require air travel, I always say "no" since I do not use airplanes. They strike me as unsporting. You can have an automobile accident—and survive. You can be on a sinking ship—and survive. You can be in an earthquake, fire, volcanic eruption, tornado, what you will —and survive. But if your plane crashes, you do not survive. And I say the heck with it.

Isaac turned down so many invitations to travel that you would think he would have developed some "form letter." But all of his letters were written spontaneously at the typewriter. Here are a variety of ways that he declined to travel.

25 November 1968

It is no more likely that I will ever be in the Northwest than that I will ever be on Mars.

3 June 1969

In two words: im possible.

I do not like to travel more than six hours from home, and I do not take airplanes. That puts Texas forever beyond my horizon.

4 August 1969

Alas, alas, not a chance in Hades.

I never fly, and I don't like to travel generally. I will never in my whole life (as far as I can see it) visit Florida.

1 July 1971

Absolutely impossible for me to get to Springfield, Ill. I couldn't even get to Springfield, healthy.

16 June 1973

NO to Seattle.
NOT A CHANCE
NIL
NEVER
NOT AT ALL
NO, NO, NO
NOTHING DOING
NEVER
NO
I hope I'm not being too subtle.

20 July 1971

California is unreachable for me, and the only way UCLA can hear me is to establish a New York campus.

4 October 1971

Not even for robots would I go to Chicago. I would go to Stockholm to receive the Nobel Prize. Anything short of that, forget it.

5 June 1973

Not even if Mary Tyler Moore were to ask me (with a meaningful glint in her eye) to come to Minneapolis, would I come. Well, *maybe,* if Mary Tyler Moore were to ask me with an *unmistakable* gleam in her eye, would I come.

29 October 1977

First-class accommodations on ship and in Paris notwithstanding, I just don't want to leave home.

18 September 1978

Nothing will get me out to Wyoming by train, bus, car or oxcart.

20 June 1981

What it boils down to is getting to Hollywood.

Since I don't fly, the remaining options are walking, running, jumping, hopping, crawling, bicycling, motorcycling, pogo-sticking, horseback, automobile, bus, train or ship via the Panama Canal.

I consider none of them acceptable because they would all take too much time. Please forgive me, but Hollywood must come to me. Since I can't really expect Hollywood to do that, I must do without.

9 September 1988

I am sorry to have to tell you that I do not travel. I live on this small island in peace and serenity, and I don't like to leave it for any reason at all. The island is called Manhattan, by the way.

Fred Pohl once urged Isaac to go with Bob Heinlein and him to Japan, where they had been invited to a science fiction symposium. Pohl added: "I'll fly with you and hold your hand. I will even arrange so that you and I and Bob Heinlein are in the same airplane, so in the event that it crashes, none of us comes out with a competitive advantage." Isaac replied:

2 October 1969

A dingaling I live, a dingaling I'll die. No airplanes. No Japan. That way if the airplane crashes, I come out with a competitive advantage.

Tomorrow I have to drive 50 miles to give a talk. And I'm having to steel myself. Japan yet!

But he did occasionally travel to make speeches and to attend science fiction conventions.

11 May 1980

You have no idea how phobic I am about travel. I *must* travel because I love after-dinner speaking. I'm good at it, and I command high fees. But I try to stay close to home, and I raise my fees each year. Even so, I've got more than I can handle.

It's not that I have forgotten my origins, believe me. There's not a science fiction convention in Manhattan that I don't attend and speak at (for nothing). But it's got to be in Manhattan. For a world s.f. convention, I may go as far as Boston or Washington and speak (still for nothing, not even carfare or roomfare).

On occasion, he really regretted not enjoying traveling. For instance, he was invited to be a "celebrity judge" at the Ms. and Mr. Nude America Contest.

6 July 1981

I will be honest. I receive many requests that I judge this or that, and I use my formidable talents as a fiction writer to make up expressions of regret as I refuse. Today, for the first time, I REALLY REGRET having to refuse. You have no idea how I would be willing to throw myself into the task of judging, the amount of pains I would be willing to take. But I REALLY can't do it. The fact is I don't travel.

And there was the time that the American ambassador to the Soviet Union invited Isaac to come to the Soviet Union as his guest. Isaac replied:

30 January 1984

It breaks my heart. I have never gone back to the Soviet Union since I left at the age of three, although I have this queer urge to see my hometown someday (for all the good it would do me—I remember nothing).

The Soviets themselves, in one way or another, have frequently invited me to visit (and made my brother very welcome in my place a few years ago). I have been informed over and over that my books are very popular in the Soviet Union and that I am well known. And I am terribly flattered that you are interested in my books as well. Furthermore, I am completely in agreement with your desire to find ways to encourage good relations between the two superpowers.

Now comes the catch. I never fly. I have a phobia about travel. It takes incredible pressure to get me to go as far as Washington. There is no way in which I can go to Moscow. It sounds incredible, I know, but I am virtually pinned to the ground here in Manhattan. Please forgive me.

One fan once offered to get him a course in "autosuggestion in overcoming phobias" and promised him that he would be flying with pleasure within a few weeks. Isaac replied:

7 February 1986

As for my acrophobia, you mustn't touch it. I find it useful. It enables me to refuse to travel on legitimate grounds and without my having to lie (which I am no good at). Since I hate traveling and like to sit at my typewriter or word processor and take in the sounds and sights of Manhattan every day, you see that my acrophobia is a blessing.

Yet in the 1970s, Isaac did travel. Not by air, but on occasion by ship, train or car. It was because his extreme love for Janet was greater than his extreme aversion to travel.

14 December 1972

Just returned from a cruise, in the course of which I watched the Apollo 17 blastoff. Wow!

24 April 1973

Yes, I'm going on a cruise to Africa. It's the second one. Last December, I went down to Florida to see the Apollo 17 launch. I felt a science fiction writer ought to see *one* launch and a science writer ought to see *one* total eclipse.

I don't like it, though. I've been vaccinated, and I didn't like that. I refuse to take a cholera shot (which isn't compulsory), so when the ship makes its one-day stopover in Dakar, I do not intend to get off the ship.

But the cruise to Africa to see the eclipse did not go off as planned. Janet suffered a subarachnoid hemorrhage and was hospitalized. However, she recovered sufficiently to go home before the start of the cruise and she insisted that Isaac go alone.

13 August 1973

The trip to Africa went very well except for the fact that Janet could not come along with me. I spent 12 to 14 hours in the radio room—literally and honestly—calling her every day.

The following year, when he and Janet went to Great Britain, Isaac made sure to get his priorities straight. He wrote this letter to his host, Victor Serebriakoff, then international head of Mensa:

10 March 1974

It is now but little more than 11 weeks before I am scheduled to leave for Great Britain, and, as the time shortens, my apprehensions rise, and you must do everything you can to soothe me, or I shall blacken my face, dash into the cellar and disguise myself as a heap of coal.

One of the soothings that is required is the reassurance that the sightseeing tour comes first.

The reason for that is easy to see. If I come to London first and proceed to get all my speaking engagements and media work and people-meeting work and smiling-and-signing work over with, then, by Parkinson's Law, the work will expand to fill the time. There will always be "just one more little thing" and, finally, there will be left one minute to spare to make the ship in Southampton to go home.

As it turned out, Isaac wanted to see Great Britain.

24 May 1974

If there is one foreign nation that I would like to visit it is Great Britain. After all, I am culturally a Briton. My childhood reading was of books that were totally British. My early nursery rhymes talked of the road to Norwich, of London Bridge, of going to St. Ives. My early fairy tales were of Cornish giants, my readings of Dickens, Shakespeare, Conan Doyle, P. G. Wodehouse, Gilbert and Sullivan, all immersed me in things British. Besides which, I have been told the British people use a version of our very own American language.

My wife is also an Anglophile and for the same reasons. Unlike myself, she is even partly of English descent. When, some time ago, she was hospitalized, I promised her that if she would but make an effort and stop that nonsense, I would take her to Great Britain. Her prompt improvement was remarkable.

In Great Britain, I anticipate that my meticulous Brooklyn accent (cultivated at great expense as a longtime resident of some of the less desirable neighborhoods of that borough) will render me largely unintelligible. I have therefore arranged for subtitles to play across the magnificent expanse of my shirtfront.

And I expect to do a lot of gasping because nowhere will I go in London or elsewhere but I will come across names familiar to me from childhood. "Good heavens," I shall gasp, "Piccadilly . . . Pall Mall . . . Regent Street . . . Limehouse . . . Threadneedle Street . . . St. Paul's . . ."

22 June 1974

I sightsaw: Stonehenge, Westminster Abbey and numerous cathedrals. During five days in London, I gave three talks, 50 interviews, four receptions and so on.

3 July 1974

I saw two plays: *King John* in Stratford-on-Avon and *Pygmalion* in London, the latter with a favorite actress of mine—Diana Rigg, whom I managed to get to see backstage.

From time to time, Isaac was invited to speak aboard ships.

22 July 1978

As to talking on the *Queen Elizabeth 2*. What happened was that I was on a full-paid cruise once, when someone who was supposed to speak couldn't because of seasickness. I was in the audience and my wife instantly volunteered me. I got up on the platform and delivered an effective off-the-cuff talk. The master of ceremonies remembered that and, thereafter, I was regularly invited though I didn't always accept.

And Isaac did eventually go to California—by train.

26 July 1978

Some organization met the totally ridiculous fee I quoted them in order to get them to leave me alone. So I'll be talking at Pebble Beach on December 11. And then I'll have to go up and down the coast of California for a while to see the redwoods and the San Diego Zoo and visit Janet's brother and things like that.

14 March 1979

That trip to California was undertaken only because I had faithfully promised my wife that someday I would take her to the San Diego Zoo.

And believe me there's a spot in Penn Station that's still pretty clean from being kissed by me when I got back to New York.

22

More Saying "No"

One of the amazing things about reading Isaac's letters is to see how many invitations he received to write books, write articles, make speeches, accept jobs, attend functions or be elected or appointed to various positions.

Isaac was so overworked that he had to say "no" to thousands of projects. Over the years, he developed many explanations for why he had to decline a project. He always asked that proposals be in writing. Here's why.

28 February 1976

It is very difficult for me to say "no" face to face. It's much easier facing a piece of paper.

First, here are some letters in which he declined writing assignments.

23 October 1963

I am so buried in work, so pecked to death with it, so suffocated by it, so beaten by it, so swept away by it, so demolished by it, so strangled by it, that I am simply going to have to learn to say "no." So you see, I'm learning. No!

29 October 1963

It is strange that in an age when technological advance constantly shortens the workweek for the "working man," my own workweek constantly lengthens and yet leaves me falling farther and farther behind my contractual commitments.

20 January 1968

I wish I could write you a new story but although I haven't slept in three years, I *still* can't catch up.

13 June 1969

I am still screamingly busy. (The use of the adverb is to imply that I'm always screaming, "I'm busy; I'm busy.")

18 September 1975

I have six books in progress, two monthly articles and something like nine short pieces on order (including four s.f. pieces). I have a disease called "yesism" which has kept me to the grindstone for 25 years without letup so far, but even I can see when nothing more can be squeezed in. I *can't*.

24 November 1976

There are only 36 hours in a day; I have only three hands; and time doesn't stretch.

12 February 1977

I make my living out of my reputation for knowing everything and being able to write about everything. Every once in a while, though, I am forced to admit that I don't know *every* thing. I wouldn't be comfortable writing about religion in the future. I don't know enough.

22 February 1977

I'm a case of supply failing to meet the demand, even though I do put out a book a month, more or less.

13 June 1979

I am up to my fetlocks or my chin (whichever is higher) in all sorts of tasks, and there is nothing I can do about it.

11 August 1979

I have already said "yes" to exactly twice as many jobs of work as I can possibly do in the time allotted me. I have contracts, already signed, stretching to the horizon and I simply must stop.

21 January 1986

My writing schedule is compressed to the density of platinum already.

7 January 1987

I hesitate to start a new column. At the present moment, I am writing 52 columns a year for a newspaper syndicate, 26 columns a year for a magazine, 13 for another magazine and 12 for still another magazine, amounting to 130,000 words per year.

He declined an invitation to run for the presidency of the Science Fiction Writers of America.

13 September 1971

My temperament is such that I am utterly incapable of running any organization. I don't have the stiff fiber required for making decisions and pushing them through. I don't have the judgment required to do what is right and feasible and what is wrong and unfeasible. I get along with people entirely too well. To run an organization, you have to be able to offend when necessary and not worry about it.

In short, almost anyone (maybe quite anyone) would be better than I am for not only the presidency of the Science Fiction Writers of America but for the presidency of anything—even including the USA.

He declined a late-night radio guest appearance.

22 June 1979

I am a morning person. I am asleep by 11 P.M., and I am awake no later than 6 A.M. I do morning shows gladly, but I don't do night shows.

He turned down £20,000 (about $30,000) from a British publisher to write about the future of microchips.

24 December 1980

I ruminate over the ironies of life. There were times once when I was so eager, willing and available—and I could not persuade anyone to offer me money. Now people of their own accord wave huge batches of cash under my nose and I am helpless. My time is occupied for years in advance with a variety of projects, and there is no way in which I could add another. I retire—weeping.

He declined to be part of a search committee for a museum director.

28 February 1981

My dear wife, with tears in her eyes, has asked me to submit all flattering proposals to her, and so I showed her this one. She shook her head firmly, indicating that my judgment in these matters was notable only for its complete non-existence. Her exact words were "A klutz like you?" So I think I had better decline the honor.

He declined a request to make a speech for no money similar to a speech that he had given to the same organization 20 years earlier for free:

17 March 1982

I sounded out the various interested people in connection with the suggested talk.

My speech agent warned me that a suggestion like that made him feel like throwing me out of the window (he's on the 36th floor). He has just gotten me an engagement for a talk that carries a fee of $10,000. "How," he asks, "can I get fees like that if you go around giving talks for nothing?"

My wife warned me that a suggestion like that made her feel like throwing me out of the window (we're on the 33rd floor). She says I am 20 years older, and I keep promising to take it easy. A talk for free involves just as much hard work, she says, as one for $10,000.

My doctor warned me that a suggestion like that made him feel like throwing me out of the window (he's only on the second floor, so who cares). He says I've already had my coronary and that he has told me 100 times that I can't overwork as a favor. I'm too old. So I have to say "no."

He declined to attend a gala dance.

8 November 1988

I cannot attend the gala for a number of reasons.

It won't start earlier than 10 P.M. I'm an old man who goes to bed early, and I cannot eat dinner when my body is accustomed to sleeping.

I expect there will be a great deal of smoking, drinking and dancing at the gala. I, however, do not smoke (and detest the smell of tobacco). I also do not drink and do not dance.

Finally, it is a black-tie affair. Though I am sometimes forced, very much against my will, to don a tuxedo, I hate it and never do it if I can possibly avoid it.

The next declination summarized his views.

22 June 1984

I find that, as I grow older, I receive more and more invitations to take on honorary offices, memberships on consultation boards or advisory panels and so on.

I suppose it makes sense, for, ordinarily, as you grow older your real accomplishments fade and you have to take on posts that establish you as a "sage."

Unfortunately (or fortunately), my real work is not fading. I'm turning out 20 books a year, and I'm doing my best to fight off all the offers I get to spend my time otherwise. I've got to keep on writing.

23

Television, Hollywood and Star Trek

Friends were always urging Isaac to write for television or the movies and "make a lot of money." Throughout his writing career, however, he was not interested.

3 July 1956

The medium in which my work appears (the printed page) is under my own full control. Barring minor changes that are worked out between the editors and myself, the stories as they appear are under *my* name and represent *my* work.

Television and movies would mean adaptations. I am not anxious to have my stories "adapted" unless I can have veto power in order to make sure that they aren't adapted to death, a fate for which mere money is inadequate recompense.

Since I know television and movies wouldn't agree to that, I have made no attempt at all to search them out. If they come looking for me (unlikely, I suppose), we can try to do business on terms mutually agreeable. That may take forever, but I'll wait.

As examples of "adapting to death," I mean putting in a ridiculous love interest where I have none; tacking on a happy ending where a tragic one is called for, and, most of all, making the science ridiculous after I have done my professional best to make it reasonable and plausible.

10 September 1968

TV is a different kettle of fish altogether. It is huge, impersonal and heartless. Anyone writing for TV or any of the mass media is courting either ulcers or lost self-respect. That's one reason I don't write for the mass media.

13 April 1969

Under no circumstances will I ever sign a contract, for whatever sum of money, up to and including all the money in the world (with Raquel Welch thrown in), which will require me to consult with Hollywood concerning anything I am writing. This is not just because I am afraid of airplanes and hate traveling. I wouldn't consult with Hollywood even if they sent a man to my home for the purpose.

Anything I write is strictly between me and my editor. Hollywood might buy a story I have written, once it is written and published, and then mess it up. Too bad, but if anyone says, "What a rotten movie!", I can say, "Read the book!" Hollywood *can't* mess up my story while I write it and leave me *nothing* to point to with pride.

27 July 1973

I not only do not write for television, I most sincerely do not want to write for television. I make an adequate living writing books and stories and articles, all of which I control myself. To write for television is to involve one's self (I understand) in a creative pigsty, which is all right if you need the money (perhaps), but I don't.

11 February 1979

I do not trust Hollywood. All my experience is that any arrangements that involve Hollywood people break up for any of a thousand reasons.

31 October 1979

I have been tangentially involved with movies and television on numerous occasions. I have consulted; I have advised; I have written treatments. . . . Nothing seems to come to fruition. In the end, I spend a lot of time and get nothing on the screen, either little or big. I sometimes get a bit of money, but I can get money in other ways that give me more satisfaction.

26 June 1981

My experience with television has been a peculiar one. No matter what anyone suggests; no matter how much approval there is; no matter how much excitement there is; no matter how much progress is made . . .

Nothing ever happens!

Occasionally, he was asked to appear as a host on a television show.

11 January 1983

I've spent a week thinking about the business of being on television à la Arthur Clarke, and I've decided against it.

I can't bear the thought of five strangers in our home for the entire day. I can't bear the thought of television equipment in our home. I can't bear the thought of having to move furniture. I can't bear the thought of spending the entire day at it.

It is more than I can bear.

Isaac loved Star Trek, *both when it was on television and in its later reincarnation in the movies. But the relationship between Isaac and* Star Trek *had a rocky beginning.*

2 December 1966

I have sinned, and I repent in sackcloth and ashes.

TV Guide asked me to write a funny article on the new science fiction programs, and I watched a week's worth, blew my top at their ridiculous science and went to town.

So intent was I on being funny and on not picking on any one program exclusively *(TV Guide* had sent me a list to cover) that I found one little item to cavil at in connection with *Star Trek,* and added—but not strongly enough—that I thought it the best.

Now I am the object of enraged *Star Trek* fans—which doesn't bother me in itself. But I think they are perfectly justified and that *does* bother me.

6 December 1966

If I had had an ounce of brains, I would have realized that I've spent years boosting s.f. everywhere I could, from science fiction magazines to scientific periodicals, and here was my chance to boost *good* s.f. on the TV screen. And I muffed it.

Within a couple of months, Isaac made amends by writing another article for TV Guide. *In a letter to Gene Roddenberry, the producer and moving force behind* Star Trek, *Isaac wrote:*

21 February 1967

The article begins: "A revolution of incalculable importance may be sweeping America, thanks to television. And thanks, particularly, to *Star Trek,* which, in its noble and successful effort to present good science fiction to the American public, has also presented everyone with an astonishing revelation."

I then go on to say that *Star Trek,* in the person of Mr. Spock, has shown that "women think being smart is sexy." In other words, Mr. Spock very effectively turns on young ladies (he really does—I've checked), and it is his high intelligence that seems to make him successful in this. That, and the challenge he represents in seeming so impervious to being bowled over. The title of the piece is "Three Cheers for Mr. Spock."

Leonard Nimoy, who played Mr. Spock, loved the article. He wrote this to Isaac:

May 8, 1967

When I first came to California to start a film career, the current rage was Marlon Brando, who had just won the hearts of American females by playing a stupid, insensitive boor. Perhaps you're right. I certainly hope so. At any rate, the article was marvelous.

In a letter to Roddenberry, Isaac wrote:

22 October 1967

I'm watching *Star Trek* with great pleasure this year and worry each week about how many blasts the *Enterprise* can take without being reduced to unrepairable junk. But I have faith in you, Gene, and know you will keep it in tip-top shape.

*During the decade of the 1970s, Isaac was a featured speaker at
many* Star Trek *conventions.*

1 March 1976
Science fiction readers, unlike mystery readers, tend to be emotional, articulate and intense. Thus, there are numerous science
fiction conventions organized and conducted by the *fans* all over
the country, whereas one does not hear of meetings of mystery
readers. The *Star Trek* phenomenon, which is not precisely typical of science fiction, would nevertheless be inconceivable in any
other category of popular fiction.

By 1979, Star Trek *had become a movie. Isaac then wrote Roddenberry:*

6 January 1980
Janet and I finally saw *Star Trek—The Motion Picture* and enjoyed it very much. I must tell you that however much it pleased
me to see all the old friends of the *Enterprise,* the character who
won me over was Baldy. I came in with an invincible prejudice
and told Janet there was no way I would find myself sympathetic
to a billiard-ball female Kojak. But long before the picture was
over, she was all I was waiting for. She was beautiful.

So was my name, correctly spelled, moving up the screen. I
applauded wildly.

And Roddenberry replied:

February 8, 1980
As you have discovered with "Baldy," I am much shrewder than
you vis-à-vis the human female and what makes her excite us. I
bow to you in all other areas of science and art.

I still chuckle when I remember Paramount going secretly (they
thought) to you in order to get expert proof that Crazy Gene was
talking nonsense by insisting that machines could be alive and
that there might be more dimensions to the universe than those
we presently know. It was all made doubly funny by the fact that
so much of my thought and theory on such things came out of
reading Asimov.

I'll never forget the day that one of Paramount's young vice presidents came to my office with an astonished expression on his face as he reported that you agreed with most of the story points I had been fighting for. Ah, I'd like to have back all the energy wasted on such fights during the last four years of trying to get this film started and completed.

In a letter to a friend, Isaac explained the screen credit:

4 January 1980

Actually, all I did in the *Star Trek* movie was to answer some questions by phone and mail on whether this or that point could be made within the limits of legitimate science fictional extrapolation. It was just the work of an hour or two, and I don't think I deserved the screen credit.

And a final appraisal of Star Trek:

5 July 1990

I consider myself a good friend of Gene Roddenberry and have been an interested viewer of *Star Trek* for a quarter of a century (though by no means as devoted to it as my fanatical wife is).

Star Trek has been enduring because it was the first and continuing piece of visual science fiction to be *true* science fiction and to depend upon intelligence rather than upon shoot-'em-up special effects. People are attracted by intelligence even if they don't like to admit it.

24

English

Isaac loved the English language.

12 June 1971

I am in one respect of language a ferocious chauvinist. I want English to be a world language.

But when S. I. Hayakawa, a linguist and former U.S. senator, asked him to support a constitutional amendment making English the official language of the United States, Isaac didn't agree.

23 March 1984

I am a lover of the English language as anyone who writes 300 books in that language would have to be. What's more, I am essentially monolingual.

However, while I don't want to see our nation split into language groups, neither do I want to encourage Anglo-olatry. It is important that Americans speak languages other than English, and I have always regretted the fact that my parents (who each spoke perfect Russian) did not bother to introduce me to the language while I was young and might have picked it up easily. Yes, English is my one and only language, and I'd rather have that than any other, but I have a sense of loss.

Isaac was proud of his creation of three English words.

19 October 1990

When I was quite young (in my early 20s), I coined three words: positronic, psychohistory and robotics. They have found their way into the Oxford English Dictionary (with credit to me) and are now part of the English language.

In selecting the letters for this book, I discovered a number of instances when Isaac used periods when he should have used question marks. Apparently, even Isaac was aware of this failing.

25 May 1972

Fred Pohl was complaining about my lack of "pothooks" as long ago as 1941. I'm afraid it's an inherent vitamin deficiency or something. I *know* question marks are supposed to be there, and my copyreaders work overtime inserting them. But no human mind can catch *every* question mark I leave out.

Isaac loved to think, hear and write about the English language.

9 December 1963

The world being what it is, differences in speech and pronunciation, even quite minor ones, arouse hostility, amusement and all the latent prejudices that exist within one. Heaven knows how many votes Al Smith lost because he referred to "raddio" instead of "radio." Heaven knows how many times I curled my lip at Eisenhower because he said "modren" instead of "modern." My own Brooklyn accent stamps me as illiterate to anyone who doesn't know me.

In an ideal world, differences in dialect and pronunciation are delightful. In our miserable world, I would honestly like to see speech standardized until the human race matures (if ever).

16 January 1968

"Gymnasium" means, literally, a "place for exercise in the nude." "Ordeal" is homologous with the German word *"Urteil"* meaning "judgment." The "trial by ordeal" is really tautological. When you held a red-hot poker in your hand to see if you got burned (if you were only slightly burned you were innocent), you were undergoing judgment—*Urteil*—ordeal. The ordeal *was* the trial.

I *love* that sort of thing. I'm so glad that there are just enough nuts congruent to myself to make my books profitable enough to cause publishers to humor me.

The most frequent expletive that Isaac used was "dear me."

10 May 1962

Dear me! What would I do without that exclamation? It is not as prissy as it sounds but is a distortion of the Italian *"Dio mio!"* meaning "My God!"

Occasionally his dear friend science writer L. Sprague de Camp would sent him galleys of one of de Camp's forthcoming books. Isaac would read them not only with great enjoyment but with an eye toward finding errors if any existed. After reading The Great Monkey Trial, *he wrote de Camp:*

13 December 1967

I didn't seriously expect to find any errors in your science. (I don't recall that I have ever found that kind of error in you.) Sure enough, I didn't.

On page 478, I corrected the word "evanishment" by eliminating the initial "e," then got a little restless about it and looked it up in Webster's. Sure enough, it turned out to be another one of those cases in which you know words I don't.

Another one of Isaac's favorite correspondents was the famed geologist Stephen Jay Gould, professor of geology in the department of earth and planetary sciences at Harvard University. Isaac wrote this letter to Gould:

29 January 1983

I am reading the bound galleys of *Hen's Teeth and Horse's Toes* with completely predictable pleasure. In the very first chapter you mention that "all versions written for nonscientists" speak of *the* anglerfish.

A spasm of panic struck me. Last year I wrote a book entitled *How Did We Find Out About Life in the Deep Sea?* intended for 10- to 12-year-olds. Had I avoided the trap? I didn't remember.

I went through the book, scarcely daring to read the passage. I speak of "the anglerfish," but the plural of "fish" is "fish," you know. Then in the next sentence: "There are about 210 different species of anglerfish." Then later on: "In some anglerfish the female is much larger than the male."

Thank goodness!!! There is no one whose scorn I would less like to rouse than you.

And he wrote this about Gould.

16 October 1987

Gould is an absolutely mesmerizing lecturer, and if he'd been around Columbia when I was a student there, he might easily have made a paleontologist out of me.

But did Isaac's knowledge of the language mean that he should write a book about linguistics?

5 June 1988

I haven't written a book on linguistics because I don't know anything about linguistics. My interest in words proves nothing. I am very fond of food and of eating, but I know absolutely nothing about cooking.

25

Still More Limericks and Oddities

To the retiring president of Mohegan Community College in Norwich, Connecticut:

28 April 1981

All hail to Mohegan's old Prexy
Who should always be current, not ex-y.
 For he's wonderful, wacky,
 Delightful, by cracky,
And the damsels all think he is sexy.

To a doctor friend on his birthday:

15 August 1981

The roll call of patients of Leon
Is a very good listing to be on.
 With illness endured
 (If you want to be cured),
That's the place you can wager your fee on.

To a Mensa member:

19 November 1981

There was a young lady named Prior
Who said that sex made her perspire.
  Those who've tried her a lot
  Say the lass is quite hot,
So it's clear that she isn't a liar.

To a friend who was retiring:

1 June 1982

Let's all give three cheers for old Charlie
In steinfuls of hops and of barley.
  To Boston and arts
  He goes with our hearts,
Long before he's grown wrinkled and gnarly.

To a fan who missed seeing him at a science fiction convention:

28 August 1982

There was a young lady named Grant
Who at sex was a true dilettante,
  With her feet on the bed
  And the floor 'neath her head,
She always got screwed on the slant.

To one of his magazine editors:

11 December 1982

There once was a fellow named Jim
Who published a mag on a whim.
  He found it expensive,
  The work most intensive,
Oh, gee, I feel sorry for him.

To a woman who worked at one of his book publishers:

3 February 1983

There's a certain young lady named Helen
Who told me, alas, she's not sellin'.
      As to what I would try
      (If I managed) to buy,
It wouldn't be wise to be tellin'.

To one of the executives at Doubleday:

19 April 1983
IF I HAD ALADDIN'S LAMP

My ambition for sweet Linda Winnard
Is (after she's well wined and dinnered)
      To go to her flat
      And arrange it so that
She's thoroughly lovered and sinnered.

To a person arranging a science fiction banquet:

21 September 1983

There was a young woman named Carol
Who looked great without wearing apparel.
      It's my own great ambition
      To see that condition
And have her right over a barrel.

To a fan of his limericks:

17 April 1984

There was a young man named Hans Frommer
Who screwed a young woman all summer.
      She said (came the fall),
      "Someone else will now call!"
And he muttered, "Oh, hell! What a bummer!"

Did anyone ever predict he would be a failure?

11 April 1981

I cannot recall that anyone ever flatly prophesied that I would come to nothing. A professor once said to me apropos of one of my class papers, "The trouble with you, Asimov, is that you can't write." But by then I was already a published author on multiple occasions, and I merely laughed at him.

No one actually predicted great things for me, but I imagine everyone was hesitant at predicting failure in the face of my own evident conviction, strongly and surely held, that I was going up the mountain and did not intend to be stopped.

If he were sentenced to the gallows, what would he ask for his last meal?

30 June 1982

The truth is that if I were sentenced to the gallows, I would probably throw up if I tried to eat a last meal. So I wouldn't order one.

What was his favorite story of a word origin?

23 November 1982

To the Greeks, "chaos" was primeval matter in total disorder. "Cosmos," on the other hand, was that same matter in some appearance of order.

The creation of the universe, then, was not the creation of matter. That already existed. It was the creation of *order*. Anything that imposes disorder on matter originally in order is "chaotic." On the other hand, anything that imposes order on matter originally in disorder is "cosmetic."

And now we know what it is that a woman does when she uses "cosmetics" to "make up" her face.

What book as a child influenced his life?

8 July 1985

No book ever changed my life. A magazine did, however. The August 1929 issue of *Amazing Stories* was the first science fiction magazine I ever read, and it caught me at once. I became a science fiction reader and then a science fiction writer. It has made me better off and more famous than I could possibly have been under any other condition.

What did he think of successful young entrepreneurs?

21 October 1983

I don't admire these millionaires-by-30. They're impressive, as are all the ballplayers and rock musicians who are millionaires-by-30, but that just means they are people who give a lot of people what they want—whether it is home runs, touchdowns or chocolate-chip cookies.

The most marvelous accomplishments are those that people don't particularly want: great scientific discoveries; great experiments in art and literature; great labors in humane endeavors. Such people die poor and unknown very often; sometimes on the cross.

What is the most romantic place he ever visited?

25 November 1983

I have never traveled to any significant extent, and when forced to do so, I do not like it. So the most romantic place I have ever seen is home.

However, I do travel a great deal in my imagination and have, in this way, seen a great deal more than almost anyone. My current favorite is the planet Aurora, which is the scene of my novel *The Robots of Dawn*.

What did he wish he had written?

18 May 1984

I'm quite content with my output. It may not be the best stuff in the world, but it's the best I can do and that is all I ask.

Naturally, I would be happy if someone had told me that I was the real author of *Hamlet*, but I couldn't be unless I were Shakespeare. And I am not Shakespeare. I am just me.

Besides what kind of big deal would it be if I said, "I wish I'd written *Huckleberry Finn*"? What idiot doesn't wish he'd written it and gotten all the fame and money and literary reputation that would accrue?

I'm glad to have written what I have written. That's enough.

26

Name

Isaac loved his name.

11 April 1963

When I sold my first story to John Campbell, he suggested that I adopt an Anglo-Saxon name as a pseudonym because "the readers will find it easier to remember." This is one of Campbell's more egregious stupidities because my odd name burns itself into the fan's memories. Once it is seen twice, it is never forgotten. It becomes heavily associated with s.f. and, later, with popularized science that works strongly in my favor.

I wish I could say that I objected violently to Campbell's suggestion and gathered up my stuff to march out of the office because I was extremely intelligent and foresaw all this. But not so. I did object violently to Campbell's suggestion, and I did gather up my stuff to march out of the office (and he gave in *at once*). But that was because I was far too self-centered even to consider not getting the credit for my stories in my own name.

He hated it when either his first name or his last name was misspelled. He didn't like being addressed as Ike (although Campbell called him that in letters). He did accept "I," which both Fred Pohl and I used.

There were many occasions over the course of his career when his name was misspelled, and his letters correcting them were numerous. Here are just a few of the responses to these errors.

6 December 1967

We all have our little idiosyncrasies, and one of mine is a certain irritation at having my name misspelled.

22 April 1968

My unhappiness over the misspelling of my name amounts to a neurosis.

2 November 1972

Do you enjoy having both your names misspelled? I don't.

9 October 1974

On the envelope and in the letter, you spelled my name Isamov three times. It is Asimov, and if my books are so great and you love me so much—you should know.

27 December 1976

Your description of me as a "major writer" may be more flattering than sincere. If I were really a major writer, you would know how to spell my name correctly.

22 April 1984

I am curious to know how you can have taught science fiction for eight years with some attention to my work—without having learned to spell my name correctly.

1 November 1986

My name, with its correct spelling, gets a great deal of exposure. People who misspell it, therefore, are either terribly nearsighted or thoughtless or simply don't care about me.

But when an Israeli publisher wanted to translate several of his books into Hebrew, Isaac agreed to use a different name!

20 December 1988

I was born in Russia, and my parents named me, in Hebrew, Yitzhock. In the United States, it was anglicized to Isaac (pro-

nounced in many European languages as EE-SOCK, rather close
to the original). Now I love Isaac (EYE-zick) and would not have
it anything else *except* in a Hebrew translation. In Hebrew (and
at no other time), I want it Yitzhock.

To the Authors Guild Bulletin, *he once wrote:*

25 November 1969
Certainly members of the Authors Guild recognize the importance of recognition value in an author's name. The correct spelling of one's name is *important*. In the October–November 1969
issue of the *Authors Guild Bulletin,* the author's name for two of
my books is given as Issac [sic] Asimov. Need I say that my first
name is spelled I-S-A-A-C?

To you, it may seem a little point; to me, it is a great, big, fat
point.

To misspell Isaac argues illiteracy. Has one no acquaintance
with the Bible, where the name Isaac occurs repeatedly through
the later chapters of Genesis? And how do you spell Isaac Newton or Isaac Bashevis Singer? Well, I'll tell you, on page 24, you
spell it Issac Bashevis Singer.

Get on the ball, please!

To an Episcopal minister:

13 June 1988
I am just a little surprised that a minister of the Gospel should
not be able to spell the name Isaac correctly.

*Isaac was asked on occasion whether he was related to an
Azimov or an Asimov in the Soviet Union.*

5 July 1969
The other day I got a letter from Edwin McMillan, the Nobel
Prize–winning physicist who is now at the head of the Lawrence
Radiation Laboratory at the University of California. It seems
that five years ago, during a conference in the Soviet Union, he
had met the head of the nuclear research institute of the Uzbek
S.S.R. (one of the Soviet republics of Central Asia).

The man [S. A. Azimov] had the same name I have (but with a

"z," which is correct), and he apparently had read my books (presumably in Russian translation) and was naturally interested to know if I was one of his crowd. He said that the name was a common Uzbek name and I must be of Uzbek origins.

I wrote both McMillan and the Uzbeki that my family comes from a small town named Petrovichi on the border of the Byelorussian S.S.R., a town about 25 miles from Roslavl, and the family is of Jewish origin. I told them that my name had been made up out of the Russian word for "winter grain" in which my great-great-grandfather had dealt.

Carl Sagan wrote him a letter teasing him that one of the 72 members of the Soviet Academy of Sciences who signed a letter condemning the award of the Nobel Peace Prize to Andrei Sakharov was M. S. Asimov. Wrote Sagan: "Have you no influence on your wayward relatives?" Isaac responded:

6 January 1976

I'm convinced he's no relative. I have been told that Asimov is a common Uzbek name and that some Russians have thought I was Uzbeki on the strength of it. I suspect that M. S. Asimov is at the Kremlin's Uzbek and call on such matters.

To another person who raised the same question:

6 January 1981

About the Order of Lenin to M. S. Asimov. Apparently Asimov is a very common name among the Uzbeks since (my theory) Hassim is the family name of Muhammad's tribe. This particular one, with his first name Mukhamed, is clearly of Islamic origin. Me, I'm from the borders of Byelorussia and am strictly Jewish (by descent). No connection.

As to why the correct Russian spelling is Azimov and why we spell it Asimov:

13 February 1985

The Russian spelling of our name is A3IMOB and the precise transliteration is Azimov. The "z" was changed to an "s" at Ellis Island.

His concern about his last name even went to its pronunciation.

10 October 1969

Pronounce my name correctly (accent on the first syllable, all vowels short, and "s" pronounced like "z").

13 September 1975

My name is pronounced as though it were the three words "has-him-of," with the two h's left out and the accent on the first syllable.

27

Youth

Isaac would occasionally write about his younger years.

26 March 1969

When I was young, my family was too poor to buy books, but library cards were free. From the age of six, I have haunted the library, and the books I read educated me before the schools got their chance.

While I went to school, library books taught me what school did not and when I finished with my formal education, books kept right on educating me. If you use the library, there is no charge, either.

30 October 1962

In the early 1930s, I belonged to the Brooklyn Public Library *and* the Queens Public Library because I lived on the boundary of the two boroughs. The Queens Public Library branch was a full two miles away, but I used to walk there and back regardless of the weather every week. I once walked it when the temperature was in the single numbers and never thought it odd. It was just cold. So I bundled up. My mother let me go without a thought about it either (one advantage of having been brought up in Russia).

10 January 1959

I never had an electric train or a two-wheeled bicycle or a Hula-Hoop or any but the smallest Erector Set. But I'm lucky. When I was 11 years old, my parents listened to a suggestion I made and for my birthday got me a copy of the World Almanac. As a measure of our level of economic welfare, it cost 50 cents and my father swung a deal to get it wholesale (i.e., at 40 cents) and was greatly relieved at being able to save a dime.

I wouldn't swap that World Almanac for all the electric trains in the world. I spent hours (literally) poring over every word it contained and when I got tired reading the statistics, I got my parents to invest in a sheaf of graph paper, and I prepared line graphs and bar graphs of them.

This accomplished several things. (1) It kept me out of my parents' hair. (2) It kept me deliriously happy. (3) And thanks to my near-photographic memory (I can remember things near photographs), I salted away a mess of stuff I could use later on in stories and articles.

2 May 1965

If my parents were small-scale merchants, they nevertheless took it for granted I was going to be a "learned man." So I took it for granted, too. However, a childhood spent in "playing games" and "doing nothing" is not to be sneezed at, by the way.

While my childhood was not seriously deprived or really tragic, it was nevertheless not a particularly happy one. This was not through the fault of my hardworking parents, but entirely because I did not fit well into the society of my peers. There is a price to pay for everything.

9 September 1961

When I was a youngster, whenever I went to a movie with my father (which was rare), he always turned to me when we emerged and asked, "Well, Isaac, wot did you loined?"

22 March 1973

In the early 1930s, I used to look forward to Fourth of July the way most people looked forward to Christmas. For a week, everyone shot off firecrackers. My family was too poor to get me anything but a few strings of "half-inchers," which I could set off on the windowsill. But I could always watch the other wealthier kids set off their inch-and-a-halfers, their cherry bombs and, if I was ultra-lucky, their rockets.

2 February 1966

The 1930s were my decade. I read Krazy Kat and the Rover Boys, and I knew about the Louis-Schmeling fight.

8 April 1969

I do *not* know Hebrew. Oh, when I was eight years old, I spent four months or so in a Hebrew school and that was enough to teach me to *read* Hebrew, and since my memory is what it is, I have never forgotten. I also remember some of the vocabulary I then learned and some that I have picked up by osmosis here and there in my reading.

3 February 1977

My parents did not abandon Yiddish, but continued to speak it for years. In fact, I myself learned Yiddish and can speak it fairly fluently. I can understand it almost as well as I can understand English. At the present moment, I am thoroughly bilingual in English and Yiddish in that I can think in either without having to translate from one to the other. I can speak German fairly well, largely thanks to Yiddish. In a pinch, I could make myself understood in French if it were a life-and-death case. I have a surprisingly large vocabulary in Greek and Latin, largely thanks to my etymological work, but can't handle the words at all in sentences in either language.

11 November 1988

The truth is that I know no Russian at all. When I came here at three, my parents were determined that English would be my first language. They never spoke to me in Russian.

10 April 1985

When I was about ten years old, there were a number of books I loved. There was *Tom Sawyer*, for instance (but *not Huckleberry Finn*, which I learned to love as an adult). There were the various Penrod books by Booth Tarkington (I felt a kinship with "bad boys" for some reason); there were various books by E. Nesbit, with my favorite by all odds *The Story of the Amulet*, and the various Dr. Dolittle books by Hugh Lofting, with *The Voyages of Dr. Dolittle* my favorite.

If, however, we judge a book as favorite by counting the number of times it was read and reread, my all-time favorite was none of these. Indeed, it was not a children's book (by the usual definitions) at all. But I didn't know that. My parents were immigrants who couldn't read English at that time and who didn't know English-language literature. They obtained a library card for me but could do nothing more, and I read anything I could persuade the librarians to let me have. I tried to get the long books because they lasted a longer time. And I found *Pickwick Papers* by Charles Dickens.

I read it and reread it and reread it. It's an actual fact and not exaggeration that I read it 25 times before I was out of my teens. Since then I have read just about all of Dickens (and *Nicholas Nickleby* is my second favorite), but I have never wavered as to what is in first place. I still reread *Pickwick Papers*. I reread it, first word to last, only last month, and I enjoyed it just as much as ever, even though I can close my eyes at any point and continue reading.

9 April 1987

During my childhood as a member of an ambitious but very poor immigrant family, I did all my reading and obtained nine-tenths of my learning in the public library. It frightens me to think what I might have become—and what I might have *failed* to become—without one.

25 April 1985

I believe most of my teachers considered me a pain in the neck and did not enjoy seeing me in their classes. I was a disruptive influence and a disciplinary problem. My huge and incredibly vicious crime was that I would tend to whisper to my neighbors in class. For this I was endlessly disciplined.

There was nothing they could really do to me, however, for I was also far and away the brightest kid in the class—and the youngest. Heaven only knows what they wrote about me in the records, but it was no secret what they thought of me. The other kids could hear the teachers yelling at me. It probably saved my life. If I had been extraordinarily bright *and* a teacher's pet, the kids would probably have killed me.

I was very happy at school. I enjoyed being bright. I enjoyed baiting the teachers. I wouldn't do anything differently.

19 May 1967

When I was in my early teens, I went through a period of enormous interest in baseball. At the beginning of the season, I would buy a large notebook and prepare 154 complicated tables in which I could put a set of double-entry standings with complete scores. It was fascinating. The only trouble was that I practically never went to see any games and when I did go, it was 55 cents for a bleacher seat in the beating rays of the sun half a mile from home plate.

The most remarkable occasion of my attending a game was Memorial Day 1938 (I believe), when Carl Hubbell had won 24 games in a row and was up for his 25th. He was knocked out of the box. What a harrowing experience for me. Carl Hubbell was my all-time baseball hero. I sat there desolate—convinced that it had happened only because I was in the stands. After all, when I hadn't been in the stands, he had won 24 games. I can see him right now, walking off the field.

11 April 1981

What I enjoyed most in high school were those courses I found easiest: chemistry, history, mathematics, English. I don't think that my English teacher or anyone else (except me) saw that I was going to be a successful writer someday. Even I never guessed *how* successful I would be. But then, the surprises in life are the best part. If everything were cut and dried, how dull it would be.

10 November 1989

I have only one piece of published juvenilia. It is an essay entitled "Little Brothers," written when I was 14 and published in the spring 1934 issue of my high school literary magazine, also when I was 14.

The faculty adviser accepted it with the worst possible grace because it was the only offering that attempted to be funny. And he told me so quite bluntly.

His opinion of my writing ability was rock-bottom, and I don't know if he lived long enough to realize that he was badly mistaken. Fortunately, regardless of his opinion, I already knew, at the age of 14, that I was a great writer. So I didn't require his approval at all.

29 April 1969

To my shock and horror, I find I don't qualify for First Fandom [active s.f. fans in the 1930s].

To be sure, I have been reading s.f. since 1929 and was a fervent fan all through the early 1930s.

However, the fanship was entirely secret and private. I may have written a letter or two to the science fiction magazines, and I seem to recall being shown one, published in 1935 in *Astounding,* by Sam Moskowitz. But I have no hard details on it.

It wasn't until 1938 that I really began writing frequent letters and joining fan clubs and engaging in fannish correspondence. Then, of course, I became a pro that same year and fannishness faded away. (The short, happy fanship of Isaac Asimov.)

6 December 1969

My first science major was zoology, but in my sophomore year, I took embryology and found that nothing I could see under a microscope made any sense to me. In the same year, I took my first college chemistry course and liked it. So I switched from zoology to chemistry. Thank goodness.

9 April 1969

I never took any astronomy courses in college—or physics courses either.

I concentrated exclusively on chemistry (plus assorted junk courses). And this has made my life miserable, too. The reason is that I have written semi-texts on both astronomy and physics and have therefore had to undergo intensive self-education in both fields. And oh boy, considering how brilliant I'm supposed to be, that was *so* difficult.

7 December 1960

The first time I voted, I was concerned lest I be asked to take a literacy test. For some reason, I felt this would be humiliating. So I brought my college diploma with me. When the guy who registered me asked what I was carrying, I unrolled the damned thing and said I thought it would bear witness that I was literate.

He was horrified. "I don't question your literacy," he said. "Do you mean that you took that diploma off the wall just to bring it here?"

And I said lightly, "Oh, it wasn't on the wall. It was in the closet." And I blew some dust off it.

The look of horror deepened. He rose to his full height and for five torturing minutes, he lectured me on my callousness, my hard heart and my near-criminality on burying my diploma in a closet after my father had worked so hard to put me through college. I didn't have the heart to tell him I worked my own way through college. I just slunk away.

I refused to attend the ceremonies for either my bachelor's or my master's degree, but when it came time to get my Ph.D., I gave in. My father so obviously wanted to see me indoctrinated (if that is the word). So I took him, but obstinately and obdurately refused to put on academic robes and parade through that medieval sham. I sat in the audience with him, and when acting president Fackenthal raised his hands and let the heavenly light of Ph.D. fall upon all the candidates at once, I leaned toward my father and whispered that at that moment the divine effulgence nestled on me, too, right there in the audience. And he smiled weakly.

Imagine my horror when, many years later, a letter from the new president of Columbia University asked me to represent him at the induction of some fellow president at some minor institution in Boston, and I was flattered enough to agree. THEN I found out I would have to wear academic costume. I hired cap and robes and wore it in the sullenest way possible. To maintain a principle so long and then to stub my toe over my vanity. Well, serves me right.

16 February 1960

When I first applied for a chemistry-type job at an American Chemical Society convention, I placed at the bottom of my application: "Not interested in any job that has any connection with atomic bomb work in any fashion whatever." During the entire convention, I was not interviewed by a single person. I considered it the inevitable fruits of virtue. (Virtue is its own reward because there is no other.)

7 January 1963

I once (back in 1953) read through 25 years of *Time* issues over a space of two years. Yes, I did. Boston University had bound files of the magazine, and they gave me permission to remove one volume after another and take them home, provided I returned them faithfully after a week and took only one at a time. (The librarians spoke of me, in awe, as "the fellow who reads *Time*" and watched me owl-eyed as I worked my way through the set.) However, it was fun and gave me a bird's eye (a distorted bird's eye, of course) view of history. It inspired my most intricate novel, *The End of Eternity*.

However, it did fill me full of *Time,* and I have not been able to read it since.

2 April 1982

I read comic books in the local luncheonette while eating lunch when I was actively teaching at the Boston U. School of Medicine. Donald Duck was my favorite.

10 December 1966

I keep thinking backward to the days when I was sending stories to *Astounding* and waiting breathlessly for the news of a possible penny-a-word sale. Who cared about the money? I wanted to sell. If I could have looked forward into the future to the day when *Harper's, Playboy* and *SatEvePost* would call me and *ask* for articles and that I would sit there and say "How much?" I might have been stunned to death.

28

Parents

*The things you don't know until you start doing a book about
your brother!*

*My parents had three children, and all three used the same
names in addressing our parents but spelled the words differently. Isaac spelled it "Pappa" and "Mamma." My sister, Marcia, spelled it "Papa" and "Mama." And I spelled it "Poppa"
and "Momma." But no matter how the names were spelled, we
loved our parents. And since this is a book of Isaac's letters, I'll
use his spelling.*

*For my family, there was another wonderful by-product of
writing this book. When Isaac began thinking about writing his
autobiography in the late 1960s, he asked Pappa to write down
his memories of life and family in Russia before my parents came
to the United States in 1923.*

*Pappa wrote 20 single-spaced typewritten pages of his memo-
ries. And in my research for this book, I came across the letters
from Isaac to Pappa. But the 20 pages of Pappa's memories were
missing. We started a search for them, and Isaac's wife, Janet,
found them in her home and gave them to me. He had never sent
them to the library archives.*

*I made copies and gave them to Isaac's daughter, Robyn, my
sister, Marcia, her children and my children. I also made copies
for my two young grandsons who I suspect will be old enough to
read and comprehend it in the early 2000s. Because of Isaac's*

204 ·YOURS, ISAAC ASIMOV

foresight, Pappa's memories have become an Asimov family treasure.

My father wasn't educated in the United States. So, while he was very intelligent, his written English wasn't grammatical. He had run-on sentences without proper punctuation, and his spelling frequently was phonetic rather than correct. But he wanted to tell the story. And he did.

He started writing his memories in January 1969, and the writing stopped when he died August 4, 1969. If he lived longer, I'm sure that he would have written more about the early days of the Asimov family in the United States. But he didn't, and consequently, that history is gone.

Pappa and Mamma were brave and wonderful people. It took a lot of courage for them to leave their family and friends in Russia in 1923 and come to the United States. They never saw their family and friends again.

For 30 years, they owned candy stores in Brooklyn. Until the 1940s, they worked seven days a week and kept their store open from 6 A.M. to midnight. From the early 1940s until they sold their last store in the 1950s, they closed a half-day on Sundays. It was a hard life.

In his two-volume autobiography and his memoir, I. Asimov, Isaac described in detail how Pappa influenced him. But here are a few letters that Isaac wrote about Pappa:

18 November 1963

I was brought up by a father who got all his morals out of the Hebrew equivalent of McGuffey's *Readers*. As a result, I don't drink, smoke, gamble or use bad language. However, once shortly after I got married, I was inveigled by some evil companions into a poker game for money. It was the only time I ever played for money.

Afterward, when I saw my father, I confessed. He said, "How did you make out?" I said, "I lost 16 cents." He said, "I am greatly relieved, for you might have won 16 cents and become a lifelong gambler."

24 August 1962

My father is a great one for dignity, being quite Central European in that respect. When I sold my first story at the age of 18, he at once advised me with great seriousness that henceforth I must consider myself an author, walk with pride and dignity and be very careful not to besmirch myself with low associations. I think this was good advice in a way, but it was not possible for me to take it. I am essentially undignified, I fear, and some of my low associations among science fiction personalities have been much fun.

13 October 1959

My father (very intelligent but without a formal education) is reading *Realm of Numbers* [one of Isaac's books on mathematics] and enjoying it. He told me it has suspense. I said, "Suspense???" He said, "Yes, I'm just beginning about the square root of two. Tell me, *do* they ever find an exact solution to it?"

11 September 1963

My father just sent me a letter. He has read *The Kite That Won the Revolution* [a book about Benjamin Franklin] and this is what he says, exactly as he says it:

"Now about your book, reading it reminded me, of the mother, who had in her arms a sick child, and is about to give it a medicine, but the child closed the mouth, and don't want to take it, so the mother tickled the child under the arm, the child started to laugh, and the mother put the spoon with the medicine into the mouth. I firmly believe that 90% of high school graduates don't know the information this book holds, and never took the time to read so many books where they would be able to read in such a understanding wonderfull writing as yours, for that reason, I am sorry that the jacket states "Ages 11 up" it should have said for any body who is interested in a chapter of U.S. History as told by a *master* story teller."

My father is weak on periods, but he is very strong on commas. But he's a nice old man, isn't he? He's apparently given up on his earlier insistence on never praising me lest I get swelled-headed and quit trying. He must have decided I won't stop trying no matter what he says.

31 May 1966

I was speaking to my father on the telephone yesterday. He had just received a copy of my book *The Neutrino,* and he was disturbed that they said on the cover that I had written more than 60 books, when according to his estimate it must be 75. I explained that the book jackets were prepared months in advance of the book publication and that actually *The Neutrino* was only my 69th book.

And he said, with clear disappointment, "Only 69?" And I said, "I'm sorry, Pappa, I know I must be a big disappointment to you since I've been writing books for 17 years and have only managed to write 69." And after he thought that through for a minute or so, he actually saw the irony and laughed.

18 November 1967

In the slum-ridden poverty-stricken days of my childhood, my father was ailing but would not see a doctor. I asked him why he didn't see a doctor and he answered, "Because the doctor will say I need a two-week vacation in Florida, and I know that without him. And although he'll tell me I need it, he won't give me the money for it." I didn't realize it at the time, but he couldn't afford a doctor.

Here is a sampling of letters he wrote to Mamma and Pappa:

4 May 1965

Pappa, I just received your letter with the excellent translation of the article on Steinmetz from Russian to English. You can go into business, Pappa, you write so excellent an English. In fact, if you had been born here and had gone to school here, I'm afraid there'd be no room for me. You would have been a generation before, and I would only have been Judah Asimov's son.

8 April 1966

It's so funny. I may end up being one of the most popular writers in the Soviet Union after having left it over 40 years ago. Perhaps if we had stayed in the Soviet Union (and if I could have survived the war), I might have ended up over there as I am over here, except that I would be speaking Russian instead of English.

3 November 1967

Mamma, I know Pappa worries that my whole career is collapsing if a month or two passes without a book from me. But so far in 1967, I've had seven books, and there'll be one or two more yet and plenty are scheduled for next year. So my career is still safe.

But in 1968, he began thinking seriously about writing his autobiography and decided that he needed some help.

1 November 1968

Pappa, I have a job for you. Now that you are in Florida, a retired man, it seems to me that you might welcome a chance to devote yourself to an interesting project.

Here it is. Every once in a while, some publisher asks if I ever plan to do a biographical book. I always refuse because I think my life story is quite dull and uninteresting. I just sit at home and write. However, it is possible that if I don't do a book about my life, someone else someday might want to do one.

So I've been thinking that I've kept a diary since my 18th birthday (I still keep it, 31 years later—never missed a day), and I have a good memory for what went before. But naturally, I remember nothing about Russia and very little about Van Siclen Avenue [where the Asimov family lived from 1923 to 1925].

Perhaps, when you're a little bored, you might want to sit down and jot down your own memories of life in Russia, of your father and mother, your brothers and sisters, Mamma and her family, any stories about me when I was a baby, how you came to America, what life was like before you bought the Sutter Avenue candy store in 1926 and so on. You're the only one who knows about this, and if you don't write it down, it will be forever lost.

30 January 1969

What a surprise to get the letter with the news about how we all came to America. It is *exactly* what I want, Pappa. Don't worry about spelling or English because the way you write is not only perfectly understandable but is better than I can do.

I am absolutely amazed at the way in which you remember details that happened nearly half a century ago. There is no question where I get my brains from. Between you and Mamma, I'm no accident.

25 February 1969

Pappa, you are such a good storyteller. I see now that it would be wonderful to believe in an afterlife because think how nice it would be to suppose that your beloved grandfather (my great-grandfather) who died four years before I was born might be looking down to see how you went to a new land and had two sons who made out well there and how your oldest son became a famous scholar. On the other hand, he might be mad because I became a scholar in goyische things and he might be *very* mad over my Bible book.

So on the whole, maybe it's just as well I don't believe in an afterlife.

13 April 1969

Pappa, some people might think that the reason I am such a good public speaker is because Mamma was acting in plays when it was almost time for me to be born. But, of course, I don't believe such things.

You may be surprised to know that I remember the book of birds and animals you mention. At least I don't remember that that was what was in it. But I remember I looked through a book I loved to look through and for years I kept looking for it, wondering "Where is that book that I loved?" I had no idea that it was torn up. So I can now testify from personal memory that when a baby tears up a book, it isn't doing it because it wants to tear it up. It might actually want very much *not* to tear it up. But it can't control its hands well enough to keep itself from doing it. How old was I when I was given that book?

26 April 1969

Thanks for the information on my age when I had that book. Now I know I can remember things when I was only a little over two years old.

Pappa died on August 4, 1969, the day after an article appeared in The New York Times Book Review *about Isaac. Isaac then wrote this letter to Lewis Nichols, the author of the article:*

7 August 1969

Thank you very much for the article about myself. It meant more to me, as it turned out, than either you or I would have suspected.

When the article appeared, I took the occasion to call my father in Miami Beach, where he lives, and made sure that he would get the paper since, as you know, he is mentioned in the article. We spoke, he got the paper and he was *very* pleased.

The next day, August 4, he died.

It happens, then, that on the last full day of life, I had occasion to speak to him. And I knew he was happy, and it was because of your article. I am very grateful to you.

Because of the article, my younger brother also called my father on his last full day of life.

Several days later, Isaac wrote this letter to a friend:

11 August 1969

My father's death came as quite a blow. While he and I had been physically apart for the last quarter-century, we had always been very close in spirit. However, he had angina for 31 years, and he might easily have gone long before. He had lived to retire, to spend a wonderful last year in Florida and to see his sons completely successful.

He received news of his younger son's promotion to "assistant to the publisher" of the Long Island newspaper, *Newsday,* and of course, he read the article about me—all in the last four days.

He was active to the very last day. He went out shopping with my mother on the morning of the day he died, and he died quickly and without undue pain. We could scarcely expect more.

29

Children

Occasionally, Isaac would write about his children, David and Robyn.

15 December 1962

Last night was bowling night for David and me. I don't particularly enjoy bowling, but if I'm going to do anything, I like to have it done right. And one of the things involved in bowling right is scoring efficiently and promptly. I keep my eye on the ball, keep track of the pins and make the additions in split seconds. All is well.

However, the family I play with (who are much better bowlers than David and myself, though David is improving and is now almost as good as I—I am not improving) gets restless. Perhaps they think I am cheating or incompetent. So in the second game of the evening, I let them score. It is then I have to call the Goddess of Patience to the rescue.

In the first place, the attention span of the people scoring is limited. They cannot watch the ball and are unaware of the fact that the bowling inning or chukker (or whatever the hell it is) is over. So one must always go to them, tap their shoulder and say, "Four, Marty. Put down four." Then, every time a spare is involved which produces the problem of adding by, say, 17, there is a consultation about the scoring sheet in order to solve the higher mathematics involved.

One time last year, when I was teamed up with another family (even better at bowling than the family this year), I was treated by them as a kind of idiot to whom they were gracious and gentle. (They were very nice people actually and never showed annoyance with my low scores. And so are the people now, nice people, mind you, and I like them.) Anyway, I was quite humble about my own low scores and grateful that they didn't lose their temper with me. So I didn't mind being treated like an idiot.

Well, at the end of the session, one must add up the scores and perform various complicated procedures, and the family would get together and visibly sweat it out. So one time, I said, "Let me help," and took the card and added up the scores with my customary efficiency. They stared at me with disbelief and amazement as though I were a beagle hound who suddenly talked and said, "How come *you* can do it so fast?" And I was childish enough to say, "Magic!" However, I didn't offer to do it again. I think they liked me better as an idiot.

12 August 1963

Yesterday I took the children to a miniature golf setup and joined them in a threesome. David was pretty good at it. Robyn was all right on the drives, but her putting was indifferent. She hit the ball with only a rudimentary attempt to aim and always struck too hard so that when she missed the hole, she was as far on the other side as she had originally been on the first. She kept saying, "Don't count that one, Daddy." But I kept saying with gloomy firmness, "All strokes must be counted."

Actually, I believe that attitude should be taken more often, though ordinarily I haven't the heart. Someday children will enter an adult world in which all strokes *are* counted, and they must accustom themselves to this.

It is easy to say kindheartedly: Let them get round the dictates of the universe while they can and let us soften the wind to the shorn lamb. This is all right up to a point. But I don't think it does any good to have the child think he can *always* bend the rules. There has to be *some* contact with reality.

Oh well, I'm just trying to justify myself because I insisted on playing fair so that David got a 53 and Robyn a 70 on a par 42 course. I myself (believe it or not) got a 42, including *three* hole in ones, which my kids witnessed and which excited Robyn no end. Twice she nearly got a hole in one, missing by the merest trifle (then taking a number of putts). This downcast her, and I had the impulse to say, "Let's count this a hole in one." But I refrained.

12 August 1962

I have told Robyn that when I seem to be frowning I am really deep in thought. This morning Robyn said to me, "You're amazing, Daddy."

"Yes, I am," I said with my usual modesty. "But why?"

And she pointed to the space between my eyes and said, "Because even when you're talking, you keep thinking and thinking."

So I unfurrowed my brows and tried to look placid.

11 September 1963

David and Robyn are in Robyn's room, and there's all sorts of scuffling and giggling going on. After a while, I look up nervously from my book in the living room and say, "What's going on there?"

Robyn's voice called out, "Nothing! We're just playing being married."

The book goes flying into the air, and I yell, "Come out here, you kids." They come and I say, "Now how does the game go?"

So they show me how it goes. They link arms and walk gravely forward while Robbie intones, "Here comes the bride, all dressed in white . . ."

So we told them they could play being married—but no honeymoon.

15 November 1963

I was walking to the letterbox to mail a letter, and Robyn chased after me on her bike, yelling (from a great distance), "Daddy! Daddy! Daddy!" There was no response. So she stopped and called out, "Asimov!" and I turned at once. I may be blind to my role as father, but the magic of my name always works on me.

10 July 1965

Last Thursday I went to the gymnasium that David attends in order to have a session with him. I was told to wear sneakers, which I did. To my horror, I had to put on boxing gloves and box a little, then take off my sneakers and do some judo. I had to work out at the punching bags and shoot a rifle. All this was a source of great joy to David, who was put in the position of instructing me. To my surprise, he could box and wrestle and did both with great enthusiasm.

30 December 1965

Yesterday after ten days of rip-roaring life, our hamster (for no known reason; he'd been getting the most loving care from my little girl) decided to sicken and die. The tragedy was heartrending, and little Robyn wept her own weight in tears.

I tried to console her with some philosophy by telling her that all things must die. "In fact," I said, trying to get across what *real* tragedy would be like, "someday Daddy will die." And she said impatiently, "Well, I'll be older then," and kept on crying.

5 September 1968

The kids start school today. Robyn is very perturbed about all sorts of problems, and I tried to console her by pointing out how very minor the problems were. She said impatiently:

"Look, Daddy, when you're a small person, you may have small problems. But the problems are still just as big as you are."

I was struck very forcefully by that. I hugged her and said she was right. I had been quite obtuse and I would remember this lesson in the future.

4 March 1969

Robyn single-handedly shoveled out all the steps and all the driveway, even taking care of the pile of snow that the plows had heaped up at the edge of the road. I looked out the window when one plow passed, and I thought he was going to fill the driveway again. But he lifted the darned blades and shouted friendlily to Robyn. It's great being 14 and beautiful and having the trick of charm.

1 October 1969

Today Robyn complained of a stomachache. Maybe it's my fault. For supper last night, I introduced her to the delights of an Italian hero sandwich, large size, hot peppers and all. I ate one also, but then I have nearly twice her body mass to absorb it into and a hardened stomach.

17 June 1970

Today I gave a 15-minute talk at my daughter's junior high school. About a week ago, they asked me to give the talk, sending the message by way of Robyn, who ordered me to go. What's more, she told me this morning that she expected me to dress to the nines. So I came in with a good suit, a shirt, a tie, etc. It was a very muggy uncomfortable day, and all the students came shambling in. They were dressed in assorted, well-ventilated rags. Robyn was certainly no model of formality.

Anyway, as I sat next to the principal on the stage, highly uncomfortable, I explained to him that I was there speaking for nothing at Robyn's orders and I was dressed according to her specifications. When she finally came in near the end of the total line of better than 400, she grinned broadly and lifted one hand with thumb and forefinger meeting in a circle. The principal leaned toward me and said, "I think you pass."

17 November 1971

My daughter hasn't lost her faculty for putting me down. Last night I said to her, "I've just dedicated a book to you. I said, 'To Robyn, Best and Sweetest of Daughters.'

"Of course," I added cautiously, "I don't know if that's true."

"It's true," she said, "and you might as well take my word for it."

Undated

A few weeks ago, we were expecting some friends of ours for dinner. It was nearly time when my dear wife rushed to me with a laden bag and said, "Isaac, you haven't taken out the garbage."

"I will do it immediately," I said, for I am well trained. I opened the door, and there were our friends.

I smiled amiably and said, "I was just remarking to Janet that it was almost time for you to come, and she said, 'That reminds me! You must dispose of the garbage!'"

Whereupon Janet, not at all seeing the humor of the remark, turned a charming pink and said, "Oh, *Isaac!*"

"That's all right," said our friends. "We don't believe him."

"He just says these horrible things to embarrass people," said Janet. "Everyone is always saying, 'Oh, *Isaac!*' to him."

"Not everyone," I said. "My dear, sweet, loyal daughter, Robyn, never says it to me."

"Don't you ever embarrass her?" asked our friends.

"Certainly I do," I said, "but she never says, 'Oh, *Isaac!*' She wouldn't dream of it because she's such an angel. She says, 'Oh, *Daddy!*' "

30

Growing Older

Isaac was always aware that he was getting older, but he didn't appreciate it.

3 March 1952

Old age is your present age plus 10.

Back in 1940, when I was 20, I wrote a story in which a passage went: "He had become a middle-aged man at 30—the first flush of youth long gone."

I was 20, the editor of the magazine was also 20. The passage read fine. It was printed. At 32, I cheerfully move middle age to the "late 30s." In 1960, I shall speak of "an old man of 50." My young squirts are now 30. In 1960, they shall be 40.

21 February 1959

Middle age is, of course, a state of mind. I never expect to be middle-aged. Of course, the body gets physically weaker, but I was never the athletic type, so I've been struggling with a feeble musculature all my life and notice no difference as yet. Someday, presumably, I'll die. After that, I will be middle-aged.

3 January 1964

I may be 44 but I feel no different from the way I always felt, even as a young man of 19. I puff when I run up the stairs, but I puffed when I was 19, too, so what's the difference.

6 January 1966

I know it will be just about impossible not to think that I am 155 years old just on the basis of the writing I've done, but that's not true. I'm only 46, honest, only 46. Of course, 46 is pretty old. When Napoleon Bonaparte was my age, he had just lost the Battle of Waterloo a month before and was on his way to St. Helena.

2 January 1969

I am 49 today, and I *hate* it. Somehow I feel I ought to be a child prodigy forever. After all, that's what I once was.

4 January 1969

Day before yesterday was my 49th birthday and a surprise party was thrown for me at a friend's house, with the connivance of Gertrude [Isaac's first wife]. We went there, ostensibly for doughnuts and coffee, as we have done on several occasions in the past. And I was far too naive to wonder why so many more people were coming along this time than on previous occasions. After we parked, Gertrude deliberately stalled, pretending her skirt had hitched, her gloves were maladjusted, her back was in a sudden crick.

By the time we got to the door, everyone else was inside, the lock was firmly closed, and I was left outside, pounding on the door in the bitter cold. You can bet I was furious and when they finally let me in and started with that "Happy Birthday" I found myself neatly fooled.

Three letters came in the mail this morning (and others in recent days) from enthusiastic teenage fans from all over the nation wishing me happy birthday. It's very touching. Of course, unlike most authors, I am constantly mentioning my birthday and age in my articles. So I suppose I'm asking for it.

When our mother reached her 50th birthday, Isaac telephoned her and congratulated her on being "a half-century old." In his autobiography, he wrote: "To my surprise, she didn't find the situation humorous." That set the stage for this letter to Mamma:

2 November 1969

On January 2, I will celebrate my 50th birthday. I will call you on that day, of course, so you can laugh at me and say, "Ha, ha, now *you* are 50 and how do you like that?"

8 December 1969

All I want is my typewriter, and my only fears concerning 50 are that I am a decade closer to ultimate death at which time I am sure there will yet be books unwritten.

3 January 1970

Yesterday was my 50th birthday and the Houghton Mifflin people had promised to take me, Gertrude and the kids out to dinner last night. We went and had a very good meal and then my editor said we would go to another restaurant for some special dessert. I thought he was going out of his way to make the occasion festive and felt embarrassed about it but consoled myself with the thought that after all it *was* my 50th birthday and I deserved a little festivity.

Off we went to a hotel, up the elevator, into a function room and I stopped short at the doorway. There was my picture blown up and there were nearly 50 people there with presents and food and drinks and yelling surprise and people who had come from New York and New Jersey and old friends and everything.

Judy-Lynn Benjamin had been organizing it for three months and no one, *no* one, had let slip a word. I was caught *completely* flat-footed.

Oh, well, now I've got to face up to the ordinary everyday world of today. I suspect that last night may prove to be the happiness-highlight of my life. I dare say that if I live long enough, even more of a fuss will made for my 70th birthday (assuming I don't pass into the limbo of forgotten greatness and all that). But by then I will be feeling old and there will be too many gaps among the familiar faces. So I better savor the memory of yesterday all I can.

3 January 1972

Shakespeare died on what was probably his 52nd birthday. Considering my own writing ability, I've been worried. You know, all us great men . . . But my 52nd birthday was yesterday and I seem to be in one piece. I'm relieved.

3 January 1974

I am 54 years old and any year now I am going to get out of my youth and into early middle age.

2 August 1976

I can't give you my real birthday because I don't know it. January 2 is the official birthday but it's possible that the real one is somewhat earlier. I am glad of this because many people have cast my horoscope for January 2 and come out with something that fits *exactly*—which is itself an indication of how nonsensical astrology is.

12 July 1979

Let me tell you by personal experience that once you pass 40 you will never feel that old again. I hated reaching 40; I was indifferent to reaching 50; I look forward with great glee to reaching 60 (in 5.5 months). It will be a triumph, especially after having had a coronary at 57.

31 December 1984

In 27½ hours, it will be my birthday and I will be 65 (officially a senior citizen). And I'll have you know 65 does not mean I'm retiring. In fact, night after next, I'm throwing a big "Non-retirement Party."

6 January 1986

I am 66 and I suspect that I'd better stop describing myself as in my late youth and begin accepting the fact, as gracefully as possible, that I am in early middle age.

14 October 1986

I'm on Medicare. I tried to refuse it, but they wouldn't let me. I refused Social Security but they said once I was 70 I'd have no choice. And in a little over three years I'll start getting Social Security checks if I can't think of a way to stop it. I'm five years older than John Campbell was when he died.

About my only consolation is that I'm *still* three years younger than Arthur Clarke and 13 years younger than Bob Heinlein. Maybe (?) I'll outlive them and become the Big One.

3 February 1989

At 57, I had a heart attack. At 63, I had a triple bypass. My next birthday will be my 70th.

I have noticed that the following have now completely disappeared from the American scene, and I am told they will never come back.

Eggs and bacon	Soft drinks with sugar	Whipped cream
Chicken fat		Sundaes
Prime ribs of beef	Chocolate candy	Maple syrup
Thick filet mignon	Chocolate cake	Sugar
Hamburgers	Chocolate milk	Chocolate icing
Hot dogs	Chocolate soda	Marshmallow
Pizzas with pepperoni	Anything with salt	Hot chocolate
Salami	Pork chops	Halvah
Corned beef	Ham	Cheesecake
Pastrami	Pecan pie	Oreo cookies

I would like to see them all restored. (I wonder where they all went to.)

31

Funnies

Funny things happen to a lot of people, but Isaac would occasionally write about them.

31 May 1961

Yesterday I visited some people who live in a big, rambling house absolutely filled with antiques. It was all very informal with guests wandering about. Things were just scattered around and I saw a tarot deck of cards for the first time. Everybody was looking at it. It consists of four suits, 14 cards each, plus 22 "major trumps," for a total of 78. It is used in intricate fortune-telling and is supposed to have all sorts of arcane significance.

I spent half an hour with it and finally the hostess asked what I was doing and I said, "Putting them in order." I finally succeeded and put them in the container and put the whole thing aside so that no one could get them and mix them up again. The hostess was very amused because, she said, people were supposed to alter the course of their lives by shuffling the cards and that I had placed my life in order. And I said, "Wonderful," which tabbed me as hopelessly bourgeois.

24 June 1963

Last night we went to the Boston Arts Festival. An award was to be given to Peter Ustinov for his *Billy Budd*. They ran a scene from the picture, and the sound failed. We never heard a word.

So I said to Gertrude, "When Ustinov comes out, he will mouth his speech and carry on the silent-movie bit." She said, "How do you know?" And I said, "Because Ustinov thinks like me, and that's what I'd do."

Then I realized that my voice carries (it always carries somehow), and I had attracted attention for rows and rows. Fortunately, Ustinov came out and mouthed his speech to carry on the silent-movie bit, exactly as I had said he would. I achieved a bit of minor fame in my vicinity.

5 November 1966

Last night I was at the annual meeting of the Boston Authors Club. The occasion was the retirement of the president, Mildred Flagg, who is 80 and who is constantly looking earnestly at me and saying, "I'm in love with you, and I'm old enough to have the right to admit it."

I was given the task of making a short speech of farewell to her. Mrs. Flagg had told me during the course of the dinner that she valued a man for a number of handy things he could do around the house, like pull down the zipper in back of her dress. "And afterward?" I said innocently. So she slapped my hand and said I was awful. Then she went on to say that what she chiefly valued in a man was "whether he could *do* things *well* and if he were *big* enough for the job." And I said, dear, dear, how frank women were about those things these days, and she was covered with a delighted confusion.

In any case, in the talk I gave, I said that she had been shocking me dreadfully all through the dinner by her frank and libidinous talk, without telling them the details, and there was a great deal of laughter at the thought. Then I said I wanted to make a little rhyme about her and began: "There was once a young lady named Flagg," but that I found to my horror that the English language was so arranged that there was no permissible rhyme for Flagg, not one that wouldn't be a gross libel on our dear and respected president.

There was a kind of delayed explosion on that. First each person ran through the rhymes—bag, nag, fag, hag—and I'm sure each one exploded at some different point. So, I said, I would choose an easier rhyme—Mildred. I then said:

"In thinking of all of your talents, dear Mildred,

"I'm astonished, astounded, amazed and . . ."

And I turned to the audience, a number of whom shouted out "bewildered," and the place broke up in good-humored pandemonium. I think she loved having fun poked at her since she must have been treated with awed respect for so many years. At least she acted so. She insisted on kissing me afterward—on the lips yet—in the full view of the multitude.

30 July 1968

As those of you who have ever driven in the Boston area know, Boston driving is anarchy on wheels. But I learned to drive in Boston, and I know no better. Once I had a passenger in my car and after I negotiated my way around a "circle" while chatting in an amiable sort of fashion, the passenger, perspiring noticeably, said, "How did you avoid those six other cars?"

"What six other cars?" I asked. He got out of the car at the next red light and wouldn't get back in again.

19 July 1975

For two weeks, we had a leak through the roof that no one could locate. So naturally, there was a record two-week period of rain. Yesterday, they found the leak. Naturally, there will be no rain from here on in till God knows when. (Why waste rain on a non-leaking roof? You have to know how the universe is run.)

Someone once submitted an article to Fantasy & Science Fiction *magazine that included a pun on his name. The editor, Ed Ferman, asked Isaac's opinion and got this reply:*

6 September 1968

Randall Garrett did it much better several years ago when he had someone sterilize the exterior of a spaceship with poisonous vapors. When asked how he handled extraterrestrial germs, he said, "I gas 'em off" (Ike Asimov). No one can improve on that.

32

Favorites

Isaac was always being asked to name his favorites—books, stories, authors, etc. So here are some.

Which of his short stories were his favorites?

3 July 1980

1. "The Last Question"
2. "The Bicentennial Man"
3. "The Ugly Little Boy"

Why was "The Last Question," which was written in 1956, his No. 1 favorite?

9 June 1990

It was an idea which excited me and which I was sure had never been done before. It managed to tell the story of a trillion years of human development and computer refinement in less than 5,000 words. It was made into a planetarium show that knocked the audience (and me) right out of our seats.

Why did he like "The Ugly Little Boy," which was written in 1958.

10 October 1972

I like it even though its sentimentality is so opposed to my usual rigidly cerebral style. Well, I got tired of hearing that I can't handle human emotion, so I wrote a story intending to handle it. I cried when I wrote the last scene, and I have received many letters from people who told me they cried when they read it.

I gave a speech a year ago in which I concluded with the plot of "The Ugly Little Boy" and by God, I had half the audience in tears. Only two months ago, I told a lady this, and she wanted to know the plot of the story. I told her, and tears rolled down *her* cheeks.

Here are the five books that he most enjoyed writing.

12 February 1982

1. *In Memory Yet Green* and *In Joy Still Felt*. (My autobiography, written as one volume, though published as two.)
2. *Asimov's Guide to Shakespeare*. (Again written as one volume, though published as two.)
3. *Asimov's Biographical Guide to Science and Technology*.
4. *Murder at the ABA*. (A straight mystery.)
5. *The Gods Themselves*. (My favorite science fiction novel.)

The science fiction writers whom he respected the most.

4 July 1981

Arthur C. Clarke
Clifford D. Simak
Frederik Pohl

The science writers whom he respected the most.

4 July 1981

Martin Gardner
Carl Sagan
L. Sprague de Camp

His favorite non-science fiction writers.

12 July 1974

A tie. P. G. Wodehouse and Agatha Christie, because I can, and do, read their books over and over, enjoying them each time as much as I did the time before.

Who were the greatest living American authors?

25 September 1968

I have just voted for myself as one of the 75 greatest living American authors. I explained that actually I thought I was *the* greatest living American author and besides I *had* to vote for myself because there was a good possibility nobody else would.

His favorite television series.

6 August 1983

> *Cheers*
> *The Avengers*
> *WKRP in Cincinnati*
> *Laverne & Shirley*

His favorite cookie.

3 June 1978

When my darling wife carefully samples a new variety of cookie, makes a face and says, "How disgustingly sweet," I seize it quickly and memorize the brand name. I know it is a dish fit for the gods. "Thank you, Janet," I say.

It works the other way around when I take a bite out of an untried cookie, make a face and say, "Cardboard! Pure cardboard!" Janet claps her hands together and says, "Really. Oh, it sounds yummy." And thereafter, that cookie in numerous reincarnations is in the house to stay, and I avoid it studiously.

We agree only on chocolate chips.

His favorite quote about himself.

24 February 1973

My favorite quote is something Professor George Gaylord Simpson, the paleontologist from Harvard University, once said in a review of a book of mine that he wrote for *Science*. He said: "Isaac Asimov is one of our national wonders and natural resources."

That I like.

33

Reading

Isaac read reference works the way other people read novels.

23 November 1959

I just received a book in the mail entitled *Brewer's Dictionary of Phrase and Fable*. It consists of 1,000 pages of small print listing all sorts of things for which it gives derivations and little squibs. Like, thus: "Canter" is the easy pace at which pilgrims to Canterbury drove their horses. "Broadcloth" was originally broad cloth indeed, being woven by two men side by side and two yards wide.

It's supposed to be used as a reference book, but I'm just reading through it page by page. Offhand, I don't remember anything I'm reading, but it will all be there in my mind and at some time or another when information is required. It will come to hand easily, and everyone will say, "G'wan, it's rigged."

I once woke up early in someone's house when I was a kid and, while waiting for everyone else to wake up, started going through a copy of a dictionary near the bed. It was a very interesting one which I had never seen before—reading their little essays on synonyms and antonyms, coming across words I didn't know. It was *impossible* to explain what I was doing when they found me.

2 November 1960

Yesterday I received a 15-volume *McGraw-Hill Encyclopedia of Science and Technology*, and it is quite good. I spent the evening going quite happily through the first volume, skimming articles and stopping at those which dealt with subjects I have dealt with in my books to see if there were any new or better information I could add.

I feel responsible as a science writer to never finish writing a single one of my books. Every one of my library copies of science books is margined with notes, bringing it up to date, correcting or extending it. Even if no additional edition is ever called for, I still must do this for myself.

6 December 1962

I just wish I could find a little niche in time in which I can suspend my own aging process and the passage of time for, say, 20 years so I can use it just to fill up my head as much as possible.

20 February 1972

I *collect* facts and ideas. I *read* reference books and get pleasure out of picking up something I didn't know before. The latest is that "mayonnaise" comes from Port Mahon, Minorca.

I certainly *do* feel threatened by all I don't know. As my books take in more and more topics, I begin to feel responsible for keeping up with more and more branches of learning. Now I feel that I ought to collect jokes carefully, read books on Shakespeare and Byron and so on.

24 January 1989

My general library has about 2,000 books, virtually all reference books. My wife has at least an additional thousand.

As for my personal library, I have 406 published books altogether, and I have at least one copy of each English-language edition of each book. This means somewhere about 750 English-language books, no two of which are alike, all by me.

Foreign editions are at least as great in number, probably greater, but I can't say how many without going through my records in greater detail than I care to do. The trouble is I stopped saving them years ago because they would drive me out of house and home. I send them all to the Boston University library.

I don't collect any books but my own plus reference books I might use—strictly utilitarian.

He loved encyclopedias.

11 May 1960

I am working away at my articles for the *Book of Knowledge.* When I was a little boy, I knew some people who had the *Book of Knowledge,* but my family, of course, was far too poor ever to buy me one. Occasionally, I would be in the house of the lucky people who had it and invariably, I would sneak over to the bookcase and, if no one was looking, I would take out one of the volumes and leaf through it.

As I think back on it now, I realize that nobody could possibly have minded and that I could probably have received permission to come there and read through it at leisure if I had only asked. Unfortunately, it never occurred to me to ask, because it seemed patent on the face of it that these wonderful books were not meant to be touched by little children.

Anyway, when I was asked to do a couple of articles for the *Book of Knowledge,* my first impulse was to refuse because they gave me a very short deadline and God knows I have enough work as is. However, the thought of myself at the age of ten came sharply back to me as though the little boy were someone else with whom I could maintain contact. I was overwhelmed with the thought that somewhere the little boy existed and somehow he would know that the man he grew into was going to write articles for the *Book of Knowledge* and that he would be very pleased and excited by it.

So I agreed to do it.

24 January 1964

The New York *Herald Tribune* has asked me to review the third edition of the *Columbia Encyclopedia.* As I began to leaf through it, I found an item, bold as brass, under the heading *Asimov, Isaac.* In works of fiction, someone occasionally is "crying out in surprise." Well, I actually cried out in surprise.

21 August 1974

I have indeed heard that I am an entry in the new *Encyclopaedia Britannica,* and I wish there were some time machine I could use to go back to the early 1930s and tell a young boy I knew then that this would happen someday. It would have left him thunderstruck.

Isaac believed that the essential ingredient of education was reading.

10 September 1965

It seems to me that no one really requires urging to read more broadly; any more than anyone really requires urging to eat dessert—once he finds out it exists.

The school-required reading is something that is enforced. It is "good for you." It is intellectual steak and potatoes. Very good as far as it goes, but then you are released. If there is something that interests you and it has been let go too quickly in class, you can read about it for yourself, following your own directions and moving at your own speed. The library and bookstore are highly personal teachers with infinite patience and infinite learning.

Furthermore, school ends eventually. The steak and potatoes bow out. But dessert goes on forever and indeed becomes more important to the lifelong student than ever the main course was. Without steady renewal, school learning fades out and the college graduate returns to the natural state of illiteracy. The habit of broad, outside reading keeps him intellectually alive, culturally sharp.

Libraries and librarians were special to Isaac.

10 November 1968

Last Tuesday I lectured to a group of librarians and had a lot of fun. At the end, one of the librarians got up and said, "Dr. Asimov, I just want you to know that in our library, of all the authors we have, you are the one whose books are most frequently stolen."

What kind of popularity is that a measure of?

11 March 1972

Librarians are something special to me, not only because they buy my books faithfully and make it possible for me to be comfortable, but because in the days when I lived in Brooklyn while my father made a most precarious living in our candy store, it was the librarian and books he/she let me have that was the gateway to wonderland for me. I have never forgotten this.

5 February 1981

I can't vouch for this, but a librarian once told me I was the only writer to have books listed in every one of the ten major classifications of the Dewey Decimal System.

He was asked to state his concept of the "ideal classroom" of the 1990s.

25 October 1989

My idea of the ideal classroom of the 1990s or any period is one in which each student gets individual attention and is taught at his natural speed and according to his natural bent. This cannot be done without access to a computerized library and therefore my "wish list" for technologies for education in the future is a thoroughly computerized world library with access in the school and in the home.

34

And Still More
Limericks and Oddities

To an executive of the American Cancer Society who asked for a
ribald limerick for her father, a scaffolding engineer:

31 May 1984

From his scaffold said Abraham Ellman,
"I would jump any belle with a yell, man.
    But I won't give her name,
    That would bring her to shame,
I will not be a mean kiss-and-tell man."

To a former editor at Doubleday:

18 December 1984

There's a beautiful lassie named Stephanie,
Whose cries of delight simply deafen me.
    So, as a precaution,
    I've cut down the portion;
We make love by long-distance telephony.

To a fan who sent him a limerick, he sent one in return:

21 April 1985

There was a young lady named Joy
Who, by nature, was very un-coy.
    When she said, "Won't you, sir?"
    I replied, "I concur."
Had I not, I'd be sure to annoy.

To a fan who asked him to judge a poetry contest, he declined and sent her this limerick instead:

6 June 1986

Said a very bright lass named Joan Austin,
"Bed and blanket is what to be tossed in,
    By a vigorous male
    With the lust to impale;
That's the joy that I'd like to be lost in."

In 1978, Isaac was the sole judge in a limerick contest sponsored by Mohegan Community College that received 12,000 entries. The winner, selected by Isaac, was George D. Vaill of Yale University. A framed copy of that limerick was later hung on the wall at Mory's, Yale's famed eating club. This was Vaill's limerick:

The bustard's an exquisite fowl
With minimal reason to growl:
    He escapes what would be
    Illegitimacy
By grace of a fortunate vowel.

A doctor friend of Vaill wrote Isaac and asked if he knew how often others had written limericks in which one line was a single word. Isaac replied:

8 July 1986

As for one-word lines in limericks, I have no statistics. But I dare say it is not rare or even particularly difficult. It is only necessary

to think of a six-syllable word with accents on the third and sixth
syllables and then build a limerick about it.

Thus, on receiving your letter, I thought for two or three minutes and wrote the following:

> In most sexual matters, Doc Dave
> Would always somehow misbehave.
>> He would do it, you see,
>> Unintentionally,
> But the gals thought him rather a knave.

Had Isaac ever gotten angry with a reader?

8 June 1984

My readers are a very nice bunch of people who virtually never
impose. However, *once* I blew my top. A bookstore owner asked
if I could sign "a few" books for him. I sighed and said okay.

Next thing I got huge packing crates containing every book of
mine he had in the store, scores and scores and scores of them.
My first impulse was to throw them away and claim they never
came. My second was to keep the books for use as gifts (or to a
deserving charity).

But I couldn't do that. I had to sign them all, reassemble the
packing cases and hang them together with ropes. Then, my wife
and I had to stick them on luggage carriers and lug them to the
post office, which was several blocks away (and I'm not exactly
in my first youth anymore).

The only satisfaction I got was to write the bookstore fellow an
eloquent letter that probably singed all the hair off his head and
body.

Had he ever been scarred emotionally as a child?

19 June 1984

Nothing terrible happened to me, and I don't seem to have any
scars. I worked all my life, from the age of nine. I'm still working,
and I don't know any other life. And I don't feel bad about it.

Is he a night person?

21 June 1984

I am NOT a night person. Quite the contrary. I get to sleep at 11 P.M. and wake up at 6 A.M., without exception.

Did he like bagels?

27 June 1984

I've been eating bagels ever since I was a child. My favorite kind is a plain bagel. And I usually have one a week, preferably with lox and cream cheese. I like bagels because they taste so good. In fact, I'd like to do more with bagels, but I eat too much food as it is.

Would he autograph his Monopoly set and permit it to be displayed?

24 January 1985

It may be un-American of me to say so, and it is certainly embarrassing, but I have never owned a Monopoly set. The thing is, you see, one can write and publish 314 books or one can play Monopoly. It is difficult to do both.

Would he buy a house within five miles of a nuclear reactor?

14 February 1985

One has to ask the alternative. Would I buy a house within five miles of a nuclear reactor rather than live surrounded by no danger whatever? Of course not. But would I rather live close to a nuclear reactor or Love Canal? Close to a nuclear reactor or near a Union Carbide plant producing methyl isocyanide? Close to a nuclear reactor or to an oil refinery with stored oil? Close to a nuclear reactor or in a slum? Believe me, I would choose the nuclear reactor every time.

Is he a happy person?

4 June 1985

I am a genuinely happy person except where the outside world impinges—if I develop clogged coronaries and am threatened with death, if those I love are unhappy for good reason, etc.

When unthreatened by the outside and left entirely to my own devices, I am openly happy. The fact is that I write easily, I receive instant appreciation for my work, I make a good living, my wife and daughter love me, I have good and affectionate friends —I have no *reason* for unhappiness. And in my whole life, I have never had self-doubt. I have known exactly what I could do from the very start, and I have gone out and done it.

Where does he get his energy?

21 October 1985

Far from being high-energy, I'm the laziest man in the world. I do all my work sitting down. The only reason I keep writing all the time is that I am afraid that if I leave the typewriter even for an instant, someone will put me to work doing something that requires my standing or (worse yet) moving about.

35

Intelligence

The first time that Isaac was called a genius in print was in 1962 when Amazing *magazine ran an article about him entitled "Isaac Asimov: Genius in the Candy Store." It wasn't the last time.*

14 November 1975

I am told so many times, directly and indirectly, that I am a genius. I am in constant danger of believing it. And of course, once I believe it, I am sure to become an impossible person.

20 November 1968

I was at a meeting of the Boston Authors Club, which consists almost exclusively of dear old ladies who write occasional poems. They are very nice old ladies, and I love them dearly. They always put me at the head table. To my left was a spry 76-year-old, and to my right, another writer whom I had never met.

I asked her the name of her current book and she said, with a sigh, *"Jeanne d'Albret, Queen of Navarre,"* and I said questioningly, "The mother of Henry IV, I believe?" She sat bolt upright with a look of incredulity on her face and said, "You *know*????"

And she started talking about 16th-century France with the greatest enthusiasm, and I asked skillful questions that kept her going and she went on and on. When she was completely out of breath, she told me that she never met *anyone* who knew anything about 16th-century France except fellow specialists (she's a history professor at Tufts), and they always *argue* with her instead of listening.

Then she asked who I was and was delighted and said, "I was *told* you were a Renaissance man!"

See the advantages of intelligent listening? Now I'll have someone else going round spreading word-of-mouth propaganda about what a genius I am.

Everyone agreed that Isaac was incredibly intelligent. Sometimes he had to deal with this reality.

28 October 1966

I published a three-volume book called *Understanding Physics* and reread it. In the chapters devoted to "relativity," I had the queasy feeling of reading passages undoubtedly written by myself that I wasn't sure I grasped. Can Isaac Asimov the writer be smarter than Isaac Asimov the reader?

9 September 1969

Saying something intelligent, as opposed to saying something, is very difficult even for me. I can imagine how it must be for most people.

7 December 1969

I know less about anything *practical* than anyone else in the world. When I say I know everything, I mean everything useless.

31 January 1972

I tend to feel irritated when someone else turns out to know a fact I thought only I knew—like invasion of private territory.

22 February 1974

We all have our special temptations, and mine is that of succumbing to the widely held belief that I know everything. It is therefore particularly important to me not to be tempted into pontificating on subjects I know nothing about.

14 December 1981

I don't know what part intelligence plays in human achievement. I know that I couldn't do what I do were it not that I am enormously intelligent. But I know people as intelligent as I am who accomplish little or nothing.

Isaac was frequently asked questions by his fans. On this occasion, he was asked about a quotation.

29 February 1988

What is the difference between a computer, a concordance and Isaac Asimov?

Answer: If you give a computer or a concordance a misquotation, they are helpless. If you give Isaac Asimov a misquotation, he knows instantly from that what the correct quotation is and looks it up in a flash.

The quotation you want is: "Thou shalt not muzzle the ox when he treadeth out the corn." The citation is Deuteronomy 25:4.

Although Isaac was an international vice president of Mensa, the organization of high-IQ people, he had reservations about the concept.

2 February 1977

I have never been able to believe that the possession of "intelligence" (in the specialized sense in which Mensans define it) is sufficient in itself to make for a congenial group.

I first became aware of this in 1964 when I discovered that a surprising number of Mensans favored Goldwater. It dawned on me that my criterion for a congenial pal was not whether his IQ was higher than a certain minimum but whether he, like myself, disapproved of Goldwater.

An anti-hunting column in a recent issue of the *Mensa Bulletin* has produced precisely the same letters from Mensans that would have been produced if the column had appeared in the *American Legion Magazine* or *Playboy* or anywhere else where the readership was not confined to the "intelligent."

I have no overwhelming desire to avoid the less intelligent. Some of them are very nice people whose inability to go slashing through an intelligence test does not detract from their interest, their sense of humor, their kindness and their general congeniality.

I *do* have an overwhelming desire to avoid gun freaks, theists, mystics and so on. They have a right to their opinions, but not necessarily to my company. I will argue with them when I feel the need to; but I don't want the necessity of argument thrust upon me willy-nilly.

So though some of my friends are highly intelligent, that is not the basic criterion and some of them, as dearly beloved, aren't.

28 October 1983

It seems to me that Mensans tend to be elitist in many of their views—an attitude with which I, personally, am not in sympathy.

He was once asked for a prepublication comment on a book dealing with IQ testing. He declined and wrote the author:

24 October 1984

Over the years, I have been finding the whole notion of IQ testing distasteful, and I have been increasingly alienated from Mensa in consequence.

Your chapter on the psychology of testing, while excellent, is an example of what I mean. Through following your shrewd advice, people can raise their IQ scores, but, of course, don't raise their intelligence. Or, conversely, through not understanding the psychology of it, they can get lower IQ scores, but that doesn't make their intelligence a scrap the worse.

What then is the use of IQ testing and does it not merely produce a group of "smarter-than-thou," "IQ-proud" individuals who are one big pain in the neck to everyone about them?

Isaac tried on several occasions to resign from Mensa. Each time, he was persuaded not to do so. In 1989, he did resign.

But Isaac kept it all in perspective.

8 August 1988

If I knew how to straighten out the world, I would *really* be a genius.

36

Memory

Isaac always had an incredible memory. What he read, he remembered.

19 March 1973

I do very little research because I have been reading avidly all my life and remember virtually everything I read.

9 August 1979

As far as I know, my gift of instant recall has always been with me from the beginning. Like everything else, the more you exercise a faculty, the easier it is to keep exercising it.

But that doesn't mean his memory was perfect.

14 October 1965

A most weird thing has just happened to me. A newspaper reporter called me. He said that three Frenchmen had just been awarded the Nobel Prize in Physiology and Medicine for discoveries in connection with genes and he wanted to know if I could explain to him what they had done in layman's language. I said, humbly, that he had me. I had never heard of the three Frenchmen and couldn't tell him what they had done.

So I got off the phone and brooded. A fine memory I had! I

was certainly keeping up with genetics efficiently! I was completely crushed.

So I cudgeled my brains savagely and out of nowhere popped up the thought that perhaps the guys who had discovered that Mongolian idiocy was caused by an extra chromosome in the cells had gotten the award. It was an important discovery, opening up a whole new avenue of medical research and well worth the Nobel Prize. The only thing that remained to do was to find out who had made the discovery.

I ransacked my library and I came up with the answer— THREE FRENCHMEN HAD DISCOVERED IT!!!!!!!!

I was back on the phone in a minute, unbelievably jubilant. I had lost only ten minutes, and my reputation was saved. I *did* know everything. I got the guy and said oleaginously, "Won't you please read me the three winners of the Nobel Prize again."

I could hardly wait.

He read the list. THEY WERE THREE DIFFERENT FRENCHMEN. And I had to say, like a jerk, "Gee, I still don't know."

I still haven't recovered.

And then there was the time that Franklin and Marshall College gave him a Doctor of Humane Letters, and he forgot to take home the academic hood that symbolized the degree. He wrote the college president:

8 June 1979

I am rather ashamed that I have put you to the trouble of having to mail my hood. Generally, when I go out, Janet pins my mittens to my sleeve to make sure I don't lose them.

In 1984, a professor wrote him that Isaac had once quoted him, and he wanted to know in what written work the quote had appeared.

11 July 1984

It is with great embarrassment that I must tell you that I have not been able to find the quote in which you are interested.

The trouble is that I have published some 20,000,000 words divided into nearly 3,500 books and shorter pieces and even my supposedly fabulous memory is, through age and overwork, beginning to fail me. I know I said that about you, because I know I believe it, but to find the exact place and words is beyond me.

A graduate student once asked him how he filed his writings. Isaac replied:

27 January 1987

I don't keep any files and therefore have no system for keeping them organized. I also don't index things. I'm afraid that I rely entirely on a very useful memory. I presume that someday my brain will break down physically if I live long enough—but that evil day has not yet come.

One of Isaac's most memorable quotations occurred when Barbara Walters asked him during a taping for her television show what he would do if he were told he had only six months to live. His answer was: "Write faster." And that led to this letter:

11 April 1974

I wish I had seen myself on the Barbara Walters show. But when the time came, I forgot to watch it.

37

Errors

As smart, as bright and as intelligent as Isaac was, he occasionally was involved in incidents that we both called "my stupid brother Isaac" stories. Here's one that he wrote about to close friends:

26 June 1980

I'm so glad you liked my book. Anyway, I couldn't help but notice your letter was dated Sunday, July 22, so that it reached me from the future.

But then last Monday, June 23, I showed up at a bookstore to sign books and there seemed to be no one there waiting for me. So I said, rather annoyedly, "Where do I go to sign books?"

And I was told, "Oh, Dr. Asimov, that's on the 23rd of *July*."

In 1981, Radio Shack gave Isaac a computer in return for his acting as a spokesman for the company. After he had the computer for about a year, he sat down at it one day and it wouldn't work. He called Radio Shack, and a clerk asked him whether he had a service contract. He said he didn't. The clerk said no repairs could be made until he had a service contract.

So Isaac went to a Radio Shack store, filled out the forms and paid $1,402 for a service contract. Isaac then went home and waited for a serviceman. Several hours later, the serviceman arrived and inspected the machine. Then he walked over to the wall *and flipped the electric switch to the "on" position. The computer began to work.*

19 August 1987

I am still using the TRS-80 for my manuscripts and in seven years, it has given me no trouble at all. (Except once when I forgot to turn on the wall switch, which is a very funny story in its own right—to other people.)

Isaac once had to send 55 cents through the mail.

2 October 1987

I don't know how to make out a check for less than a dollar (another piece of minutia that escapes me since I am not very bright). I enclose 55 cents' worth of stamps. Please accept that as payment of this debt I owe you.

But while Isaac may have been a genius, he wasn't a genius at everything.

23 June 1969

Once again (I am periodically talked to), Doubleday had to explain to me (very gently) that I was to confine myself to writing and was never to try to do any business because though my IQ might be 200+ in general, it hit −40 as soon as anything practical came up.

3 October 1972

I am very stupid. This morning I was on a television talk show and was told exactly what kind of shirt to wear. I concentrated so hard on putting on the right shirt, I forgot to shave. That's me.

Then there was the time that I asked him to sign some important family legal document. I gave him explicit instructions. He wrote this letter to me.

23 May 1973

Despite your careful instructions and the precisely placed initials, I managed (owing to my well-known high IQ) to begin signing in the wrong place. I hope this doesn't screw up the whole document.

When anyone writes as fast as Isaac did, errors are bound to occur. And his readers had no hesitation in letting him know about them. Here's how he responded:

29 February 1968
Far from minding gentle corrections, I am very grateful for them. They are my bread and butter, for my articles must appear in book form, and I count on my Gentle Readers to keep me sounding intelligent.

29 August 1969
The error in *The Universe* is an inversion in an equation. I managed to get the correct results by using the correct equation in my mind, even while I had the wrong one on paper. (Don't ask me how that's possible. We geniuses are a law unto ourselves.)

21 September 1987
Unfortunately, my typing fingers have minds of their own and sometimes interpret my thoughts in terms of their own perverted senses of humor. I have frequently thought of firing them, but I know (and they know I know) I can't do without them.

Occasionally, some of his errors really bothered him.

14 September 1962
In *The Intelligent Man's Guide to Science,* there are several bloopers, of which one is really *bad.* (It is in an illustration, which I wasn't responsible for, but which I should have looked at more closely.) Well, in advertising the book, the publishers photographed it open—and it was open to the page of the blooper. No one could see the details, but *I* could and my heart bled.

22 March 1966
There are certain subatomic particles called "bosons" because they follow "Bose-Einstein statistics." Well, everyone knows who Einstein was. But who is Bose? Searching my library, I finally came across a Jagadis Chandra Bose, an Indian physicist, who

died in the 1930s. Could it be he? He died a little too long ago for comfort, but how many Indian physicists named Bose could there be? So I took a chance and put him down in my physics book. Well, after I sent off the galleys and indexes yesterday, I sat down to read the *World Book Year Book*.

I didn't really *read* it, but I looked at every page and read what I felt like. At the very end, I came upon several pages of new words for the *World Book Dictionary*. There was "boson" and the name of the Bose who was responsible—a *different* Bose who was born in 1904 and is still alive.

Everything went black. I had to write a quick letter to the editor to change that name.

8 October 1969

I am particularly embarrassed about killing Cain instead of Abel. I always find it easier to bear with errors that arise out of ignorance than those which arise out of carelessness. After all, one can't help not knowing everything, but one ought to be able to help being slipshod.

Sometimes he even made an error outside of his published works. Once he was scheduled to be in Rochester and told one of his correspondents that since he was already in the city he would consider making a speech to the correspondent's organization. But after a further exchange of letters, he realized his error.

17 October 1968

Every once in a while, even the best of us must own up to an embarrassing piece of foolishness, and I am very far from being an example of "the best of us."

I will be in Rochester soon. There is only one trifling catch. I had meant Rochester, *New York,* and was too damned stupid to notice that you were writing from and I was answering to Rochester, *Minnesota.*

But out of all of his errors, one stood out.

13 March 1976

From a million gaffes, let me choose one. In my book *Realm of Numbers,* I spoke of an "equilateral right triangle." I meant an "isosceles right triangle," for there is no such thing as an equilateral one and well I know it. The mistake escaped me at every stage of the preparation of the book.

Eventually I got a letter from a 13-year-old who wrote that his teacher had said there was no such thing as an equilateral right triangle and that he had answered, "If Isaac Asimov says so, then it's so." He asked me to write a letter to the teacher, enlightening him.

I was forced to write a letter to the youngster, telling him that his teacher was right and that his idol was human. Very embarrassing, but that was the first time the error was called to my attention.

I corrected it in later editions, but there must still be copies of the book in existence with that phrase there and I wince every time I think of it—like now.

38

Modesty, Honesty and Other Traits

Isaac had a reputation of being vain and immodest. Although being his brother might make my view biased, I can say that he wasn't. And Isaac didn't think so either.

19 June 1970

My appearance of being "obviously conceited" is entirely a matter of carefully constructed image, like Jack Benny's cheapness. In reality, I am lovably modest and incredibly sweet.

5 February 1972

I am not as vain as my public image is. A good deal of my vanity is my trademark, like my dark-rimmed glasses and my habit of kissing every girl in sight. If we get down to reality, I am *not* vain; not in the least. It is to my non-vanity that I attribute my success.

A vain person overestimates himself and constantly tackles things he cannot do as well as he thinks he can. I do not. I know exactly what I can do and what I can't. And I know exactly how well I can do what I can do. It all comes out exactly right.

I don't consider myself a good scientist or a good human being. I *do* consider myself a good writer, a good lecturer and a good teacher—in all three classifications, among the best in the world.

That is not vanity; that is an honest estimate of the situation. There is quite enough agreement from the outside world to make me quite certain of my judgment.

5 October 1989

If someone wants to attain an education in the fundamentals of science in a single book, he can try my book *Asimov's New Guide to Science*. I'm sorry if I sound immodest, but I have a horror of lying. And I won't tell lies just to seem modest.

Isaac was scrupulously honest. Here is the reason.

3 August 1989

My father brought me up to be strictly honest, which causes me a great deal of inconvenience.

On one occasion, he inadvertently pasted a nameplate on an envelope instead of a stamp. The recipient of the letter returned the envelope and teased him about cheating the government. Isaac replied:

30 October 1968

You well know that I put my nameplate on the letter in place of a stamp out of sheer oversight. After I got the envelope back, I went to the post office, told them the story and paid them six cents. I don't cheat—at least not knowingly.

His honesty extended from his tax returns to returning overpayments from his publishers.

17 May 1968

I have a thing about preparing an honest tax return. So I get the usual reward of virtue—a large tax. Fortunately, enough is left to keep me from want.

13 April 1969

I don't subscribe to the thesis "Let the buyer beware." I prefer the disregarded one that goes "Let the seller be honest."

24 November 1969

There's no way you can know that I won't cheat you unless you're prepared to take the word of someone who knows me— *anyone* who knows me.

8 January 1970

As for the expenses, I will send you a carefully itemized and non-inflated bill. We all have our little hang-ups, and integrity in money matters is one of mine.

8 April 1971

I have just received a check for $825.28. The original agreement was that I receive $750. While I would be very pleased to receive more, I am afraid that I must consider the quantity of $75.28 to be *not mine,* unless you write and say you have deliberately paid me more for some reason. If, on the other hand, this is a clerical error or a mistake in bookkeeping, then please tell me at once, and I will remit to you my own check for $75.28 immediately.

It was an error, and the $75.28 was returned.

23 January 1970

I have always operated on a very simple principle. People I like and who like me aren't going to cheat me in any way. And it's worked. I suppose it leaves me wide open for the skillful con man (or con woman) but, as far as I know, I've never met anyone I liked who turned out to be a con man (or con woman). And I've hardly ever met anyone I haven't liked. Isn't it a nice world?

As one of the most successful science fiction writers, Isaac always felt a sympathy for his fellow s.f. writers who were having financial problems. So he became a one-man loan society.

19 May 1982

I have yet to refuse a science fiction person a loan of reasonable size for a worthy purpose. So I am enclosing a check for $900.

The total money I have lent out stands at a present balance of $7,350, and all except yours are long past due. I do not know when or if any of it will be repaid, and I do not dun anybody or charge interest. As long as I don't need the money, I won't embarrass anyone. However, if you can pay it back, please do—if only for the novelty of it.

His speech agent, Harry Walker, once came up with a potential $10,000 speaking engagement on a date for which he already scheduled a speech to science teachers for a lower payment.

17 December 1977

Harry, once I make an agreement to give a talk to a certain person on a certain day—that's it. I can make a change for reasons of health or family problems or professional necessity. What I can't do is to make a change just because someone else offers me more money. To me, that is unethical behavior, and I can't do it.

My word is firm, and I won't change it for money. If I could cheat the science teachers, I could cheat you. And as far as I'm concerned, I don't cheat anybody.

Dun & Bradstreet, the credit-rating organization, once asked him to fill out a credit questionnaire. Isaac declined and gave this reply.

23 February 1975

I do not owe one cent to any person on Earth. Nor have I ever owed one cent to any person on Earth longer than it took me to make out a check. Everything I buy in the way of my "business," I pay for on the spot—from typewriters down to stationery. I have never been behind in my rent for even as much as one day, and no one has ever had to wait for payment from me any longer than it takes the post office to deliver the mail.

So with all that in mind, I don't see who the hell can be asking you questions about me. Whoever it is, tell them to stop worrying. If they wait until I cheat them, they will be waiting forever.

How did Isaac view himself?

17 June 1963

In my younger days, I was never likable. And now I am rapidly becoming the Schweitzer or Pope John of s.f.: beloved by all. Maybe all this love makes me lovable, I don't know. In the spring of 1959, when I started working on *The Intelligent Man's Guide*, I must have bumped into an ocean of love and found myself transformed. I am *so* grateful.

12 December 1965

I am essentially an ear-man rather than an eye-man. I explain by words rather than by pictures. I am the world's worst artist and have difficulty making visual conceptions.

8 August 1966

I *can't* swim, and I admit this is dangerous. However, I do my best to stay off the water and confine my peregrinations to the land surface of the northeastern quadrant of the United States— and not much of that, either.

11 July 1967

On Friday, between 7:30 and 8 A.M., I was on television. I was interviewed on the *Today* show by Hugh Downs on life in the future. (I didn't tell my friends because I didn't want anyone in the position of having to wake themselves early enough to watch on the pain of seeming disloyal otherwise.) I was so ebullient over the *Time* article [a laudatory profile] that I forgot to assume my pose of dignity and gravity. I did everything but put my feet on the table. As a result, I have received a number of comments to the effect that this was the first time I'd ever seemed myself on television.

19 December 1967

Oh my, the word spreads around the entire publishing industry that I am easily won over by flattery. Now, every editor I meet flatters me and leaves me helpless.

8 August 1969

It is part of a writer's makeup that he can swallow indefinite quantities of the most outrageous flattery without even the slightest pang of nausea.

12 August 1968

I am optimistic because it suits my personality to be so and because I am an essentially happy person who is fond of people.

31 July 1972

I am very sympathetic to the notion of accepting people as they are—for the very selfish reason that I insist on being accepted exactly as I am. However, accepting people as they are is different from associating with people as they are.

I'll accept someone whose big thing in life is to avoid the use of deodorants, but will not willingly allow him within smelling distance. I will pass no laws against him, but I will avoid him.

18 July 1977

I'm essentially a recluse. I sit facing my typewriter, almost all day, almost every day. When I do get away (more or less forcing myself), there is no way on Earth I can make myself be serious. With men, I can only joke and with women, I can only flirt—and that for relatively short periods of time. With my typewriter, and *only* with my typewriter, I can be serious.

What did he think about his creativity?

17 June 1976

If you are not creative, there are no easy setting-up exercises that will make you creative. The fact that I'm creative doesn't give me any particular insights into it because I was always creative and I never did anything about it. It was just there.

There are two things I feel about creativity:

1. What militates against creativity most of all is peer pressure. By definition, that is creative which seems new and novel to most people. People distrust the new and novel and prefer the tried and true. Therefore, the creative person is a pain in the neck. Any person with tendencies toward creativity quickly finds out he is having trouble socially. Since many people would rather be popular and one of the boys than anything else, they stifle those tendencies. And creative people *are* irritants and pains in the neck. How many of them do we want, for heaven's sake?

2. It is easy to confuse creativity with correctness or truth. In art, literature and many other fields, where there is no correctness or truth, but merely accepted critical opinion, anything new and novel is as good as anything tried and true and will be accepted after a while as critical opinion slowly adjusts itself to lead from behind as it always does. However, in science, where ideas are judged by their ability to match the universe, it is perfectly possible to have a brilliantly original thought which is completely wrong.

I don't want to encourage creativity because I firmly believe that creativity and social popularity are mutually exclusive, and I don't want to do anything that will encourage people to be misfits. If they *want* to be misfits without my encouragement, that's their business.

Nor do I feel guilty about this. I don't feel it would be a better world if there were more creative people in it. I think it would be an unhappier world. Prima donnas are hard to get along with, and we need more spear carriers who don't feel they've been done dirt because they're not prima donnas.

39

Likes and Dislikes

When Isaac liked people, he said so in letters to them or about them.

New York Times *science writer Walter Sullivan, who received the 1969 James T. Grady Award from the American Chemical Society after being nominated by Isaac, was praised in this way.*

25 September 1968

He is not only a great science writer but also a great guy. And he is good-looking enough to be Hollywood's conception of a science writer, too.

24 May 1974

Anyone who reads his news articles in the *Times* is aware of how skillfully he can bring even the most abstruse scientific concepts to the news-reading layman. Anyone who has met him personally knows his keen intelligence, his sweet nature and his delightful personality.

To an editor asking him to write an article, he wrote:

29 November 1966

Are you not the Samuel Grafton, whose column in the New York *Post* during World War II was my wartime bible? If you are, I'm so pleased to make your acquaintance and so flattered that now you read me in turn.

> 10 December 1966

Thank you for the news that you are *my* Samuel Grafton.

About science writer Martin Gardner, he wrote:

> 21 April 1975

He is part of the small group of rationalists (of whom I am another) who maintain the fight for science and sanity against the growing hordes of mysticism and folly. He is a philosopher, a religious novelist, a magician, a chronicler of pseudoscience and the author of the long-running and much-beloved column on "Mathematical Recreations" in *Scientific American*.

He has written on relativity and on nuclear physics and whenever he writes, he does so with such panache that you can swear you understand it even if you don't—and enjoy it, too. He has annotated *Alice in Wonderland, The Hunting of the Snark,* "The Rime of the Ancient Mariner" and "Casey at the Bat." He has no limits.

> 30 September 1975

He opens a world to people that but for him would remain closed. Funny thing. People think I know everything. But I know I don't, and I know how easy it is to make it *look* as though you know everything. But I think Martin knows everything.

To longtime friend Bill Boyd, he wrote:

> 17 July 1978

Thank you for getting me into the Boston University medical school. Thank you for getting me into the textbook. Thank you for getting me into popular science writing. Thank you for a million pleasant conversations. Thank you for letting me share part of your life.

To William H. Lazareth, pastor, Holy Trinity Lutheran Church, New York, he wrote:

24 December 1984

I must tell you that I enjoyed, most of all, your sermon. You not only have a pleasant voice (both speaking and singing), but you have a sense of humor and are not without courage. My wife, who is more up on these things than I am, sternly forbade me to applaud when you were done. But it distresses me that you are deprived of the immediate sense of audience approval, and I felt, therefore, that I would write you this letter.

To actor Kevin Kline, after a performance at New York's Public Theater, he wrote:

3 March 1986

I was in the audience with my wife at the March 1 matinee, watching you do Hamlet and loving it. You moved me to tears in more than one place, and it was the first time I ever heard the audience laughing in all the right places. Thanks for not playing Hamlet as a vacillating neurotic.

To Washington correspondent Elizabeth Drew, he wrote:

11 September 1990

I borrowed your *Washington Journal*. As a writer, I know darn well I should not borrow books but buy them. However by the time I found out about this one, it was out of print. I enjoyed it tremendously, but without surprise, for I also enjoy your comments in *The New Yorker* and enjoyed your TV work at the time of the Iran-Contra affair in which Bush (in my opinion) showed himself to be a magnificent liar.

What kind of music did Isaac like?

2 March 1979

I have no musical sense whatever and know only what pleases me and nothing else. In short, 19th-century European schmaltz.

19 January 1976

Goddamned rock offends my ears. Modern music, in the sense of electronic music, also offends my ears.

30 October 1979

My musical mania happens to be Gilbert and Sullivan. My favorite operetta is *Iolanthe*, but my favorite single piece is "Expressive Glances," from *Princess Ida*.

The symphonic composer I am most likely to react to is (who else) Tchaikovsky, especially his Fifth Symphony and 1812 Overture. I like anything by Beethoven or Bach; I like Mozart's *Eine kleine Nachtmusik*. I like the short movement (second?) of Shostakovich's Fifth. I like von Suppé's Poet and Peasant Overture and Enesco's Rumanian Rhapsody No. 1.

I like anything from *Kiss Me Kate* or *Oklahoma!* or *My Fair Lady*. I like Irving Berlin's "What'll I Do?" and almost any popular song from the '20s and '30s that is in the minor.

What did Isaac do in his spare time?

24 August 1978

As it happens, I don't really have time for hobbies. But I am a fiend at Crostics. I have the Doubleday Crostics #1 for instance (I bought it; I didn't scrounge it), and I intend to get every additional volume as it comes out. Crostics don't have the public that crosswords do, because Crostics *seem hard*. They aren't, and they're infinitely more interesting than crosswords.

21 January 1974

My brother called Saturday afternoon and said, "Hello, 16 across." Naturally, I said, "What? Who do you want?" Then he told me that I was the answer to a definition in the *Times* crossword puzzle. So I got the puzzle and solved it.

Why did he wear sideburns?

8 January 1987

I grew sideburns at a time when facial hair had grown popular. As it happens, I like them. They save shaving time, and they make me recognizable. This gives me more charisma and sells my books a bit more. To those who say they are out of date, I have a two-word answer.

Isaac hated smoking.

5 January 1979

I don't smoke. I have never smoked. The reason is simple. I don't like the smell.

I took a puff once and didn't like the taste or any part of the sensation. I perfectly understand that if I try it enough, I will learn to love it. But there are enough things I love at once a priori, so I don't have to go through unpleasantness in order to *learn* to love. The fact that smoking increases the chances of heart disease, lung cancer, birth deformities, etc., is not a factor. I wouldn't smoke even if smoking had no adverse effect on health at all. I still wouldn't like the smell.

Why is it I don't like others smoking in my presence?

I do not object to a person's private vices if he has been told the consequences and decides that the game is worth the candle. However, they have to be *private*. If he wants to drink and ruin his liver, his liver is his to ruin and none of the alcohol gets into my blood. (Of course, once he gets behind the wheel of a car, his vice is no longer private. And to his wife and family, it may never be.)

If he wants to engage in indiscriminate sex, it is not my bloodstream in which the spirochetes collect. If he wants to use heroin, it is not my body which suffers the bad effects. It is not that I am selfish; it is that I don't want to impose my way of life on another, lest he or she feel free to impose his or her way of life on mine.

When someone smokes in my presence, however, his vice is not private. His foul emanations find their way into my lungs and bloodstream. His stench becomes my stench and clings to me. His effluvia make their mark on me. To be sure, he gets intense pleasure out of it. But that is no excuse for victimizing me. And, of course, he raises my chance at heart disease and lung cancer for *his* pleasure.

Let him (or her) smoke by all means, but only in private or in the company of those who do not object. I would not deprive him (or her) of lung cancer if he (or she) wants it dreadfully. I just want a chance to avoid it myself. If he feels he *must* smoke and that by objecting, I am depriving him of his freedom, then would he be willing to bear with me if I feel I *must* kick him in the groin and that by objecting he would deprive me of my freedom?

Or, let's put it this way. Your freedom to smoke ends where my lungs begin.

Isaac didn't drink or use drugs.

29 September 1981

I sometimes wet my lips with sweet wine because I love it, but no more. The reason is simple. If I drink one small helping of wine, I am high; two, and I am drunk. I cannot carry my liquor, and unlike many who are in my unfortunate (?) position, I know better than to try.

6 November 1984

Cocktail parties are not my cup of tea. I do not drink.

3 October 1987

As to drugs, all I can say is that drugs destroy the thinking process. Since I must think to write my books and make a living, I take no drugs at all (not even alcohol). If anyone else values being able to think, they should take no drugs at all, either.

He was once offered $25,000 to endorse a brand of liquor.

21 March 1990

Not even for $25 million would I endorse whiskey.

How did Isaac feel about George Orwell's 1984?

15 October 1983

About ten years ago, an editor said to me, "It is only ten years to 1984, so please write an article on the subject of *1984* and where we stand."

Nine years ago. Eight years ago. Seven years ago.

I am so tired of George Orwell and his stupid book and have been dreading the approach of the fateful year precisely because I will be expected to talk and write of nothing else.

Isaac was a casual dresser and hated formal clothes.

11 January 1962

I will have to wear a tuxedo, and I have just called a tuxedo-renting place. I will go down there and see if they have anything in my size. They talked about shirts and studs and cummerbunds and collar buttons. And it just turned black before my eyes.

I hate that sort of stuff. I'm just a simple little city boy raised in the slums and contented with my backward little role in life. All I ask is a small apartment in Manhattan, a simple dinner, attractive and pleasant company (not much of that, one person other than myself would do quite nicely), and the rest of the world can go by. I won't even watch it go by.

13 January 1962

I have rented a tuxedo. I walked somberly into a "formal dress" store and said, "Can you fit a tuxedo to a fat man?" Whereupon the proprietor said, in an aggrieved tone, "I don't consider you fat," and walked from behind the counter, revealing a shape precisely like mine. I tried on a size 46 regular jacket to see how much adjustment would be needed, and it fit like a glove. I tried the trousers that went with it, and they fit like a glove.

Imagine, me in a tuxedo. (The word, by the way, comes from a summer resort, Tuxedo Park, where this type of suit first became popular. It got its name from the fact that it was on Tuxedo Lake, which got its name from an Indian word for the tribe that inhabited the area.)

To a program arranger, he wrote:

6 July 1971

I have just received your letter, and I am in an absolute panic. What is a white dinner jacket? I have never worn such a thing. I have never worn hardly anything except crummy, ill-fitting business suits. Please send a list of exactly what I'm to wear, and I'll try to get it.

Oh my. I think I'll go somewhere and shoot myself. In case I don't shoot myself, answer at once!!!!

Isaac got a prompt reply that outlined all of the clothing requirements as set forth in Esquire's Guide to Modern Etiquette.

13 July 1971

As near as I can make out, a white dinner jacket just replaces the black dinner jacket in the tuxedo. Right? I think I have a tuxedo, and I think I can figure out how to get it on me. So I'll go out and buy a white dinner jacket somewhere.

The etiquette involving men's dress clothes dates back, you understand, to the time when the only men who were expected to dress in this fashion had valets. We live in an age when valets don't exist, and fellows of essentially low-class origins are expected to ape the manners of Victorian English gentlemen. If I were a Martian, I would laugh. But as I am merely a human being forced to wear one of these ridiculous uniforms (sometimes it is even academic costume), I can only weep.

He used any excuse to avoid going to formal occasions.

11 November 1971

I am afraid that I am a rather simple soul, first-generation immigrant and the son of a candy-store keeper. I am not at ease in formal dress, and I would feel terrible coming without charge to a dinner to which others were coming only at the cost of $250.

9 March 1973

I am not sure that I would attend since I imagine that it would involve wearing academic robes, and I have principles against wearing that silly medieval costume. I'll have to give it more thought, but meanwhile perhaps you had better pick some representative better-looking, more dignified and generally worthier than I myself am.

16 January 1974

My new wife, Janet, in a fit of enthusiasm went out and bought me a half dozen expensive shirts—not realizing that they had French cuffs and that I abominate French cuffs.

"That's all right, dear," said this new husband, making mental notes that now he would need cuff links and deciding to go out and beat up the first innocent stranger he passed. And now I have cuff links.

8 July 1976

Since having married into a western family, my earlier penchant for ready-knotted bow ties was greeted with such scorn and contumely that, when I refused to go back to four-in-hands, I was ordered forward (with many a kick and blow) into bolo-tiedom. Now I wear nothing else.

9 January 1980

I'm a little taken aback at the fact that the dinner is black tie (which I hate), but I will pack my tuxedo with a sigh.

9 June 1989

For me to be in a non-tuxedo in the midst of a sea of tuxedos would make me ill at ease, and putting on a tuxedo would make me ill at ease.

Personal postscript. Despite his aversion for formal affairs, Isaac had to go to a number of them. Over the years, he lost weight. As brothers, we had the same build. After his death, I inherited his tuxedo.

40

Reviews, Criticism and Interviews

Isaac generally received good reviews for his books, but he was not a fan of reviewers.

14 May 1962

I have never really learned to accept bad reviews without bleeding. For one thing, there have been so few that I have never had the chance to develop calluses.

11 May 1963

The new issue of *Science* contains a double-barreled review of my two books *The Genetic Code* and *The Human Body*. It is a very generous and kind review that warmed my heart. Its first line was "Isaac Asimov is the Lenny Bernstein of scientists who write." I think I shall have that line blown up and framed.

23 March 1967

I am trying to be philosophic about a business in which anyone who wishes can say rotten things about you in print and in which you are not allowed to answer back.

25 May 1970

A fan magazine came out with a very nasty review of *Nightfall and Other Stories*. The reviewer admitted I had never written a bad story. But he said time had passed me by because I had never improved and gone on to write the terrifically poetic, artistic, mind-blowing novels written nowadays.

So I called up Doubleday to ask how it was doing. Well, in the first seven months of its existence, it has sold 9,000 copies, been sold to a paperback firm for a $15,000 advance (!) and sold French and Italian translation rights. Not bad for a collection of old, oft-reprinted stories. (Hell, "Nightfall" alone has been anthologized nine [!] times.) So I wrote to the fan magazine to say that I agreed that time was passing me by, but not the audience.

2 September 1970

The first review of my Shakespeare book is apparently by an (unnamed) Shakespearean scholar who takes umbrage at the fact that a mere science fiction writer should dare write about Shakespeare. If I knew his name, I would write him a two-word postcard. I imagine everyone knows the two words I mean. The second is "you."

18 May 1971

I am extremely sensitive about the quality of my writing, and I do not take to adverse criticism kindly—whether it is justified or not. I just don't. I recognize the right of anyone to maintain that my stories stink, but I also recognize my own right not to like him or her very much when he or she does so maintain.

23 May 1977

People have a right to disagree, and what is one man's classic is another man's trash. But then where is the value of the critic? What does a critic do but express his own personal opinion, guided as it may be by likes, dislikes, worship, envy, euphoria, indigestion. And why should anyone want to be a critic except for the opportunity it gives him to become godlike in his own eyes and to hurl thunderbolts at those who in real life he would be nervous about approaching.

12 April 1984

Rotten reviews are the lot of the writer, and selling well is the best revenge.

Isaac was occasionally asked for copies of good reviews.

268 · YOURS, ISAAC ASIMOV

5 May 1984

I finally found a few reviews of *The Gods Themselves* and *Nightfall and Other Stories*. You'd think someone as vain, conceited and egocentric as myself would keep all favorable reviews carefully coded for instant revelation. But apparently I don't. Can it be that I'm not vain, conceited and egocentric? Impossible!

Or occasionally for copies of bad reviews.

11 May 1987

Like all writers, I fume at them, and a fellow writer, Lester del Rey, once gave me some very good advice. "When you read a review," he said, "at the very first unfavorable adjective, read no more and throw it away." I have done that faithfully and, as a result, I have no bad reviews to send to you. I also throw away good reviews, by the way, but I read them first.

Isaac liked praise. He didn't like criticism.

11 June 1973

David Frost said that the author's idea of constructive criticism is 6,000 words of closely reasoned adulation. And I have never read a criticism of my own work that was long enough, closely reasoned and, most of all, adulatory enough. No doubt my obituary might come close on all three counts, but I won't ever read that, will I?

13 November 1980

If I were to be angry with all who criticized me, my list of enemies would be enormous.

16 May 1969

Censorship is a bad thing even in times (such as ours) when literary freedom is abused. I'm afraid we must all agree that censorship of criticism is also a bad thing, even if that criticism is abused. And I say this even though I happen to be extremely sensitive to adverse criticism myself and almost never suffer in silence under its lash.

Isaac hated interviews.

17 October 1966

It's as American as apple pie to want publicity, I know. But the more publicity I get, the more of these things I have to do and the less time I get to write—which is the only thing I *want* to do.

8 March 1969

Two nights ago, there was a phone call late at night, and it turned out that some talk show in Los Angeles was calling and asking me if I would be so kind as to hang on for a few minutes because the talk-master wanted to interview me for 10 or 12 minutes. So I said okay (it was almost 1 A.M. but, of course, only 10 P.M. Los Angeles time).

And while I was waiting I realized I hadn't asked *about what,* and they hadn't offered to tell me. Apparently, I was considered and, what was worse, I considered myself, to be a "universal interviewee" ready to talk on any subject without notice. Fortunately, he asked about the Apollo flight and the usefulness of going to the Moon and stuff like that—about which I could talk fluently if wakened from a sound sleep.

Robyn told her friends at school about my having to go on the radio in Los Angeles at 1 A.M. and apparently impressed them. She came back and said, "Gee, every once in a while I sit back and think: My daddy is famous. Most of the time I never think about it." I tried to tell her that was because I was so humble and unassuming, and for some reason, she burst into wild laughter.

13 April 1974

I am afraid that as I get older, wearier, creakier, tireder, benter, moroser, grayer, curmudgeonier, worn-outer and all the other "ers" you can imagine, I get more and more reluctant to give out interviews.

My work piles up faster than I can do it. Even a short interview makes it worse since there are many people who are after me for short interviews.

17 January 1976

Even when it's only one hour at a whack, 25 interviews a day is 25 hours a day.

20 July 1987

I have already been interviewed so many times I know all the questions by heart. I also know my answers by heart.

17 June 1988

I was just interviewed today (television), I will be interviewed tomorrow (radio), I will be interviewed Sunday (television) and I will be interviewed twice on Monday (once personal and once television).

I must put a stop to this or I will go mad. I have decided to accept no more interviews for the duration of the summer. Perhaps in the autumn, I will be able to endure the sound of my own voice again. Perhaps.

12 August 1988

I'm becoming one of the sights of New York. Last Saturday, it was a guy from Australia; last Tuesday, a guy from California; and time has been reserved for a guy from Poland and one from China. These damned jet planes bring in people from all the world and right after the Statue of Liberty and the Empire State Building, they come to stare at me. When am I supposed to do my work?

Isaac was unconcerned about publicity.

3 August 1972

I am the despair of publicity departments. I am indifferent to publicity, even if told it will sell books. I hate to travel. I conceive it my first duty to *write* books and even small amounts of promotional business would seriously cut into my writing time, and I can't allow that.

28 July 1976

I was on the *Today* show this morning. They had a feature story on me in Tuesday's Washington *Post,* and I'm in a news item in this morning's New York *News.* You'd think I had a publicity person working for me. But if I did, I would fire him. All this nonsense keeps me away from my typewriter.

18 May 1979

My talks—even commencement addresses—are all extemporaneous. I am distressed that this may discommode some media repre-
sentatives, but I will do my best to rise above the distress. After
all, if they are really desperate, they can actually attend the cere-
mony and hear me. Surely, this would not violate the First
Amendment.

21 October 1980

Let the newspeople attend the talk if they want material. If they
don't come, I'll joyfully do without the publicity. I'm not running
for office.

41

Evolution vs. Pseudoscience

Here's how Isaac dealt with evolution.

26 March 1966

I gave a lecture at Regis College, a Catholic woman's college near Boston, and had a very good time. I was surrounded by a huge gaggle of nuns, all of whom fawned gently over me and I liked it. I was so circumspect that only once in the evening did I forget myself and call one of the nuns "dear." Fortunately, she didn't seem to mind.

At any rate, they praised my books highly, and one of them said she used *Wellsprings of Life* constantly in her classes. I said in surprise, "But that book takes on a strongly evolutionary view."

And she said, "We all firmly believe that evolution is essentially correct as far as the development of man's physical body is concerned and that the answer to the problem of man's development lies with science and not with theology. We say only that whenever and however man developed, God was there."

This warmed me, coming as it did before I gave my talk (which had a strongly evolutionary view as a result).

In the 1960s, Isaac became involved in writing a series of science textbooks. In 1969, the publisher told him that California might no longer buy textbooks that teach evolution as a fact. He replied:

> 31 May 1969
> I am writing *Evolution* and I have every intention of talking about evolution as a fact. What's more, I don't intend to as much as mention Genesis. If this means writing off California, so be it. I don't have to be a millionaire. I *do* have to have my self-respect.

No change was made but in 1973 the publisher again suggested some "modifications" dealing with evolution. Isaac replied:

> 24 October 1973
> I think you are making a terrible mistake in trying to compromise with the superstitionists. I am the author of the sections on biological evolution, and I will not allow this kind of change. I will not permit the word "evolution" to be taken out and "biological change" substituted. I will not permit the section to be weakened and watered down.

Again Isaac won. But the issue arose a third time in 1978, and he wrote the publisher:

> 13 June 1978
> The reason that you wanted me to do "Energy and Life" was to omit "The Differences of Life" and get any mention of evolution out of the book. I can't go along with that. I have long been embarrassed at being associated with a product that depends for its success on catering to the prejudices of ignorant school boards. I fought rather hard against removing mention of evolution five years ago, and I'm certainly not going to help you do it now.

This time Isaac lost. So he wrote:

> 25 December 1978
> Thank you for removing my name from the books.

Isaac was a strong supporter of science and rational thought. He was an adamant opponent of pseudoscience and irrationality.

14 December 1967

I will believe in extraterrestrial visitors when one makes his appearance in an incontrovertible manner and not until then. I don't think I am being reactionary in this. I extend the same attitude toward angels, demons, poltergeists, Valkyries and the spirits of the dead—all of whom have been believed in far longer and with far more numerous eyewitness reports than flying saucers.

13 January 1972

The layman's real awareness of science is mysticism. The average layman thinks astrology is a science and that telepathy is an established fact.

21 May 1975

How much faith should one put in astrology?

About as much as in knocking on wood and in wishing upon a star.

There is no evidence that the positions of the stars and planets have any effect on your financial decisions, the nature of your mate, your emotional makeup or anything of the sort.

If there were something to astrology, ten different astrologers, given a place and time of birth, working independently, should come up with the same results; or, if given a particular person and all necessary information concerning him, should come up with his or her place and time of birth. There are many experiments that could be conducted but never will—and never need be.

For every sane person on earth, there are now and will continue to be thousands of firm believers in astrology—and in knocking on wood—and in wishing upon a star—and in every feeble fancy that the sick imagination of mankind has ever invented.

1 March 1979

As someone once said, "Astrology was born when the first knave met the first fool." You can substitute any other kind of crap for astrology and the statement will remain true.

24 August 1985

I find myself incapable of growing accustomed to the way in which undoubtedly intelligent people will believe in nonsense that is, on the face of it, nonsense.

On the West Coast, there was a city plagued by a mysterious hum. Investigation finally showed that it was the mating sound of a certain fish that gathered in the city's harbor.

A woman living in the city was asked what she thought of the explanation. "I don't believe it," she said. "I'm sure it's a Communist plot." It would never occur to her to wonder how the Communists did it or why. It's "belief first; evidence later—or never" with all these people.

29 May 1986

Individual scientists are human beings with all the foibles, faults and weaknesses of human beings. I know this well, as do all scientists. However, science, as a *belief system,* is self-correcting and scientists who go wrong, for whatever reason, are eventually corrected by other scientists.

In pseudoscience, I encounter no such correction by pseudo-scientists, whereas attempted corrections by scientists are met with deadly hostility. To put it as briefly as possible: Science gets somewhere given time, and pseudoscience does not. I consider this a huge difference.

Isaac, both a scientist and an atheist, disliked creationism and creationists intensely.

13 June 1980

These fools are unreachable by reason. We all have our own way of meeting this challenge. My personal method is to treat them with contempt and amused ridicule, and when they howl (as they always do), I know I have nicked them.

13 January 1987

My satisfaction is that if the afterlife is as I think it is, none of them will go to heaven because it doesn't exist. On the other hand, if afterlife is as *they* think it is, they will all go to hell for the sins of lying and hypocrisy.

42

Overpopulation and Women's Rights

Isaac felt strongly that one of the major problems in the world was overpopulation and that the future depended upon bringing population growth under control.

1 February 1966

Which is the greater danger—nuclear warfare or the population explosion? The latter absolutely!

To bring about nuclear war, someone has to *do* something; someone has to press a button. And the immediate terror of the event inhibits the pointing finger. Khrushchev didn't dare at the time of the Cuba missile crisis, for instance. It is not certain that no one will ever be insane enough to push the button, but there is at least a fighting chance that no one will.

To bring about destruction by overcrowding, mass starvation, anarchy, the destruction of our most cherished values—there is no need to do anything. We need only do nothing except what comes naturally—and *breed*. There are 3 billion people on Earth now. There will be 6 billion perhaps in 2000. Nothing we can do short of nuclear or biological warfare of an extreme all-out nature will prevent that, *if* we do nothing.

And how easy it is to do nothing.

16 December 1968

Any biologist, any practitioner in the medical sciences whose work is in any way likely to extend the life span must consider it his duty, his *sacred* duty to fight desperately for birth control. It doesn't mean that there must be no babies, but we must simply see to it that there must be no more than two babies per couple on the average, however extended their lives, with an upward adjustment made if necessary for deaths before maturity, homosexuals, asexuals, steriles and impotents, etc.

3 May 1968

The economically depressed often have higher-than-average birthrates because they lack sophistication and education: (1) They do not know of birth control methods. (2) They do not have the time or leisure to develop sophisticated sexual practices that bring satisfaction without conception. (3) Sex is the only pleasure that is always available and costs nothing. They view any attempt to modify it as a threat.

8 March 1970

Chestnut Hill College in Philadelphia asked me to talk about population. So I prepared my usual diatribe against relentless breeding and my usual impassioned support of any and all means of birth control.

So when I got there I found that it was a Catholic girls' college and simply overrun with nuns. My mouth fell ajar, and I said to the student who was in charge of me: "I didn't know this was a Catholic girls' school. What do I do with my speech on population?" She said firmly, "Give it exactly as you would give it elsewhere. We need it." So I did.

On television a couple of months ago when David Frost asked me about the future of birth control, I said with considerable equanimity that there were many sexual practices that gave full satisfaction without the slightest chance of conception and without expense and without any conceivable side effects. Frost mopped his brow and changed the subject.

At another occasion, I said much the same thing to a bunch of young executives at a speech at the Harvard Business School and ended by saying, with an absolutely straight face, "Have you ever thought what the most efficient oral contraceptive really is?" And there was a tremendous roar that began slowly and built up. One could see the word "fellatio" sparking from mind to mind. (Or perhaps the Anglo-Saxon equivalent, for these were business-men.)

How does homosexuality fit into the overpopulation issue?

1 December 1962

I see nothing "wrong" with homosexuality and, what's more, nothing dangerous either. I am not a homosexual myself, but the population explosion is so dangerous that any device that cuts down the birthrate without doing significant harm should be pos-itively encouraged and defined as a "right." Homosexuality is one of these.

Should we teach about birth control in the schools?

24 November 1972

The most humane solution to overpopulation is to teach every-one the use of simple contraceptives in some course on sex given no later than junior high school.

What about abortion?

20 June 1977

The only possible way to be against abortion is to propose some better and more humane way of population control. My own way is through contraception and the best way of practicing con-traception, in my opinion, where chemical or mechanical proce-dures are absent, is to teach the vast variety of sexual practices that give complete satisfaction with no possible conception possi-ble—i.e., oral-genital contact.

Should the U.S. limit immigration to keep population in this country down?

2 January 1976

I entered this nation as an immigrant in 1923 at a time when we still had an open-door policy. The quotas were established in 1924 and thereafter my family would not have been able to get in. I cannot, under such circumstances, support a harsh policy toward immigration, however I might sympathize with the rationale intellectually. I *cannot* take the attitude: *"I* got in and the hell with the rest of you."

But as strongly as he felt about overpopulation, he couldn't bring himself to offer an endorsement of a book glorifying parents who have only one child.

19 February 1977

Today is the 22nd birthday of my *second* child (I only have two), who is the light of my life. I might also have a little trouble facing my younger brother, who in all family crises was stuck with the dirty work, leaving me free.

Isaac was a feminist before the women's movement.

17 June 1963

I made a stirring plea for women in science at a recent conference in New York. Several days later, the Soviets put a woman into orbit, a feat over which I am in ecstasy. I notice that some American official has already labeled the Soviet action "a publicity stunt." (We ourselves, presumably, are too proud to engage in publicity stunts.)

Margaret Mead, however, says that if the Soviets put a woman into orbit, it is because the Soviets have able women who can qualify for the purpose, and if we shrug that off, so much the worse for us.

What it amounts to is that Soviet women contribute healthily to the Soviet economy, whereas we persuade our women to maintain the role of consumer for the most part. The average woman is not as physically strong as the average man. She has a different biological function. And she may have different emotional tendencies (a difference which may be cultural rather than physiological, however).

But the fact remains that the average woman is potentially as intelligent and as creative as the average man, and we have no right to ignore that. If the Soviets don't, then their population of creative individuals (the only ones that count in the type of war in which we engage nowadays) is, at once, more than twice ours.

And if the Chinese take the same attitude, their population of creative individuals will be eight times ours. We simply cannot afford to double the odds against ourselves in this way.

12 November 1974

If civilization is still flourishing in 2000, it will be because we are striving successfully toward a low-birthrate world.

This means that motherhood will be downplayed and that women must have something else to do than to bear many children. This means they will have to be allowed to participate in the work of the world on an equal footing with men. This means that for the first time in history, we will be tapping the brain-power of the other half of the human race.

We will double our mental capacity without doubling our numbers. And if that isn't great, what is?

27 December 1974

Women's rights are a necessary prerequisite to solving the population problem, and a necessary consequence of solving it.

9 September 1975

A woman who has no role whatever in the world cannot possibly occupy her mind and must make do with children. A woman who has a great deal to do that fulfills her as a human being may have children, but surely not many. Otherwise, she will spend too much time being pregnant and taking care of them to engage in anything else. (Undoubtedly, there are exceptions. But we're talking about two billion women, not the total of two dozen exceptions.)

15 August 1978

I *favor* passage of the proposed Equal Rights Amendment because women are human beings in every sense of the word. The fact is that through history women have *not* been treated as human beings but as a variety of other things, occasionally as pampered pets, usually as domestic animals.

It's time they were treated as human beings and no worse— and not better, either. In order to make sure that they have a complete legal right to such treatment, we need a constitutional amendment.

4 January 1980

The two great arguments for marriage are the need for security for women and the need for security for children. With women economically independent and with the number of children decreasing, I anticipate that the 1980s will continue to see divorce increasing in popularity.

This doesn't frighten me. The alternative—unhappy marriages held together by social force, social repression, enslaved women and unwanted children—frightens me much more.

4 August 1983

I wrote a strong article on women's liberation before the phrase was coined. The article was entitled "Uncertain, Coy and Hard to Please" and was published at the end of 1968. I have been repeating the attack on male chauvinism in both written and spoken form ever since. And I shall continue to do so in the future.

Isaac was criticized by one woman when he wrote an article that identified two female mathematicians as "Voltaire's mistress" and "Lord Byron's daughter." Isaac replied:

13 April 1988

I have a good friend, David Brown, who is always identified as "Helen Gurley Brown's husband." I am sure that a certain obscure Mr. Thatcher is always identified as "Prime Minister Thatcher's husband."

When I attend a function at my wife's institute, I identify myself as "Mr. Janet Jeppson."

Scrabbling around for little things is no occupation for a feminist. Why don't you concern yourself with the miserable fact that so few women go out for mathematics? That is roughly 75 million times more important than identifying a female by a much more famous male relative.

43

Censorship

Over the years, would-be book-burners tried to remove several of Isaac's books from their local public or school libraries.

In 1978, a Tennessee community that was the scene of the Scopes "monkey" trial in 1925 had a dispute over Isaac's Treasury of Humor. The local school board refused to eliminate the book from the school library after some community members complained that the book contained some objectionable language.

9 November 1978

Anyone who reads the book carefully will find not more than two or three jokes in which objectionable words appear, and in those for a specific reason. The whole tenor of my discussion is that jokes should be no "dirtier" than they have to be and that the "dirtiness" that does exist have a purpose. The proof of the fact that the book is *not* dirty is that it has not become a best seller. For people who want to read dirt (and there are millions), this is *not* what they are looking for.

In 1981, a Birmingham, Alabama, teacher was suspended and faced dismissal for giving a graduating senior the book Limericks: Too Gross *by John Ciardi and Isaac. The local school board said the book contained "offensive, lewd, and highly suggestive material."*

3 September 1981

The book consists of 144 limericks written by me and 144 written by John Ciardi. The limerick is a well-known verse form, which has been written by any number of people from great poets down to many with no poetic talent at all. Almost all limericks are humorous or witty; at least that is the intention. What's more, by custom, almost all limericks deal with what have until recently been taboo subjects, notably sex.

Until recently, it has not been possible to publish such limericks openly in this country, so that limerick-writing has been a more or less underground sort of activity. In the atmosphere of greater literary freedom now prevailing, it has become possible to publish them, and Ciardi and I have taken advantage of that fact.

Most of the limericks in the book deal with sex. There are, however, numerous ways of dealing with sex, and a *good* limerick does so lightly, humorously, wittily. It is this lightness which serves as the redeeming social content of a good limerick.

Sex, after all, is an almost universal activity, and is not far from the thoughts of most people, especially the young. To cover up sex, to hide it, to treat it as some terrible secret, gives it, all too often, the glamor of "forbidden fruit." It lends it an aura of excitement and taboo and gives it all the dubious glory that mystery will cast upon anything. Take sex out into the open and treat it with a good-natured smile, and the value it retains is only the value it really has—which is enough.

For instance, here is one of my limericks from the book:

> There's a man who is named Isadore
> Who has never made love to a whore.
>   It is not that he frowns
>   At the ups and the downs;
> He just thinks paying cash is a bore.

There is no question that this limerick deals with prostitution, that it uses the vulgar term "whore" and that it even refers tangentially to the mechanics of the sex act. But I cannot believe that any reasonable person would consider this verse to be prurient. It does not appeal to lechery, but to a sense of economy, and the only rational response is a smile (if not a laugh).

The case involving the teacher went to trial, and the teacher won reinstatement, back pay, attorney's fees and $7,500 in damages. After Isaac heard that the teacher had won her case, he sent her lawyer a postcard with the following limerick (which the lawyer framed and hung on his office wall):

23 November 1981

Don't you mess round with lawyer Ed Still,
For he puts those opposed through the mill.
    Twelve good men and true
    Will frown upon you,
And then wait till you find out the bill.

44

Final Limericks and Oddities

To a friend at the bookstore Murder Ink, he wrote this limerick about an editor of Ellery Queen's Mystery Magazine:

15 January 1987

Sixteen years I've pursued Eleanor
Round the chair and the desk, through the door.
    Although I have sought her,
    I haven't yet caught her.
She remains a bright dream evermore.

To a woman connected with the Mystery Writers of America who met Isaac briefly and expressed disappointment at not receiving a limerick:

23 April 1984

There was a young woman named Susan
Who ardently wanted to loosen
    Her conscience (too tight)
    And her urge to do right.
What she wanted, you see, was to *do* sin.

To the executive secretary of the Mystery Writers of America who never had a limerick done with her name:

10 May 1984

In encounters with Mary A. Frisque,
Be prepared for a terrible risk.
    If to screw you aspire,
    You'll be set all on fire,
For her motion's exceedingly brisk.

Several years later, Mary Frisque challenged him to write a limerick that would include the name of a friend, Stanislaw Skrowaczewski. Isaac replied:

17 March 1987

My dear Mistress Mary A. Frisque,
You will find that my answer is brisk.
    To what you ask of me
    I do hereby agree,
But S. Skrowaczewski, tsk, tsk.

To a fellow participant with Isaac and Janet at the Rensselaerville Institute, he wrote:

20 July 1988

There are pleasures, my dear Diane Zito,
That I'd like to perform incognito.
    But, alas, I'm afraid
    I would not make the grade
In the face of dear Janet's stern veto.

To a fan who sent him some whimsical writings:

7 February 1989

I HATE COMPETITION

An ingenious young fellow named Tigard
Has shown that he isn't a niggard.
    At word-play that's quaint,
    He displays no restraint,
And he's funnier than I had figured.

Did he have a quotation displayed in his office?

16 December 1985

The following is displayed prominently in my office:

"The search for truth is in one way hard, and in another easy. For it is evident that no one can master it fully nor miss it wholly. But each adds a little to our knowledge of nature, and from all the facts assembled, there arises a certain grandeur."

—Aristotle

I heard someone quote it in a talk and, at my request, he sent it to me. Unfortunately, I don't remember who that "someone" was.

How does he relax?

25 June 1986

People expect to hear I take a slug of booze, listen to rock or go up to the roof and sunbathe. But I write. That's how I relax. For me, "work" is not being busy at the typewriter.

To a publisher of a book about Brooklyn that described candy stores, he wrote:

29 June 1986

I worked in my father's candy store in Brooklyn for 16 years prior to World War II. We never called it an "egg cream," however. I never heard the phrase. We called it a "chocolate soda." Oh, boy. The gods and goddesses can keep their nectar. I had chocolate sodas unending, a heaping gob of dark, rich chocolate syrup with seltzer. The few "egg creams" I've sampled since I left my father's candy store have been nothing but illegitimate cousins of the real thing.

What character in history would he most like to travel with?

10 May 1989

I have always felt a kinship for Benjamin Franklin. (Whether he would feel a kinship for me is another story, but he is dead and cannot defend himself.)

Franklin had a wide-ranging curiosity and was interested in everything from postal service to electricity to ocean currents to politics. And I, in my way, have a similar wide-ranging curiosity as is shown by my 424 published books (so far). He had a sense of humor and so have I. He was interested in young ladies even in old age and so am I. He was highly intelligent and so (I believe) am I. And there would be no language barrier between us.

I would like to travel the country with him and explain some of the things that have happened to it in the two centuries since he died.

Had he ever received a "Dear John" letter?

12 July 1989

I'm sorry, but I have never received a "Dear John" letter, or anything even remotely like it. On the other hand, I'm not sorry.

In a debate on sex vs. money, which side would he take?

17 July 1989

Naturally, I'm on the side of sex. But had you made it sex vs. work, I would have chosen work.

How would he say hello to mark World Hello Day?

27 September 1989

I like to think that my books, which often display my devotion to world peace and to understanding among peoples, which have been translated into over 40 languages, are a way of saying hello every single day of every single year.

To those, however, who have missed my books, and, of course, they must number in the billions, I add, "Hello, to all of you. Friendship and Peace."

Does he remember his dreams?

31 December 1973

The trouble is I virtually never remember any dreams. My sleep seems to me to be a period of unconsciousness unmarked by anything. When I do remember dreams, there are only momentary impressions which don't last long.

I don't think I have ever dreamed anything that I could make a connected story out of without inventing. What serious psychological maladjustment this means I don't know. Maybe I spend too much time dreaming when I'm awake.

What kind of lifestyle does he lead?

4 October 1975

I am not one of the beautiful people.

I have just finished reading *Mathematical Carnival* by Martin Gardner and the latest Peanuts cartoon book.

As for music, I listen to WQXR [a classical music station] while I am typing, in those rare minutes when they're *playing* music instead of talking stupidly about it.

I watch TV, mostly the more outspoken situation comedies and occasional thrillers such as *Columbo*.

The last movies I saw and enjoyed were *Love and Death* and *Return of the Pink Panther*. I rarely go unless I can be sure there is neither raunchy sex nor grisly violence in the film and that excludes almost everything.

I don't take vacations voluntarily, and I spend money on what I need. I eat as I always have. I relax at my typewriter. I worry about anything that might happen to keep me from my typewriter. I trust everyone to deal decently with me as long as I deal decently with them. I am happy I am alive.

Isaac was once asked where he was on several historic occasions.

9 April 1979

Pearl Harbor Day, December 7, 1941 — I was 21 years old. I had just finished a short-short science fiction story, "Time Pussy," and felt sufficiently relaxed to turn on the radio. I turned it on just in time to get the flash. I listened dumbfounded and ran to wake up my father. "Pappa, Pappa," I said, "we're at war." It was the only time I ever was sufficiently irreverent to disturb my father in his sleep. He did not complain.

Atom bomb dropped on Hiroshima, August 6, 1945 — I was 25 years old, working in a navy yard, and my draft status was in one of its many moments of uncertainty. My wife and I were getting ready to take the train to New York, where I meant to inquire if, and when, I might expect to be inducted. The radio was on (my wife was ironing; I was reading Durant's *Caesar and Christ),* and the announcement came. "Hmm," I said, "I wonder how that will affect my draft status?" It didn't. I was inducted on November 1.

Sputnik, October 4, 1957 — I was 37. On that day, I received the devastating news that Doubleday had rejected the very first straight mystery novel (as opposed to science fiction) I had ever written. It was the first time Doubleday had ever rejected a book of mine and (as it happened, though I did not know it at the time) also the last. I heard the news of Sputnik on the radio while sitting in my living room in a state of shock. In my diary, Sputnik took second place to the rejection.

Assassination of John F. Kennedy, November 22, 1963 — I was 43. I was visiting New York (I was living in Boston at the time) because that night I was to give a talk to the New York division of Mensa. I was in the Metropolitan Museum of Art at about noon when I overheard someone talking assassination. I walked over and asked, "What the hell are you talking about?" And he told me. I tried to get out of giving the talk that night, but it was too late. I had a full house, and the talk was unusually successful. Everyone was trying to forget.

Man on the Moon, July 20, 1969 — I was 49. I had driven to Connecticut on that day to visit my son, who was at a boarding school at that time. I drove home through a light rain and then spent the evening at the television set, waiting for the initial step on the Moon. Unlike the other four items, this one did not come without warning.

45

Being a Liberal

Politically, Isaac was a liberal—and proud of it.

31 August 1968

I'm a New Deal Democrat who believes in soaking the rich, even when I'm the rich. But I can't stand the thought that it's going for the war in Vietnam instead of for the slums, for conservation, for un-pollution and so on.

12 February 1981

I was a great admirer of FDR when he was alive. I voted for him in 1944, and I revere his memory.

3 December 1981

The "Moral Majority" (so called) is a deadly enemy to science and to free thought. I think that, at the moment, they are more powerful and more dangerous than people calling themselves Nazis.

23 November 1982

I'm a lifelong liberal, and I get uneasy when "liberal" is used as a dirty word.

Representative Newt Gingrich, the conservative Republican congressman from Georgia who is now Speaker of the House, was one of Isaac's fans. In December 1982 he visited Isaac in New

York at Isaac's apartment. Several months later, Gingrich sent Isaac an advance copy of a letter that he was distributing about what Gingrich called a Second Millennium project. He asked Isaac's opinion of the letter. Isaac wrote Gingrich this reply:

18 June 1983

The letter is fine. But if you're going to rally the people of the world, for goodness' sake, you must place yourself above partisan politics. Resist poking fun at "liberal Democrats." There are a lot of them who might be on your side if you can avoid deliberately antagonizing them.

You were quoted in the New York *Times* as saying that for liberal Democrats to stand in horror at a budget deficit is like a saloonkeeper favoring Prohibition (or words to that effect).

Well, considering that no Democrat ever had a deficit even *half* as big as Reagan's, it is certainly peculiar that conservative Republicans who routinely faint at $20 billion Democratic deficits are cheerful as Punch at a $200 billion Republican deficit. It's like a hard-shell Baptist preacher getting drunk and chasing girls.

In his later years, he became a spokesman for a number of liberal organizations.

28 February 1986

I am president of the American Humanist Association and fundraising letters have gone out over my name for the AHA, the Americans for Democratic Action and the American Civil Liberties Union. In other words, I am an outspoken liberal Democrat, and I am hissed by the Radical Right. Personally, I am delighted to have the crackpots of the Right mad at me.

As much as Isaac disliked America's Republican Presidents, he liked the Democratic candidates who lost to them. Here's a letter to Walter Mondale:

15 October 1984

In a way, you can't lose. You will, at worst, join the list of candidates who have been the better people even though they come in second. You will be remembered as, for instance, Adlai Stevenson and Hubert Humphrey (both Democrats, of course) are remembered—as Presidents America was not shrewd enough to deserve.

Virtually everyone would be extremely honored to be invited to the White House for dinner. But not Isaac when the President was Ronald Reagan. He did not like Reagan or his policies. He told friends and family that he would feel like a hypocrite if he accepted such an invitation.

In 1984 and 1986, he received invitations. But Isaac respected the presidency. So here is a declination that is the model of decorum.

7 March 1984

I am greatly honored that my wife and I are invited to dinner on April 10, 1984, on the occasion of the visit of His Excellency, the President of the Dominican Republic.

It is with regret that I am compelled to inform you that I am unable to be in Washington that day and must therefore decline the invitation.

Isaac was a strong opponent of the Vietnam War.

18 May 1965

The bombing of North Vietnam has been stopped since its continuation was getting us nowhere but world unpopularity. It would take us 120 planes to bomb out two trucks, a price the North Vietnamese could well afford to pay for the terrific propaganda beating they were handing us in the world at large.

The slogan "my country, right or wrong" is not so bad. You can forgive your country being wrong. What about a new slogan, "my country, smart or stupid." It is hard to forgive stupidity. Napoleon once had a political enemy kidnapped from neutral territory. The furor that followed led Talleyrand to remark, "It is worse than a crime; it is a blunder."

27 October 1967

Some protesters against the Vietnam War plan to refuse to pay the 10% surtax if it is passed by Congress despite the risk of jail. (I am not one of these; I don't have the bravery to risk jail.) However, I would be greatly impressed if there were a solid movement on the part of the war-approvers to pay the 10% surtax voluntarily if Congress doesn't pass it.

Such a substitution of the pocketbook for the mouth would so impress me with the dedication of the American people in favor of this war that I would suspend my opposition to it.

4 December 1967

The United States would be considered a villain by some no matter what it did. But many of its actions in Vietnam *are* villainous by our own standards as applied to other people fighting their wars.

Non-Americans may fail to see the force of the argument: "Well, it's all right when *we* do it." Nor would they see the force that our conception of our national security justifies all. *That* argument would have justified Hitler.

7 February 1968

I hope recent events in Vietnam have penetrated the thick skulls in Washington, but somehow I doubt it. Given the choice of admitting a mistake or ruining the world, it's ruin by a length and a half.

In 1986, Isaac was asked whether he would write a short essay on what the United States learned from the Vietnam War. He declined.

23 August 1986

I don't consider myself an expert on the subject, and I don't want to be wise after the event. So I'll leave the punditing to others.

Besides, it's my candid opinion that my entire essay could be written as follows: "We have learned nothing from Vietnam."

The short Reagan foray into Lebanon was even more farcical and disgraceful than Vietnam was. And Reagan's mad panting for Nicaraguan blood will come to no good. Of course, if we can find enemies small enough, we can flex our muscles safely. We managed Grenada, and I suggest the next target be Monaco.

Isaac believed in the need for world peace and good relations with the Soviet Union.

29 July 1964

If anyone asks me if I'm for coexistence with the U.S.S.R., my answer is yes! What do they want? Nuclear war? We're coexisting with Russia right now, and we have to keep it up or we're all dead.

18 November 1965

My greatest desire is that the day will come when all suspicion and unfriendliness between the United States and the Soviet Union will cease, and we (and the rest of the world, too) will live together in brotherhood and peace.

20 February 1982

I would like to see a government in the United States and in the Soviet Union which will combine to destroy all nuclear weapons and to agree to a policy of external peace.

19 October 1985

The need for peace in the world today is so overwhelmingly great and the consequences of war are so overwhelmingly evil, that all good people should unite in preaching the need for peace. In this great cause, we can all of us find common ground.

1 October 1986

I think the continuation of truly independent nations is an impossible concept from here on in. The world is a single economic unit, and I think we'll have a global society by 2087 with the United States the cutting edge, I hope. But it won't be the old-fashioned U.S. we know.

9 December 1986

The desirability of peace and justice and freedom and security remain values I would keep forever. The nation-state is obsolete. We need a federalized world government.

An ideal 21st century is one in which computers and robots do routine work, a space-centered society is developed to the fullest along peaceful paths and a cooperating world tackles the real problems of humanity. What should we do? Reduce arms to a minimum and cultivate friendship and cooperation among all parts of the world.

The Soviet Union frequently had his books translated, but occasionally there were some problems.

27 January 1966

Today I got another request for anthologization (intended for Canadian high schools) of "The Feeling of Power," my satire on a computer-ridden future in which a little fellow discovers (rediscovers, rather) computing by pencil and paper and sees it turned to war use and kills himself.

The Russians have translated that story, along with a long commentary (which I had my father translate), which describes it as a savage, but hidden, satire on American capitalism and claims that I would have made it plainer if I had dared speak freely. They describe me as a "progressive" writer, with the same implication we use when we describe Boris Pasternak and others as "liberal" writers.

Well, well, we find in a work of art just what we want to see. I am merely the writer.

2 March 1966

Today I got a bundle of reading material from the Soviet Union. As I went through it, I found that each one had something of mine in it. They publish me in all their popular science magazines apparently.

My correspondent also sent me a copy of the Russian translation of *I, Robot* and talks about how good it is. He ends with "In Soviet Union we read all of yours and love you." He also said he hated to part with his copy, but "I want to do to you only good and the pleasure."

Is this an example of the godless, atheistic Red-Fascist Communist Terrorists who eat little children alive? (Or is he just softening me up so I will become Soft On Communism?)

21 May 1968

I received in the mail a Latvian edition of *I, Robot* together with a translation of the introduction and, dear me, the introduction makes me sound like a kind of storybook Communist. In my introductions to the anthologies *Soviet Science Fiction* and *More Soviet Science Fiction,* I discuss the differences between American and Soviet science fiction.

I talk about how pessimistic much American s.f. is and how "anti-Utopian." I also say that Soviet science fiction is optimistic but state clearly that it would scarcely be safe in the Soviet Union to be pessimistic about the future since that could be taken as a criticism of the Communist philosophy.

Anyway, the Latvian translator apparently quotes me as saying that I must be pessimistic in my s.f. since I am living in a capitalist country and if I were only a Soviet citizen, I would be optimistic and things like that.

What's more, the person who translated the introduction for me is planning to publish the translation in a fan magazine. So I quickly wrote him a letter telling him that he must, in that case, also include a statement from me to the effect that I was not responsible for anything anyone *said* I said. I would stand by only those remarks that appeared in print under my own byline.

I suppose that one of the hallmarks of fame is the privilege of being misquoted, but I don't like it any more than anyone else does, I guess.

In 1990, Isaac was invited to the Soviet embassy in Washington for a luncheon with Mikhail Gorbachev.

10 June 1990

I'm glad I bestirred myself to go to Washington for the Gorbachev luncheon. It was very pleasant and exciting, and I gave him, into his own hands, a copy of my book *Asimov's Chronology of Science and Discovery.* He said his daughter was a fan of mine, but I suppose that means my science fiction.

When Isaac returned from his Gorbachev luncheon, he told me that he was fascinated by the experience. "Sixty-seven years ago," he said, "Pappa, Mamma, Marcia and I left the Soviet Union in poverty to come to the United States. Now, I've had lunch with the head of the Soviet Union. Pappa would have been proud."

46

Honors

Isaac received many honors over the course of his life. But he was not eligible for membership in Phi Beta Kappa as an undergraduate. Although he took the bulk of his college courses at Columbia, Isaac was a student of the university, not the college. And since only the college had a Phi Beta Kappa chapter, he couldn't be a member.

21 March 1969

The Boston University chapter of Phi Beta Kappa asked me to speak to them this year, and I said, "Unfortunately, it would be embarrassing to speak at the initiation as I am not a member of Phi Beta Kappa." And they said, "Oh, we don't mind."

And I said, in my firmest tones, "I don't care whether you mind or not. *I* mind!!!!!"

They said, "We'll call you back." Within a few hours, they were back on the phone and said they had voted me in and I would get my key along with the rest of the initiates. A little polite blackmail, I suppose, but I deserve it.

19 June 1986

They must be figuring I'm not long for this world, for my name has been put into a cement slab ("Celebrity Walk") in a path in the Brooklyn Botanic Garden as a Brooklynite of fame, and

Mayor Koch is about to give me (and a group of others) some kind of medal.

He received 14 honorary degrees in his lifetime but never forgot his first one.

19 December 1980

It was at Bridgewater State College in Massachusetts a decade ago that I received my first honorary degree, and though I have received others since, nothing in any category equals the first. Certainly, never have I given a commencement address which was met with such enthusiasm (and at a time when some commencement addresses were being booed down).

He was very proud of being named one of science fiction's Grand Masters.

2 March 1987

I'm thinking so much about the Grand Master award, and I'm so pleased with it.

8 June 1987

Just a month ago, the Science Fiction Writers of America threw in the sponge and let me be a Grand Master. So I announced that I was the first Jewish Grand Master. Whereupon Bob Silverberg said, "And what do I say when it's my turn?" I said, "Announce yourself as the first handsome Jewish Grand Master." And he was all smiles.

24 September 1988

The longer a person lives, the more reasons people think up for handing him awards, and I can't seem to stop falling for it. Vanity, I suppose.

In his science fiction writing career, Isaac received five Hugos— the equivalent of the Hollywood Oscars. He told the story of receiving the first Hugo in 1963 in his autobiography. Because he was master of ceremonies of the 21st World Science Fiction convention in Washington and presenting the Hugos, he was sure that he was not going to receive one. But the final Hugo went to

Isaac for "putting the science in science fiction" in his Fantasy & Science Fiction *essays. As he wrote in his autobiography:*

"There wasn't any question that I was surprised. The day never existed when I could fake that look of stunned astonishment on my face. The audience roared; it roared for ten minutes."

Isaac later asked George Scithers, who was in charge of the convention, why he had been chosen to be master of ceremonies when he was going to receive a Hugo. And Scithers said: "The committee decided you were the only writer in science fiction who could give himself a Hugo without being embarrassed."

Isaac was very proud of his first Hugo, as he wrote several days later:

5 September 1963

I have now placed the Hugo on the end table to the right of the living-room couch, close to where I usually sit, so that I can reach out and touch it whenever I wish. It is right next to my boxed copy of *Intelligent Man's Guide* and a little bit below and to the right of my Steuben Owl on the mantelpiece. We might call that corner of the living room the "honor corner."

Columbia University, which he attended both as an undergraduate and as a graduate student, honored Isaac on several occasions in the past 25 years.

13 May 1970

Oh, if I had the gift to go back in time some 30 years and walk from faculty member to faculty member and administrative official to administrative official and say to one after the other: "Someday I will be recognized as one of our university's proudest products."

The gale of laughter I would leave in my wake would be enormous, and with luck, I might create two or three apoplectic strokes.

17 May 1983

I'm about to head off for Columbia University to get an honorary Doctor of Science at the commencement exercises. This is a great thing for me since when I went to Columbia for my regular degrees they always seemed a little unhappy that I was there. For one reason or another, I don't think they thought I was a credit to them.

Now they seem to have changed their minds.

For more than half of his life, Isaac was connected with Boston University, and he was proud of that association.

28 February 1968

I was introduced to a number of Boston University faculty members, and one of them said something which really pleased me. He said he had frequently heard of me but had never met me. And I said (modestly) that I could only hope he hadn't got tired of hearing of me because I spread myself so thickly and widely. And he said, very seriously, "No, no. You have an aura, and I use the word advisedly, which I am delighted to have part of the university."

I couldn't help but grin foolishly because remarks like this fit in with a theory I have that the BU faculty suffers constantly from an inferiority complex because Harvard and MIT are in the same town. People who meet a professor from Boston invariably assume he's at one of the two institutions. And if he says, "I'm at Boston University," there's a letdown that is unmistakable. I've felt it myself.

Well, my megalomaniac feeling is that my mere presence at BU single-handedly raises it a notch: that there's a kind of impressive notoriety it gets because I'm there and that other faculty members feel this and are relieved by it. When they say they're at BU, they feel that their audience knows that BU is where that guy is and they don't miss Harvard so much.

And if it's not true, then it still makes me feel wonderful to *suppose* it is true.

13 July 1979

I was back in Boston for a day, and it was absolutely necessary because after 24 years (!!!!) they finally promoted me to a full professor. So now I am Isaac Asimov, Professor of Biochemistry. Naturally, I had to celebrate.

47

Clubs

Isaac wrote many Black Widower mystery stories, which were inspired by his membership in a club called the Trap Door Spiders.

8 June 1972

The club is almost 30 years old and was started originally to avoid a wife of someone who was himself popular with the boys. It is stag. It meets once a month with two volunteers serving as co-hosts (and meeting all the expenses). Each of the co-hosts can bring a guest and usually does. Each guest is grilled after dinner.

Two unusual rules I know of are that every member is formally addressed as "Doctor" by virtue of his membership and each member agrees to have his membership in the Trap Door Spiders mentioned in his obituary.

We generally meet at 6:30 P.M. and drink and talk for an hour (which is rough on me since I don't drink). By 7:30 P.M., all have gathered who are going to be there, and we generally have a dozen people present. After dinner is the grilling, and we break up about 10:30. All we do is talk, singly and together, in separate conversations and general, with no holds barred.

Many of us are writers, and we are all articulate and opinionated. In fact, the general atmosphere of the Trap Door Spiders is very much as I have described it in my Black Widower stories.

The individuals in my Black Widower stories are vaguely based on the Trap Door Spider members as far as physical description is concerned *and nothing else*. I myself am not included in the stories as one of the characters, though I may introduce myself someday.

It is important to emphasize the *differences* between the Black Widowers and the Trap Door Spiders. In my own experience, there has never been raised any mystery of any kind at any of the meetings. We don't meet invariably in one place. We don't have any waiter who plays any significant role. In fact, Henry is the one part of the Black Widower stories that is my entire and sole creation and has no analog, whatever, in reality.

For the last 20 years of his life, Isaac was a member of the Dutch Treat Club, a luncheon club in New York City consisting of publishers, editors, writers, television and radio commentators and executives as well as people in the allied arts. At each weekly meeting, there would be a speaker and an entertainer. On one occasion, the entertainer didn't arrive, and Isaac filled in.

20 April 1985

I sang all four stanzas of "The Star-Spangled Banner" for the group, each of the stanzas (inadvertently) in a different key. They applauded anyway.

Isaac was modest about his performance that day. William Morris, the syndicated language columnist and another Dutch Treat member, wrote about it in one of his columns.

July 4, 1983

Asimov launched into a rendition of "The Star-Spangled Banner" unlike anyone anywhere ever heard before. First he set the scene, telling his listeners about the circumstances involved in the bombardment of Fort McHenry in Baltimore Harbor in 1814.

Francis Scott Key was on a boat in the harbor, negotiating for the release of a doctor the British had taken prisoner. It was the prisoner who repeatedly asked, "Can you see that our flag is still there?" When dawn finally came, Key was able to reassure his friend and they made their way to safety while Key scribbled the words of what was to become our national anthem on the back of an envelope.

"So far, so good," you say. "I thought everyone knew that." Perhaps, but Asimov proceeded to sing all four verses, explaining the special significance of each.

When he finished, everyone in the club was on his feet applauding and even cheering. It was a demonstration unlike any even the oldest member could remember. And it was more than that, it was an outpouring of genuine patriotic fervor the likes of which we experience only a few times in our lives.

In 1985, he became president of the Dutch Treat Club, and he wanted to address one of the problems about the club that had always bothered him—the exclusion of women.

11 December 1985

I have only been president for a few months, but I have already brought up the subject. The difficulty is that the older members are so far adamant and dream about how it used to be in the great old days of their youth. My mild comment to the effect "But the world has changed" seems to bring out the worst in them. "For the worse," they yell (meaning they are no longer young).

10 March 1986

The Dutch Treat Club is purely social, except for how friendships made here affect business outside. It's because this sort of thing does happen that women rightly object to being excluded. I am fighting to allow qualified women to enter.

14 November 1990

As long as I am president, I must tell you that I intend to keep on expressing myself strongly. I am not a contentious individual and I don't look for fights, but some things mean a lot to me, like women members in the club.

In 1991, Isaac finally won. The Dutch Treat Club began to admit women.

48

Shakespeare, Humor and Autobiography

Isaac adored Shakespeare. And here's why he wrote his annotations.

23 March 1968

Richard II is a beautiful play, and some of the speeches are so haunting that you can love them even if you don't have the slightest idea why everybody is acting as they do. Who cares who John of Gaunt is when you read his panegyric to England or who Richard II is when you read his speech about telling sad tales about the death of kings.

And it is possible to attend a performance of *Richard II* and be deeply moved even if you don't know who the devil Gloucester is or why everyone is making such a fuss about his murder or why Bolingbroke takes so long in killing off Richard or how come Bolingbroke gets the crown instead of somebody else and so on.

The original audience for whom Shakespeare wrote (at least the educated portion of it) knew all the characters in the play very well and could follow events in the same way we could follow a play about Lincoln, Douglas, Grant and Lee. The modern audience, however, no matter how educated, usually knows very little about medieval and early modern English history and loses a lot because of that. It misses many of the fine points.

I want to supply the lack. I want to go over *Richard II*, for instance, stopping to quote whatever lines I need and explain enough English history so that they can follow every scene and see the need for it, not just dramatically, but *historically*. In doing so, of course, I am discursive, as I was in my Bible books, and talk about anything that interests me (always taking for granted that I can talk about anything that interests me in such a way that it will interest the reader).

Sometimes he envied Shakespeare.

5 June 1969

In *Henry VI,* York has the chance to make one last speech, and he begins with a phrase that has ever since characterized Queen Margaret of Anjou in history. He says, "She-wolf of France . . ."

Oh, what a damning phrase. Oh, the power Shakespeare had of making the whole world see history his way.

Later in the speech, he apostrophizes her as: "O tiger's heart wrapped in a woman's hide!"

How perfect. Spoken by some actor with a strong voice and capable of making it drip hatred, contempt and horror, how that line could chill an audience! And how envious it makes me. If I had written the line, I would certainly have made the obvious mistake and said, "O tiger's heart wrapped in a woman's skin!" This would have killed it. "Hide" is the outer wrapping of an animal, and the use of that word in place of "skin" doubles and trebles the picture of Margaret as a wild and feral beast. And Shakespeare probably said "hide" out of pure instinct and without pausing to think.

It just isn't fair!!!

But Isaac never stopped praising Shakespeare.

5 October 1989

If there is one book someone *must* read before calling himself educated, it is *The Collected Works of William Shakespeare.* There is no writer like him, and probably never will be, for infinite insight into human beings and for ringing out the music of the English language. If any of it is lost on the individual reader, I suggest he keep at his elbow my book *Asimov's Guide to Shakespeare.*

And he had an easy way to tell friends the last four digits of his telephone number.

25 May 1982

Easy to remember: 1564 is Shakespeare's birth date.

Isaac wrote two books of jokes. In 1971, Isaac Asimov's Treasury of Humor *was published. Shortly afterward, John Ciardi suggested a sequel entitled* Asimov Laughs Again. *But all of his other writings interfered, and it was not published until the month that he died in 1992. It was the last published book of his that he saw.*

Here is how he described humor.

24 June 1977

My definition of humor is the emotion aroused by a sudden and unexpected change in a point of view. The more sudden and the more unexpected, the keener the sense of the ridiculous and the louder the laugh. Thus, this happened to me in honest truth.

I had been on a syndicated national television talk show for the first time and was rather proud of the fact. I was with a group of people later, and someone mentioned having seen me on the show. I smiled and said, "Yes, that was I on the show."

A young man who was part of the group asked jokingly as to what I had done on the show. "Did you read advertisements?" he asked.

"No," said I, sarcastically, "I demonstrated sexual techniques."

"Oh?" said he, softly. "You remembered?"

Suddenly, there was a change in point of view of myself from a competent lover able to teach the art to a doddering old man barely able to remember it. Everyone laughed. Even I laughed.

A story that is not funny at all? One that hurts someone and is *meant* to hurt someone. Once when I was young, I decided to grow a mustache. After the better part of a week, something was visible on my upper lip. A swarthy young woman, noticing this, said to me contemptuously, "Are *you* trying to grow a mustache?" Feeling she was casting doubt on my virility, I eyed her narrowly and said, "Why not? *You* did."

She burst into tears, and I was ashamed. It was not a witty retort at all. It was merely a cruel one (although it was true).

I like humor at which all can laugh and which will make no one ashamed. Perhaps the best humor is humor directed at oneself. Jack Benny spent 40 years in comedy, and all his humor was at his own expense. He was one of the best-loved comedians who ever lived. Not only his humor was loved; *he* was.

In the 1960s, a number of Isaac's readers suggested that he write his autobiography. He kept saying "no":

23 January 1964

It is hard to conceive of a life less dramatic than mine. Although writers traditionally have had exciting lives, traveling extensively, and trying their hand at many glamorous occupations—none of this is true of me. I have quietly completed an extensive education, settled down to a thoroughly conventional middle-class life and occupy myself entirely with the writing of many books. I am simply not biographical material.

In the late 1970s, Isaac did write his autobiography.

27 July 1977

I'm not just skimming through my diary, *I am reading every bloody word on every bloody page* (a hard job).

31 January 1978

It will tell everybody a lot more about me than anyone can want to know, although I have been careful not to say anything nasty about anybody. (After all, they can't answer back in books of their own and how can I be sure my version is the correct one?)

30 May 1978

In 1979, Doubleday is publishing my autobiography (640,000 words of it) in two volumes. It is all done and in press. If you ask me how on Earth I can talk for 640,000 words about myself when nothing of significance has ever happened to me, my answer is: I don't know.

31 March 1979

It makes me a little nervous to know that thousands of people are going to know all about me. But if I didn't want that to happen, why did I write the book?

Fifteen years later, he wrote I, Asimov, *a memoir.*

4 April 1990

My recent flirtation with death made it necessary for me to write a retrospective autobiography before I pass on to the great word processor in the sky.

10 June 1990

I spent my hospital time writing a new version of my autobiography (a quarter of a million words), which is now finished and at the publisher, and I have to return to my history of the world, which I had to put to one side in order to be ill. It is almost completed (half a million words) and all but the final hundred pages are at the publisher. And then I have to start a new novel.

49

Being Jewish

Isaac was Jewish and totally non-religious.

27 March 1959

I carry the front name of Isaac. I come complete with a full stock of Jewish mannerisms, which I make no attempt to hide. I refer freely to the fact that I am Jewish and accept with resigned indifference any social or cultural barriers that are put up about me. It is only in the ethereal heights of theory that I maintain I am no Jew at all, either by race, by religion, by cultural heritage or even by inner feeling. I am a Jew only because other people say I am. And this satisfies no one.

Fortunately, it satisfies me. It deprives me of identification of group feeling, of the comfort of the herd. It gives me only the cold and bleak advantages of independence. But since this is the way I like it, this is the way it is.

31 March 1966

I am the son of immigrant parents. So are millions of others, and I make no special claim to hardship on that account. However, my parents' native culture was far removed from the American and was not even a dominant culture in its native habitat. Quite the contrary. They managed to adjust to the American way of life in the sense that they made a living, brought up respectable children, formed worthy, useful members of society who were never a burden on the taxpayer in any way.

I myself needed and could earn even more—and earned it. But in very important respects, I had to do it without the help of my parents.

I had to learn American culture on my own, and it is difficult to explain to someone who has not gone through it what this means. As a simple example, I was not taken to restaurants when I was young; indeed I did not go to a restaurant till I was an adult. Even if I had been taken to a restaurant when I was young, it would have been to a cafeteria or to a Jewish dairy restaurant or a delicatessen. Even if I had been taken to a fine American restaurant, my parents would not have known the nuances of necessary behavior, and I would have absorbed their uneasiness.

Yes, I can eat in any fancy restaurant today. But I suspect (I cannot *know* without changing places with another personality) that I can never enter one, sit down, study the menu and order food with that same automatic comfort and ease of one who has been used to it from childhood.

In short, I was a cultural orphan (like many others) and "speak the culture with an accent."

The accent shows up in all sorts of ways. For instance, to take a far-fetched example, in theory I know that one buys flowers for a girl and it would be my intention to do so—but it never occurs to me in practice. The transplanted culture in which I passed my childhood, and rebelled against, was not a flower-buying culture. I cannot help feeling odd if I walk into a flower shop to buy flowers.

In a hundred little ways this shows up. I sing in public, for instance, when feeling gay. I talk too loudly and with too much animation. I lack the Anglo-Saxon sangfroid, and so on.

If all this sounds as though I am sorry for myself, I am *not*. My parents supplied me with a great deal, even if they were unable to supply me with an American cultural pattern. They gave me love and a feeling of great worth. I have accomplished a good deal, and my accent is by no means as great as it might be. In fact, I feel rather good at having achieved as much as I have despite an accent. This accentuates (forgive the pun) my feeling of worth.

17 March 1969

I am Jewish in the sense that if an Arab wanted to throw a rock at a Jew, I would qualify as a target as far as he was concerned. However, I do not practice Judaism or any other religion.

Isaac was once the subject of a Bar Mitzvah sermon.

6 May 1980

I have never before been the object of a Bar Mitzvah sermon. It may confuse God. He will listen and say, "Who is this Isaac Asimov who himself has never been Bar Mitzvahed." Well, perhaps your merits will intercede for me and help give me a portion of the life to come.

In 1988, Isaac was invited to lead a Passover seder during a science fiction convention.

29 April 1988

Oy, vay. Have you got the wrong fellow!!!

I'm an orthodox, practicing atheist and have attended a very few seders strictly as an outsider. I have no more knowledge on officiating at a seder than I have on officiating at a mass.

3 November 1983

"What makes you proud to be Jewish?"

That's a difficult question. I am proud of the things I've done that I think have been worth doing and have been useful and pleasurable to other people. I am proud of having written useful books and having occasionally done kind things and being a loving husband and father, and things of that sort.

But being proud to be Jewish? I haven't done anything to be Jewish. I have just happened to be born to a father and mother who were Jewish. That is no credit to me, and it is nothing that I should personally be proud of because it might have happened to anyone.

Let us be proud of what we *do* and not of the accident of birth.

What about the problems faced by Israel?

Nobody owns anything on the Earth. Everybody holds what they can grab, and it is force that counts. The Americans took the land from the Indians. Do you think the Americans will ever give it back? Every land is occupied by people who took it from someone else.

Before the Israelites were the Canaanites, and even when Abraham came to Canaan, there were already Canaanites there. God gave Canaan to Abraham, the Bible says, but it's the Jews who say that about their own God. Not everybody believes in the Jews' God, and I don't believe in any God.

Listen, the Israelis and the Arabs both claim the territory, and it will go to the one who is stronger. And frankly, no matter how long Israel stays Israel, there will always be millions and millions of Arabs in every direction. To me, in the long run, it looks bad.

Maybe God will protect the Jews, but He has done a very poor job of it up to now. For my part, I wish He would go and protect some other group of people for a few thousand years and let us alone to assimilate.

50

Being an Atheist

Isaac was an atheist with a sense of humor.

7 September 1969
I was just on a David Frost television talk show (it had been taped three weeks earlier). They had asked what I wanted to talk about, and I had replied, "Oh heck, tell him to ask anything he wants and I'll answer." Which made me a sitting duck, of course.

He asked me if I believed in God, and after I vainly tried to twist out of it, he said severely, "Surely an intelligent, curious, questing man like yourself would have tried to find God." And I answered fliply, "Well, He's smarter than I am, let Him try to find me." Everyone laughed, and I was just superstitious enough to be nervous.

It so happens on the morning of the day that the program was to appear, I had my worst kidney stone attack of all time—nine straight hours of absolute agony. I kept staggering about, clutching my abdomen, and shouting, "All right, you *found* me, you *found* me!"

But He wasn't finished. Last night He tried another little trick, but in such a way that I could see He really loved me. Walking into a Long Island motel, I tried to step through an opening in the wall which turned out to be a clear glass panel. The glass

SHATTERED under the impact, and I was *showered* with a thousand pieces of razor-sharp silicate. The *only* damage I suffered was a few superficial cuts on my left hand and right knee.

And as it happened, at the very moment I staggered to the desk for help, a policeman with a police *ambulance* happened to be there on utterly coincidental business, and he promptly took care of me.

All was well, but next time anyone asks me on television if I believe in God, I am going to be very polite in my answer. I suspect the Good Lord lacks a sense of humor.

23 January 1967

I attended services at a Unitarian church yesterday. All of the hymns and recitals had a science fiction motif, and the sermon consisted of the reading of one of my short stories. (I attended anonymously and enjoyed myself enormously.)

31 December 1979

I may be a Jewish atheist, but I am not bigoted about it. I spend two hours on Christmas Eve singing Christmas carols, and I'd sing Hegira carols, too, if there were such things.

> *He hastened out of Mecca on a rickety dromedary,*
> *And they said, "Don't come back, you bum.*
> *Then we'll keep our Kaaba merry."*

28 December 1981

Although I am an atheist and was interviewed on a program called *Equal Time for Atheists* on 25 December, I then afterward sang Christmas carols. I like the tunes and I like the festivities and we had a good time.

24 January 1989

I am an atheist, which is probably the only reason I have lived this long. God won't have me.

Although Isaac was an atheist, he wrote a number of books that dealt with the Bible. In a letter to Pappa, he wrote:

23 November 1962

Pappa, did you ever think your son would be a Bible scholar when you didn't even send him to Hebrew school or get him a Bar Mitzvah?

Here are some of his views on the Bible:

18 May 1963

My interest in the Bible is purely literary. I am a lover of the English language.

22 February 1966

I'm working on my Bible book. I've just reached the part where the Israelites have been seduced into apostasy by the Moabite women (in the Book of Numbers), and Moses gets all self-righteous about the wickedness of the women who deliberately seduced the poor, innocent Israelites (except that Moses ordered the slaughter of all of the Israelites without mercy).

Properly read, the Bible is the most potent force for atheism ever conceived.

28 October 1966

I have done the Old Testament and the Apocrypha and am working away on the New Testament, and I must say that I stand amazed at the highly intelligent people who have taken so much of the Bible so seriously.

1 November 1966

Luke and Matthew both give material on the birth and childhood of Jesus, and they do not correspond AT A SINGLE POINT. Whatever one says the other doesn't say. Nobody but a dedicated Christian could possibly read the gospels and not see them as a tissue of nonsense—at least the legendary and miraculous material in them.

19 November 1966

I once heard Billy Graham explain that the Bible was full of "straight talk." It called "a spade a spade." It said "hell" and "damn" and "whore" (although *he* didn't say "whore"). What Billy doesn't seem to know, though, is that the Bible contains

more euphemisms per square yard than any other work of literature in my opinion. Heavens! The King James Version says
"Lord" instead of "Yahveh" about a thousand times and *that's* a
euphemism.

                                            22 December 1967
I just saw the movie *The Bible*. I knew it was a bad picture,
having carefully read the reviews which unanimously panned it.
But I couldn't believe my eyes when I saw how bad it really was.
The first half of Genesis was approached with such literality and
hidebound reverence that there was no chance of creativity. The
letter was there, and there, and there, but the spirit was utterly
lacking.

I kept thinking bitterly of *The Green Pastures*, which presented
the Bible as seen by illiterate Negroes, with the crudest anthropo-
morphism and with the anachronisms played for laughs. *The
Green Pastures* was a noble rendition that caught the spirit,
breathed true reverence and was all the Bible ought to be. This
thing by John Huston was just trash.

                                               23 April 1968
I just had a call from Doubleday. At a sales conference of all the
sales managers (Doubleday variety in the U.S.), one and all
turned thumbs down on the title *Everyman's Guide to the Bible*.
Without a dissenting vote, they all insisted on *Asimov's Guide to
the Bible*.

I objected with considerable horror that this would sound awfully arrogant and conceited. I said that Doubleday would have
to stand ready to admit, at all moments, that the title was at their
request.

                                             4 December 1968
The Bible contains legendary, historical and ethical contents. It is
quite possible to consider them separately, and one doesn't have
to accept the legends in order to get the ethics. Fundamentalists
make a grave mistake to insist on the letter of the writings because they drive many away who can't swallow the Adam-and-
Eve bit.

12 January 1971

Actually, my Bible books are not scholarly works and are meant for the general public. My resource materials are various Bible dictionaries and encyclopedias to which all have access, and I add to it only (1) my ability to organize, (2) my ability to write and (3) sometimes my ingenuity.

26 July 1973

My interest in the Bible arises out of my interest in history. The Bible is the oldest history book we have, and my book on the Bible treats it from the standpoint of secular history and not from the standpoint of either religion or ethics.

Isaac felt that science did not support the tenets of religion.

14 November 1962

All those who say that you cannot look at the sky (or at a leaf or at a gazelle or at a mountain) without realizing that God must exist, don't consider that the hypothesis *has already been put in their minds.* As children they are taught that God exists and that they will go to hell if they doubt. If their parents don't tell them, their teachers or their playmates do. (Lots of children learn about God from the gutter.)

When they grow up, they seize upon any seemingly rational excuse to make their beliefs non-superstitious. The real test would be to take someone who has grown up in a completely materialistic philosophy and who has never heard of God. Let him look at the heavens (or a turtle or a delicate rose) and let me hear him say, "Why, there must be some supernatural power that has created us all."

If he does, I will be shaken, but I am perfectly confident he will say, "My! Look at the heavens or turtle or rose; how pleasant to know a little about astronomy or zoology or botany so that I can truly appreciate the marvelous natural phenomenon."

22 August 1963

I would not be satisfied to have my kids choose to be religious without trying to argue them out of it, just as I would not be satisfied to have them decide to smoke regularly or engage in any other practice I considered detrimental to mind or body.

1 January 1970

No scientist in speculating on the origin of the universe offers the answer "God made it." He searches for an answer of another kind on the (usually unspoken) assumption that the existence of God is irrelevant in this context.

27 March 1976

Religions may have been actively involved in the easing of the human condition, but I am more aware of conversion by the sword (the first case being that of the Edomites by the Jews in Maccabean times) and of burning at the stake and of Inquisitorial suppression of dissent. The benefits are a matter of theory; the harm is clear and present.

I am prejudiced against religion because I know the history of religion, and it is the history of human misery and of black crimes.

28 October 1987

The star of Bethlehem was in all likelihood merely a pious wonder tale to mark the birth of Jesus. But of course the Bible tends to be believed, so that rational people have tried to find a rational explanation.

There was a close approach of the planets Venus and Jupiter in 2 B.C. They were at the closest near the western horizon, so that to observers in Babylonia they might seem to be a fuzzy, very bright star hovering over Judea in the west. But if so, such close approaches take place periodically. The star of Bethlehem will shine many times except that we will know it is a planetary occultation, and we will lose the sense of magic.

1 December 1990

I have written on religion and science and have never made any secret of the fact that I am an atheist. My feeling is, quite simply, that if there is a God, He has done such a bad job that He isn't worth discussing.

In 1985, Isaac was elected president of the American Humanist Association. The humanists believe that since human beings created society's ills, human beings (not some supernatural being) will have to cure them.

11 January 1983

I have never had to develop my humanist beliefs and ideals against a surrounding religious belief since I was brought up without any religion whatever. The result is that a rational, secular view is as natural to me as breathing air is, and nowhere inside me, no matter how deeply one probes, is there any conflict about it, any hidden shame or fear. The result is that I have never had to *think* about my humanism or find any system of apologetics for it. It just *is*.

He was once asked to support "Jewish" humanism. He declined.

21 June 1985

I want to be a human being, nothing more and nothing less. It's no good having humanism split into every ethnic, religious and geographical splinter imaginable. Why bother calling it *human*ism then? I don't suppose we can ever stop hating each other, but why encourage that by keeping the old labels with their ready-made history of millennial hate?

51

Health

The major health problems that Isaac faced in his lifetime were a series of kidney stone attacks, a thyroid operation in 1972, a heart attack in 1977, a bypass operation in 1983 and deteriorating health in 1990 and 1991.

During the course of writing tens of thousands of letters, Isaac would occasionally mention his health.

5 January 1957

A couple of months back, I experienced a queer steady pain in my chest just over my heart. I am a terrible hypochondriac and secretly diagnosed heart trouble and instantly started having psychosomatic trouble in breathing, became afraid to walk up stairs, started wondering if I'd wake up when I shut my eyes to go to sleep.

It turned out to be indigestion, I'm glad to say. But before the diagnosis, I spent a lot of time evaluating my life. I came to the conclusion that I had two regrets: (1) that I hadn't written enough books and (2) that I wouldn't see my kids as adults.

1 November 1961

I just returned from my internist, whose primary interest lay in my kidney stones. He lectured me very carefully on the urinary system, using charts. He pointed out the kidneys and pronounced the word "aorta" in fully rounded tones. He explained about the renal arteries and veins, what the kidneys did and what the ureters were. I sat and listened like a good little boy and didn't say that I had written a whole chapter on the subject recently because it would have hurt his feelings. I am trying to live up to people's opinions of what I ought to be like.

22 December 1969

I have periodic prostatic examinations. Last time I was told I had the prostate of a 25-year-old. I said, "Tell me his name, and I'll return it," but that merely confused the doctor.

The first major health problem that Isaac had was in 1972. He had cancer of the thyroid, and he went through an operation to remove the cancerous growth. Here's how he described what happened.

20 February 1972

Well, to begin with, I survived the operation after all. I was under the knife for four hours. It was a very humorous experience. They shot me full of tranquilizers prior to the operation in order to eliminate fear and anxiety. And, as it happens, when fear and anxiety are eliminated within me, that leaves the only other emotion that exists in me—hilarity. So they rolled me down to the operating floor while I was singing at the top of my voice and swinging my arms in time to the music. And I heard one nurse say to another: "I *never* saw any reaction like *that* to medication."

Then they decanted me onto the operating table with the light overhead, and my surgeon approached with his green mask and smiled comfortingly at me as he prepared for the incision in my throat so that he could operate on my thyroid. Seeing him, I galvanized into activity, grabbed his arm and chanted:

Doctor, Doctor, in your white coat,
Doctor, Doctor, cut my throat,
And when you've cut it, Doctor, then
Won't you sew it up again?

And I went out like a light while the surgeon (he told me afterward) stood there shaking with laughter and wondering if he could guide the scalpel accurately. Now I always say that I'll do *anything* for a gag, but accosting someone about to cut into my throat and saying something funny that will unsteady his hands is, I think, the peak and pinnacle of idiocy.

The operation barely put a dent in his work pattern.

2 March 1972

It was quite humiliating to be ill, and I refused to give in. I took a typewriter to the hospital with me, wrote a short mystery story the day before the operation, sent it to *Ellery Queen* and had it accepted before I left the hospital. Two days after the operation, I was back at work. A week after, I was on full time again. But I have a scar on my neck now from ear to ear and visible evidence that I, too, am mortal and that my organs, too, break down with time.

19 March 1974

I ran a fever yesterday, and Janet insisted I stay in bed. Today, however, she had to see patients (that's what comes of being a psychiatrist). So while she was busy, I snuck away to my office. I don't believe in being sick.

Then came the heart attack.

11 June 1977

It was a mild coronary, and I was hospitalized over my wild protests because I had a commencement address to give two days later at Johns Hopkins and they wouldn't let me go.

I am out of the hospital now and am under house arrest for a couple of weeks. But they tell me I can sit at the typewriter all day if I want to, so I am very contented.

15 June 1977

Do you know I have lost ten pounds so far and last night I had a big dinner. I felt so rotten and guilty that I now realize I will never be able to eat a lot again. I've got 20 more pounds to lose. I'll get down to 154, the weight I had when I married the first time in 1942. Considering my top weight in 1964 was 210, that's something. It is 175 right now.

324 · Y O U R S , I S A A C A S I M O V

Isaac's internist was Dr. Paul Esserman, whom he admired and appreciated greatly. But that didn't prevent Isaac from giving Esserman the needle when Esserman planned to visit Sri Lanka, where Arthur C. Clarke lived. Isaac sent this introductory letter to Clarke:

4 July 1977

This is to introduce Dr. Paul Esserman, my internist, who saw me through my recent mild coronary. He's the guy who brought me down with a flying tackle after the coronary and had me held down on the table for an EKG over my protests.

He then said that I had had the coronary although I insisted the EKG was normal. He then put me in the hospital and personally saw to it, at enormous fees, that I came through with flying colors.

Here I am, about as healthy as I can be (but very poor), and I think you'll find Paul a fascinating fellow. In fact, now is the time for you to be sick for he'll pull you through anything. And he'll send the bill to me.

Did Isaac's life change?

11 October 1977

My doctor said I must cut down on my workload and that is so difficult I don't see how I can manage. I feel like Jack Benny.

"Your workload or your life."

"I'm thinking. I'm thinking."

22 November 1978

Since my coronary last year, I have retired from everything but my 6 to 12 books a year and my 30 to 50 talks a year.

11 March 1979

I'm the queasiest person in the world. I double up whenever someone says, "They drew blood from me yesterday." I all but go into a faint at the sight of a hypodermic. My wife (a physician) can't engage in medical small talk to anyone in my hearing.

29 May 1979

I never smoked or drank, so that I didn't have things to give up to help me after the coronary. I did overeat, and I have lost weight and am engaged in a continual struggle to keep it off. It's not just a matter of losing weight. That's easy under the stress of necessity, and there's exciting triumph in watching it go down.

Once it's down, there's nothing but dull, dull, dull weariness in keeping it down. But you have no choice.

Next came the bypass operation.

4 December 1983

I survived my angiogram with flying colors, but the news (as I surmised) was bad. The alternatives are living on medication, always on the edge of angina, and the strong possibility of heart attack and death—or a triple bypass.

I chose the triple bypass instantly.

Less then a month after the bypass operation, he wrote this letter to Ed Ferman, editor of Fantasy & Science Fiction:

8 January 1984

As I promised you last month, I intend to continue right on without missing an issue. This is, in fact, the first piece of creative writing I've done since the bypass 3½ weeks ago. It deals with heart and blood vessels (naturally), and it is my 310th essay.

Within weeks, he was fully back to work.

13 March 1984

I have recovered virtually completely. I put in a full day's work, and I make my rounds in the old way. The scars are still there and the knowledge that I have substitute vessels in my chest will undoubtedly permanently destroy my feeling of immortality. But had I not undergone the operation, my life expectancy would have been short indeed. So I accept the alternative I have chosen.

26 February 1985

The triple bypass has been very successful, and I feel great. However, I have just turned 65 and between that and the patched-up plumbing, I cannot help but feel that most of my time is past and very little time is personal future.

I have therefore made a cool assessment of what I want to do —and what I want to do is write. I have therefore cut my speaking engagements to the bone.

Isaac never wanted to retire.

20 March 1981

I will not flag or fail. I will go on to the end. I will work in my office. I will work on trains and ocean liners. I will work with growing confidence and growing strength at home. I will defend my typewriter whatever the cost may be. I will work on the beaches. I will work in the mountain resorts. I will work on Sundays and holidays. I will work during vacations. I WILL NEVER RETIRE.

15 October 1989

I am a writer, and although I am now almost 70, I have not retired. I am busier than ever. I will never retire. NEVER. Perhaps three days after I am dead, I will retire—but certainly not before.

But within months, his health turned bad again.

9 January 1990

I'm sorry to say that my 70th birthday came and went under the most miserable conditions.

For the first time in my life, I am suffering a long siege of illness with no end in sight. The natural vein of pessimism in me tells me that I am on the downhill slide. The doctors swear it's not serious, and I will recover. But I feel sufficiently rotten to wonder if that's good news.

21 April 1990

I have a defective mitral valve, and the doctors decided not to operate but to chance having me live on under medication, care and hope. So here I am with a leaking heart and with my physical equipment working at only part-level.

Fortunately, my mind is not affected, so that I am working as diligently as I always have.

21 November 1990

I *am* defeated. I have physical ailments that won't go away and can't be cured. I imagine my life expectancy is low. Mind you, it doesn't mean I have given up. I am writing as briskly as ever (did a short story today—a very funny one) and even if I die this minute, I will end up with nearly 500 books, which isn't bad.

One of the last letters he wrote was in response to a friend who praised his short story "Gold."

18 August 1991

I am delighted that "Gold" pleased you. It may be my last story. If so, at least I ended with a bang.

52

Death

Isaac felt that only death could stop him from writing.

31 July 1964

If I am indeed a writing machine, then the trouble is that it has sealed controls and I cannot be stopped manually. I suppose what will stop me eventually is death or senility, whichever comes first, and I'm not sure that senility will stop me from writing—only from publishing.

13 September 1969

If I were in heaven, I would do exactly what I am doing—which consists, mostly, of writing books.

20 February 1972

I am dreadfully aware of the fact that I get one day closer to death or senility (rather the former than the latter) each day I live and that no matter how I pack my brain with facts and ideas, it will wither and decay and come to nothing at last. That is one of the reasons I am doing my best to discharge its contents onto the printed page as quickly and as entirely as ever I can. The products, I hope, will live on even if the source doesn't.

29 July 1972

I would be interested to hear of any premonitions concerning anyone, but I DO NOT WANT ANY PREMONITIONS CONCERNING MYSELF. If I am to die, I do not want to know about it and, besides, such predictions can be self-fulfilling.

About 20 years ago, Isaac was asked what he would like to be remembered for after his death.

20 September 1973

What I *will* be remembered for are the Foundation Trilogy and the Three Laws of Robotics. What I *want* to be remembered for is no one book, or no dozen books. Any single thing I have written can be paralleled or even surpassed by something someone else has done. However, my total corpus for quantity, quality and *variety* can be duplicated by no one else. That is what I want to be remembered for.

If there were life after death, who would he like to meet?

28 January 1974

I would, on arriving in that section of heaven reserved for writers who tried to enlighten mankind, ask to see such great satirists of the past as Martial, Swift, Voltaire, Dickens and Twain. I would ask them humbly if I might sit at their feet.

But he didn't expect to meet them.

9 April 1975

The soul, spirit, ghost, essence, etc., of a person is, I am sure, an invention of mankind to counteract the fact of death. I do not believe it exists. I believe the feeling of "self" depends on the intricate arrangement of the brain cells and that this vanishes with the loss of the arrangement in death.

As he got older, death was not far from his mind.

13 May 1985

The kids I started with, who were my eager young friends then, are all old men, as I am (and, in some cases, old women), and are beginning to die off. One of them died as long ago as 1958 at the age of 34 and another that same year at the age of 43. But now, each year, half a dozen die.

There's nothing to be done about it. Death is the greatest democrat in the world. It gets us all in the end, rich or poor, smart or dumb. The only thing to do is to relish the gift of life while it exists and to live each day to the full.

5 June 1988

I feel rather grim. In the last seven months, three Grand Masters have gone to the Continuing Convention in the Sky. Bester, Simak and Heinlein, all three friends of mine.

11 October 1988

As to the third volume of my autobiography, my wife is after me to get it started lest the Angel of Death surprise me too soon. (I'll make a Faustian deal with it. The moment I say, "I'm tired of writing; I will stop," he can have me.)

16 September 1989

Tomorrow is the 11th annual "New York Is Book Country." The general theme (for the first time) is science fictional, and I am the most important of the New York-based s.f. writers. So they're going to make a big fuss about me, especially since this year I am celebrating 50 years as a professional writer.

So I'm going to be honored. I'd feel better if I didn't know that these honors accumulate with age and that they reach a high pitch in anticipation of death.

In his last year of writing, Isaac knew he was dying. And it was causing him one final problem.

27 September 1990

As I approach the end of my longish life, I have made my peace with regard to the necessary parting with my loved wife and daughter. I have always known this was inevitable and I am ready. However, I have never managed to get it through my head that I must stop writing, too. That strikes me as going too far. Why should a little thing like death put an end to my writing? If I am willing to give up everything else, why can't I continue to write? It doesn't seem very much to ask.

Afterword

About the time that Isaac had written 80 books, someone walked up to me and asked how many books had I written. My answer was:

"Isaac and I have averaged 40 books each—80 for him and none for me."

Over the years, the question was repeated many times. The answer changed only to reflect Isaac's increasing number of books.

While this book means that my book count will soar to one, it also counts as another book for Isaac. After all, they are his letters.

While I am not a dawn-to-curfew writer in the fashion of Isaac, I worked long hours on the book. I'm grateful for the loving patience of my wife, Ruth. She was the editor's editor, and a superb one at that.

My daughter Nanette, a reporter on the San Francisco *Chronicle,* spent her vacations helping me read Isaac's letters. She also reviewed the final manuscript. I appreciated her editing.

My son Eric is the Styles Editor and a restaurant reviewer at the New York *Times.* His first two books have already been published. They are compilations of his reviews. My oldest son, Daniel, is a mathematician with NASA.

Isaac used to tell the story of Nathaniel Benchley, an excellent and widely known novelist, who will forever be known as the son

of Robert Benchley, the humorist, and the father of Peter Benchley, the author of *Jaws*.

So I'm not only happy to be Isaac's brother. I am happy to be
known as the father of Nanette, Eric or Dan.

Some other thanks are necessary. In late 1991, while Isaac's
health was deteriorating, I wasn't doing well either. I have a
blood disease for which there is no cure, and I needed regular
blood transfusions that seemed to provide fewer and fewer benefits. Isaac and I spent the winter of 1991–92 checking on each
other's health with frequent telephone calls.

Isaac died in April 1992, and at virtually the same time, an
experimental drug that I was taking for my blood ailment began
to work for me. It drastically reduced the number of transfusions,
restored my energy level and enabled me to resume near-normal
living.

For this renewal of life, which enabled me to do this book, I
want to thank Dr. Lewis Silverman of the Mount Sinai Medical
Center. And thanks, too, to his always cheerful nurse, Barbara
Rawlerson, and to the many people at North Shore University
Hospital on Long Island—Dr. Vincent Vinciguerra, the treatment
room nurses, the blood technicians, the blood bank staff and
everyone else who have treated me with compassion, gentleness
and kindness.

One last note. It was a privilege to read Isaac's mail. I was his
brother, not one of his Gentle Readers. So while I knew how
smart and good and nice he was, I was casual and accepting of
these traits—as a brother should be.

But these letters told me that he was REALLY SMART and
REALLY GOOD and REALLY NICE. I will be forever grateful
for the opportunity to read them.